LABOR AND TECHNOLOGY:

Union Response to Changing Environments

Edited by

Donald Kennedy
Charles Craypo
Mary Lehman

Department of Labor Studies
The Pennsylvania State University

C-112

Preface

The major purpose of this publication is to contribute to the body of knowledge which is coming to be known as Labor Studies. A corollary outcome is the promise of enriched instructional materials for use in Labor Education. University labor educators have an important stake in seeing both these purposes through.

According to some, university labor educators inhabit a marginal occupation at best. They package and survey information for their union clients with a high degree of skill and versatility, but they really are "generalists" and command no specific knowledge base.

There are those university labor educators who sensed the need for such a base before this charge was made. They knew that the most readily available materials which they were adapting for labor education programs were originally conceived in a non-labor context: answers to problems posed by management, labor economists, and industrial relations specialists. And it is not necessarily impugning anyone's scholarship to say that when a specialist investigates a problem that occurs to a manager, the outcome, by the very nature of the motivating perspective, will be a management solution, however scientific the examination.

This publication represents a step toward intellectual autonomy. University labor educators, together with their counterparts in union education and research are now determined to define their own problems and to seek the answers to their own questions in as objective a fashion as their joint resources permit. It is in this spirit that this publication addresses the impact of new technology and changing corporate structure and provides an increment to both Labor Studies and Labor Education.

HELMUT GOLATZ, *Head*
Department of Labor Studies
Penn State University
December, 1981

CONTENTS

INTRODUCTION

In 1980 General Electric employed approximately 37,000 assembly line workers. By 1990 nearly one-half of those workers may be replaced by industrial robots, according to company estimates. If large computer manufacturers enter the market as expected, the number of robots introduced yearly in U.S. industry will reach approximately 200,000 by 1990. Some industry analysts estimate that 65 to 75 percent of today's factory jobs could be done by robots in 1990. In addition to the robotics revolution, other new technologies are restructuring nearly every workplace. Researchers estimate that new technology will affect as many as 45 million jobs — about half of which are currently held by union workers. Of this number, approximately 25 million workers will be affected in the most drastic way — their jobs will be eliminated.[1]

Yet technology is not a natural immutable force with its own inner dynamic. There is no "correct" way to automate or mechanize any industry. Instead there is a range of options from which to choose. The form, rate and direction of industrial innovation result from calculated decisions made in the privacy of corporate offices which are far removed from the actual scene of the change. Because businessmen select new technologies, their values are expressed in the choices — productivity, profitability, and control of the workplace. But the social costs of unemployment and the erosion of industry-based communities are not found in profit and loss statements and therefore not taken into account in bottom-line calculations.

Unrestrained technology is neither neutral nor random. It is not neutral because its introduction benefits and damages some of us more than others; it is not random because individuals consciously determine the pace and extent of innovation. Nor has government policy in the matter been neutral. There are few public constraints regarding

---

1. "Robots Join the Labor Force," *Business Week*, June 9, 1980, pp. 62-76.

industrial decisions on technology. Absence of regulation in effect, then, is support for the decision-makers instead of protection for those adversely affected by the decisions. A lack of federal commitment to full employment, for example, or a policy preference to combat inflation with recession-level interest rates, means that job-displacing innovation normally occurs in the face of moderate to high levels of joblessness in the economy.

Historical Development

Discretionary control of technology, unaccountable corporate structures and a "hands-off" public policy are issues of commanding importance for workers and unions today. Historically, however, workers have faced similar challenges. In his important study of Lynn, Massachusetts shoe workers, Alan Dawley analyzes the origin of industrial factories. Production of shoes under the pre-factory system was limited by the availability of journeymen stitchers in the city and semi-skilled binders who finished pre-stitched shoes in their rural households. This fragmentation minimized employer control over labor and hampered product standardization, resulting in undisciplined, uneven production flows.

Management's solution was the factory system. Huge regimental structures were built to house the steam-driven machines operated by large numbers of semi-skilled workers. This deliberate technological adaptation gave employers the industrial control they sought.

> The factory system resolved the contradictions and conflicts of the household era in favor of the manufacturers. It gave them the means to make the employees act in the employer's interest. Under the new industrial discipline, workers pursued their own momentary enjoyments at the risk of a head-on collision with the boss or his foreman and the loss of a job. Order, therefore, rested on the power of the manufacturers and harmony in the beehives of industry was founded in economic compulsion, rather than on some instinctive dronish desire on the part of wage earners to cooperate among themselves for the owner's benefit. The manufacturers were eager to take charge of the new industrial army, and, like other men on horseback, they were confident of their right to command and convinced they were astride the forces of progress.[2]

Technological innovation in this instance was an automatic stitcher which enabled the operator to sew 80 pairs of shoes in the time a journeyman could do the seams on one pair. The machine benefited employers in two ways. It reduced labor costs per unit of product and it increased managerial dominance over the workplace. Technology was power and therefore control over the pace and form of technology was a source of power.

---

2. Alan Dawley. *Class and Community: The Industrial Revolution in Lynn.* (Cambridge, MA.: Harvard University Press, 1976), p. 92.

The president of Western Union knew this in 1918 when he admonished his managers to introduce automatic teletype machines in place of Morse hand telegraphers so that the skilled workers "should not be the important factor in the transactions of the telegraph business."[3] Not only did the machines substitute semi-skilled, low-wage typists for craftsmen, they also monitored the work pace. An automatic lever attached to each machine notified supervisors when an operator slipped below the prescribed rate of transmission. The same pervasive supervision exists today in telecommunications and, as before, it is accomplished through design choices in new technology.

Historically, workers formed unions to match the power of management. They tried to protect previous gains, preserve whatever status they had achieved and insulate their power at the workplace from erosion by threatening industrial and economic environments. Once again, labor faces rapid and fundamental change and a collective and coordinated worker response seems necessary in order to protect hard-won standards.

The 1981 Technology Conference

The articles in this paper were presented as working papers at a Conference on Labor and Technology held at The Pennsylvania State University in November, 1981. The Conference brought together staff members of union research departments, university educators from various disciplines, trade union members and officers, and labor studies students. It was motivated by a belief that the problems confronting labor in the 1980s are not specific to particular industries but are similar in all sectors, and that the strategies and solutions developed by one union can inspire others.[4]

Unionists cannot be concerned only with events in their own industry, nor can labor educators communicate only with other labor educators. If they do, labor's progressive voice becomes fragmented and ineffective. These papers are published, therefore, in order to share the events, apprehensions and responses discussed at the conference and to stimulate further discussion and sharing of ideas and experiences. Exploring a common predicament enables us to comprehend more fully the impact of change and respond effectively to it.

3. *Labor Studies Journal*, "Special Issue: The Impact on Labor of Changing Corporate Structure and Technology," 3(Winter, 1979) p. 295.

4. A working bibliography of selected books and articles which explore changing environments and labor's responses is appended to this volume.

Forces of Change

The articles in this book present various aspects of labor response to the current environment. At issue are the inevitability of technological change, the accelerated pace of technology as a result of changes in corporate structure, the impact of new technology on workers and organized labor, and labor's responses to employer initiated shifts in production processes and business structures.

From Dawley's shoeworkers to the present, technology has had a momentum that appears unstoppable. But the underlying forces of change are more complex today than in the past. Technological innovation historically was fueled by employer desire to control the work process, the competitive need to lower production costs, and the desire — with or without competitive pressures — to widen profit margins. In those industries dominated by one or a few firms — where price competitive product markets were absent — the desire for worker control may have been the stronger motive; in those industries characterized by large numbers of price competitive firms, the need to reduce costs would have been paramount. In either case, there were strong and direct incentives for employers to adopt labor-saving technology.

The introduction of technology is accelerating today in a business environment that combines industrial concentration and fierce product market competition. In the post-World War II years concentrated industries such as telephone and auto became sluggish and unresponsive to consumer needs. Price and product competition have now been introduced, however, in these and other industries through deregulation, development of new products and services which merge previously discrete industry sectors, and trade incursions by foreign corporations. Many companies are belatedly gearing up to meet the unaccustomed competition by massive investment in technology.

The combatants in these changing markets are industrial heavyweights. The retail food industry, for example, has become a market battleground for both European and domestic corporations. Competition in telecommunications involves some of the nation's biggest firms, including IBM, AT&T, and EXXON; companies which have the resources to technologize more quickly than most others. As one firm adopts technical innovations the others must either follow suit or retire from the battle. The rate of technological change is thus increased. In addition, capital mobility accelerates the pace at which technology engulfs entire industries. Gregory Giebel's description of commercial printing, for example, shows how large national companies have moved into smaller geographical markets, forcing existing firms to match their technology or go out of business.

If there is an ideal business environment for rapid technological advance, it is probably the combination of concentration and competition which exists now. Within this environment, a few pieces of technology have been developed with revolutionary potential in a wide variety of industries. It is possible, therefore, that the widespread automation predicted for decades will now arrive virtually overnight, with both workers and consumers unprepared for the magnitude of the change.

Diffusion of microprocessors — tiny computers etched onto silicon chips — profoundly affects other industries, as George Kohl says in his paper. Changes in telecommunications are at the heart of expanding technological capability in a variety of other sectors. Large communication networks in which a small host computer is linked to several remote terminals are now available to serve industry. In addition to providing the means for decentralizing work, this innovation paves the way for electronic funds transfer in banking, electronic postal services and data systems for home and business. Other changes include the expansion of satellite communications, digital transmission, computerized systems for maintenance and testing, and the automation of switching and billing. Elsewhere, the article by Judith Gregory predicts that the office workplace of the future will include computers, advanced word processors and new equipment and techniques to store, retrieve and transmit data through microfilm and electronic mail networks.

The Impact of Technology

The impact of technology on workers varies depending on the industry, firm, workplace and job. The industries dicussed in this volume, however, reveal patterns of general importance for labor such as the wave of job elimination which is likely to accompany new industrial processes. In retail food, William Burns describes how scanners will be programmed with price changes, eradicating the jobs of many clerks. An estimated 10,000 meat processing jobs were lost between 1974-1980 as central cutting plants were either closed or converted to boxed-beef warehouses. In Lydia Fischer's description of the current auto crisis, she mentions that 300,000 auto workers have lost their jobs. The United Automobile Workers (UAW) estimates that because of the introduction of new technology only one-third of these workers may ever be called back to employment in the industry. Telecommunications and printing, two traditional growth industries, may experience job losses for the first time. And, Judith Gregory predicts that the number of jobs in the service industries may not be sufficient to offer employment to workers displaced from other sectors. That new jobs will be created by technology is probably true, but the number and types of positions and who will be hired remains unclear. The authors in this book suggest that the number of jobs eliminated may be greater than the number created.

Another industrial dynamic is producing job losses in conjunction with new technologies. Plant, store or office closings often occur when a firm is acquired during a period of increasing ownership concentration. This outcome is particularly frequent in retail food, where foreign-owned multinational conglomerates have closed many domestic stores.

For workers who keep their jobs or are displaced by machines but find new work, the impact of technology may well be that their jobs become deskilled, simplified, devalued and less fulfilling — in other words, more machine-like. Popular publicity surrounding the introduction of robots suggests that machines will take over only the dull, routine tasks which workers dislike. However, this is not always the case. As the case studies in this book show, particularly those involving the Machinists' Union as described by Leslie Nulty, dull routine jobs are being created by the new technology as it breaks down and deskills existing jobs. People who did skilled work will now simply feed material into machines or, worse, spend their days watching machines work, ready to step into the production process only in the event of a breakdown.

Lowering of required skills logically leads employers to pressure unions and workers to accept lower wage rates. Such downward pressure on wages has already affected meat packing plants and clerical offices and threatens to do the same in other industries experiencing a diffusion of new technologies.

Corporate demands for concessions at the bargaining table not only demonstrate labor's declining power, but ironically, may also speed technological change. For example, auto worker concessions, granted in the midst of a sharp economic slump and increased foreign penetration of domestic markets, may in fact, help subsidize a massive introduction of robots by the Big Three. Therefore, even when recovery does occur, the industry may experience large and permanent job losses; and the union's bargaining power may never be fully restored.

In the midst of this technology-induced challenge to its bargaining power, labor may also have to contend with employers who are more flexible and elusive. Telecommunications and new information processing equipment allows firms to transfer work almost effortlessly from one setting to another in response to union demands. Centralized corporate control of diverse, far-flung, often multinational enterprises presents a strong challenge to labor when it is combined with technological change.

Union Responses

Technological change is inevitable, as is some subsequent social impact. But the design, implementation and pace of change can be jointly determined by employers, workers and society in order to minimize the socially harmful effects of technological innovation and enable employees to adjust to shifting labor force needs. The cases discussed in this volume represent a variety of union responses to the technology challenge. They demonstrate that bargaining, organizing and political approaches occur, at both the national and local levels, and that they are ongoing rather than conclusive responses because of the evolutionary nature of environmental change. The issues raised are never settled decisively and forever.

Collective Bargaining

Because they have national, company-wide contracts, unions like the UAW and the Communications Workers of America (CWA) respond at that level. The UAW historically has not stood in the way of technological change in the auto industry. Instead it pursues other means of protecting workers against job erosion. At the bargaining table it tries to win assurances that outsourcing will be minimized and domestic plants kept open. As for CWA, it negotiates income maintenance, job rights and anti-subcontracting provisions, on a company-wide basis. Joint union-management committees in each of the various AT&T divisions deal with technology and job issues at that level. The union hopes these committees will evolve into worker participation agents that cut across corporate structure and, in this way, union representatives can have input, influence and even veto power at each stage of decision making involving technology. Historical experiences suggest, however, that considerable union aggressiveness will be needed to realize these hopes in that or any industry. Indeed, without full union representation, such committees may actually hinder the emergence of a collective bargaining solution.

The Graphic Arts International Union (GAIU), the United Food and Commercial Workers (UFCW) and the International Association of Machinists (IAM) all supply their locals and intermediate bodies with model contract language aimed at establishing some control over the introduction of technology that could adversely affect bargaining unit members. In addition, the GAIU, following a tradition in the printing industry, has established funds and programs that enable its members to stay abreast of new equipment and methods.

Four case studies of technological change in IAM plants show the importance of local union awareness, initiative and imagination in meeting the threat, both in local and national contract bargaining settings. They also identify the sources of local union bargaining power in technology disputes as: (1) workplace information networks; (2) contract language that defines the bargaining unit and describes job classifications; (3) the formal grievance procedure and (4) workers' intrinsic skills and knowledge. Of particular significance in the Machinists' experience is the union goal of redefining the bargaining unit in order to include all of the employees who control a new technological system — e.g., computer programmers.

Another advantage of joint determination may be drawn from the Machinists' experience. If management allowed workers with years of shop-floor experience to participate in the design and implementation of technology, more productive processes would often result. Surely, the workers would gain by using and improving their skills and knowledge, retaining their wage levels and performing more interesting work; but management would gain too by tapping this "human capital" pool in order to design a more productive system. Theoretically, consumers also stand to benefit through more efficiently produced goods and services.

In general, the cases examined here show that workers and unions need greater job security, more advance warning and detailed information about pending technology change; and that they want a stronger voice in the planning and installation stages of new production systems. In addition, there is the question of who will bear the cost of retraining workers for new jobs. All of these are goals which may have been or may be achieved through collective bargaining. However, since existing contract language is usually inadequate to protect workers, unions need to negotiate stronger language in anticipation of the introduction of new technology.

Other unions are responding to the change in bargaining opponents resulting from increasing corporate concentration in their industries by organizational mergers which strengthen their bargaining position. Examples included in this collection are the Graphic Arts International Union and the United Food and Commercial Workers. Should industrial concentration continue to dominate workplace settings, and new technology threaten to weaken the ability of unions to represent their members, merger talks are likely to be a more prominent part of labor response to the changing environment.

Organizing

In addition to collective bargaining, labor also recognizes that new organizing is a vital response to environmental challenges. Effective technology agreements that protect worker job rights are best negotiated in industries where a high level of unionization gives workers bargaining leverage. Because rapid technological change threatens job losses almost indiscriminately, labor needs to organize in every workplace. Ironically, technology may be a positive force in this regard, orienting some workers towards unions for the first time. Office automation, as Gregory and Mathews point out, leads to business offices which resemble factories, and the change may well encourage clerical workers to embrace collective bargaining as a remedy.

Other changes coincidental with technology add urgency to the job of union organizing. Deregulation, to cite one example, is moving traditionally stable, unionized industries such as telecommunications into competitive and often non-union surroundings. Kohl shows how this jeopardizes established union wage levels and benefits. Rather than equalizing conditions by lowering union standards, labor's appropriate response is to organize those working in the sub-standard firms. In the unregulated segments of telecommunications, Kohl anticipates more job-displacing and craft-deskilling mechanization and automation as employers try to reduce their operating costs and become less dependent on and accountable to organized labor during a period of great change. This effort may indeed undercut previous CWA gains and undermine its hard-won national bargaining structure in telephone.

A third area of change that prompts increased organizing efforts is industrial relocation. Movements or threats to move to traditionally non-union areas such as the sunbelt can only be countered by organizing workers and raising economic standards in these new locations. A number of unions, recognizing their mutual challenges, have joined together in AFL-CIO coordinated organizing drives in sunbelt locations such as Houston, Texas and Tupelo, Mississippi, cities whose recent industrial growth mirrors the economic decline in northeastern communities.

Political Strategies

U.S. labor can also explore innovative political strategies. In other countries organized labor has gone well beyond economic bargaining when confronting new technologies and changing business structures. As Steven Deutsch explains, some Western European labor movements have won national legislation guaranteeing the rights of advance information on new technical change and of employee participation in planning for such change. These laws enable both workers and industry to adjust to the potential impact of change. In this way European labor mixes legislative initiatives and collective bargaining in its attempt to protect workers and society.

In the first article in this collection, Markley Roberts calls for political action by unions in support of a national plant closing law to protect employees and communities from the devastation of economic dislocation. He also wonders whether a careful examination of U.S. tax policy would show that business is encouraged to close profitable plants in order to enjoy favorable tax write-offs. This raises the possibility that tax reform could be an important part of labor's political solution to technical and structural change.

The remedy for the well-publicized troubles of the U.S. auto industry may be in part political. As Lydia Fisher's paper shows, other industrialized countries legislate local content requirements or impose tariff and non-tariff restrictions or have export requirements for firms which do business in their economies. The Japanese government, in particular, offers tax and non-tax subsidies to its own auto industry and pursues additional policies to limit foreign producers' sales. By contrast, U.S. policy minimizes such trade barriers and requirements.

There are several political strategies in the United States and other countries from which labor can choose. They range from narrow, self-interested orientations to broad-based labor parties. When all the potentially harmful effects of new technology and corporate change are considered, however, U.S. labor may be drawn into the political arena more fully than it has in the past. This may be necessary in order to make full employment and extensive job retraining and relocation rights national economic priorities. Active organizing efforts, strategic bargaining demands and national full employment are essential ingredients in a labor agenda aimed at protecting workers and communities during the technological revolution of the 1980s.

The Impact of Technology on Union Organizing And Collective Bargaining

Markley Roberts

Challenges to American Labor

Robots in the factory, word processors in the office, scanners at the check-out counter, push-button banking, gene-splicing in the laboratory, and computers in the home. These are a few indicators of the ongoing technological revolution which is changing the American economy, the nation's job structure, the number and location of job opportunities, the nature of work — and challenging American Labor unions once again to demonstrate their vitality and relevance in the workplace and in society. Changing technology is not the only challenge facing trade unions today. They must respond to new forms of corporate structure and new patterns of international trade. They must deal with the geographic shift of jobs to traditionally non-union areas. And, they must solve these problems within the atmosphere created by an increasingly unsympathetic public policy.

Industry and occupation changes have contributed to pronounced shifts in the workplace itself. The average American worker is now performing a different job, and is probably employed in a different geographic location than he or she would have been twenty years ago. Employment in manufacturing has declined from 26 percent of the workforce in 1955 to 22 percent in 1980, while service sector employment is up from 20 percent in 1955 to 28 percent in 1980. Using a traditional distinction, "white-collar" employment is now up to 50 percent of the labor force, compared to 43 percent in 1960 and "blue-collar" work is down from 36 percent in 1960 to 32 percent in 1980.

Markley Roberts is on the staff of the Department of Economic Research, AFL-CIO.

However, as technology leads to increasing automation in "white collar" work, the distinction between "white-collar" and "blue collar" jobs becomes blurred and may eventually become irrelevant in discussions of the modern labor force.

As job content changes, so does job location. The number of manufacturing jobs in the industrial North dropped between 1966 and 1977 — down 12 percent in New England, 19 percent in Middle Atlantic States and 7 percent in Great Lakes States — while growing 18 percent in the Southeast, 40 percent in the Southwest, 39 percent in the Rocky Mountain States, 10 percent in the Plains States and 8 percent in the Far West.[1] This suggests that new plants with new technology are in historically non-union or anti-union states, while some areas of traditional union strength are left with aging, obsolescent plants and equipment. Technology transfers from U.S. multinational corporations to other nations also have drastic effects on job opportunities for American workers.

There are, as noted, a variety of factors influencing the new workplace. The impact of technology, however, stands as one of the key issues requiring immediate attention from both labor and government in the United States. Technology is changing the way goods and services are produced and distributed. For all its potential benefits, including the creation of new jobs and reduction of occupational safety and health hazards, technology can also have destructive effects on workers and their jobs. It is entirely logical and reasonable, since workers and their unions have a vital interest, that they should have a voice in determining how technology is introduced in the workplace and in society. Unions must make sure workers and ordinary citizens are not scrapped, ignored and tossed aside, that equity is given the same attention as efficiency, and that human values prevail in this new workplace.

Technological progress usually involves labor-saving operations — increased production with the same number or fewer workers. New jobs may be created, but the major impact of changing technology is to eliminate some jobs, to redefine the content of others, to lower skill requirements, and to alter the flow of work. Many workers will monitor and maintain, instead of operate equipment. Although some U.S. jobs will be upgraded in skill and pay by technological change, many will be downgraded.

---

1. Thomas Kochan, *Collective Bargaining and Industrial Relations,* (Homewood, Ill: Richard D. Irwin), pp. 74-75.

Government is not neutral on technological change. Public policy encourages the introduction of new technology through "accelerated depreciation", research and development allowances, and government procurement policies which affect the pace of technological change, and the structure and availability of jobs.

More information is needed on the effects of new technology on workers. A clearinghouse could be set up through the federal government which would continually gather information about technological change and its effects on jobs, skills, training needs, and industry location. Through this clearinghouse, the federal government could provide unions and employers with comprehensive information and services and, upon request, could help develop labor-management solutions for the complex problems related to the impact of technological change at the workplace. With more and better information, we would be able to devise more effective public and private adjustment programs.

Labor's Responses

The strength and continued vitality of American labor will be determined in part by its ability to produce innovative and effective responses to these changing conditions. New forms of corporate structure have created huge concentrations of private economic power. Unions are attempting to match this structural change through the processes of merger and amalgamation, thereby enhancing their power to organize and bargain collectively. Through the merger process, workers in declining industries retain their individual unions as merged segments of a larger organization which is better able to serve its members. Every merger broadens and strengthens the entire labor movement resulting in fewer, stronger, and more diversified unions.

Organization

The success or failure of labor's attempts to organize more workers will be a key element in strengthening the capacity of unions to deal with changing conditions. Union organizers today, face difficult problems not the least of which is a new wave of business hostility marked in many cases by sophisticated management consultants conducting well-financed anti-union campaigns. In addition, union firms are opening new operations as non-union and trying to eliminate the unions at older, organized locations. This has long been true of the printing industry. It is becoming more and more apparent in the building and construction industry and in manufacturing. Plant closings and relocations outside the United States have disproportionate effects on domestic unionized operations.

But I am convinced that American Workers will join unions in increasing numbers in the 1980's to maintain dignity and self-respect, as well as to improve wages and working conditions in the future. Workers look for ways to protect their jobs in periods of high unemployment and economic uncertainty. To the extent that women and minority workers suffer disproportionately from adverse conditions, they will, I believe, join unions in increasing numbers.

National Labor Relations Board election statistics show intensive union organizing activity in the private sector has continued over the past 20 years. From 1959 to 1978, AFL-CIO unions won bargaining rights for 3.15 million workers.[2] This does not include the tremendous organizing achievements during the same period in the public sector, where a substantial portion of union membership growth has occurred.

Total U.S. membership in national unions and employee associations increased by 2 million members from 20,721,000 in 1968 to 22,757,000 in 1978. As a percentage of potential union members — both private and public production and nonsupervisory workers — union membership dropped from 32.2 percent in 1978 to 30.4 percent in 1980.[3] But the scope of the American labor movement is not determined by union membership numbers alone. Many workers — particularly in so-called "right to work" states, and in federal, state and local government — are protected by union contracts and bargaining activities and enjoy union benefits without being union members. There are few hard figures on numbers of workers represented, as compared with union membership, but it would appear that some 25 percent more workers in private industry are covered by collective bargaining agreements than maintain membership. For government workers at all levels, this representation covers an additional 33 percent. Therefore, the effect of union contracts is far greater than the absolute number of union members would indicate. Union membership statistics also understate the impact of unions on the political and social environment in America. There are no adequate numbers or analyses on the active role of unions in grass-roots political action and on union lobbying on social, economic, and political issues in the halls of Congress, state legislatures, county governments, and city halls throughout the nation.

---

2. AFL-CIO Department of Research, *Union Membership and Employment, 1959-1979,* February 1980.

3. U.S. Department of Labor, Bureau of Labor Statistics, "Corrected Data on Labor Organization Membership — 1980," press release, September 18, 1981.

Signs of serious interest in unions are growing in the financial sector. This suggests that many unorganized workers will join or organize unions, if they have the chance. This view is supported by Thomas Kochan who reports that if all workers who want union representation (one-third of the unorganized work force) were organized, the size of the labor movement would double.[4] Kochan goes on:

> The greatest source of potential growth appears to be among non-whites; a two-thirds majority of non-white workers prefers to unionize . . . In addition, none of the growing segments of the labor force exhibits an inherently negative view of trade unions or to the prospects of joining a union. Younger workers, women and higher educated workers are no less willing to join a union when their job conditions warrant it than their older, male or less educated counterparts . . . Even the common stereotype of the anti-union Southern worker does not show up in these data. Therefore, the changing regional and demographic composition of the labor force should pose no new barriers to organizing.

Cooperative organizing drives give promise of bringing unionism to more workers in the South and other parts of the country where unionism has been relatively weak. The AFL-CIO Department of Organization and Field Services and the AFL-CIO Industrial Union Department have conducted such campaigns. The Los Angeles-Orange County Organizing Committee, with some 200 full-time organizers, brought 400,000 workers into unions over a 20-year period.

In October, 1981, a massive, 20-union organizing drive started in Houston. This drive is aimed at all major industries in this metropolitan area which has a population one-third black and 20 percent Hispanic. The Employment Relations Report for September 30, 1981 noted:

> Financial projections for the drive call for a $1.7 million budget, including $500,000 for media and other communications aimed at getting the union message to the public. The AFL-CIO will coordinate the campaign, assisted by organizers assigned by participating unions, who will also contribute to the organizing budget. The industries specifically pinpointed in a campaign organization chart are manufacturing, health care, public employment, construction, retail and wholesale and other services . . . As one of the nation's fastest growing cities, with a broad base of industries, Houston was selected as the major test for a new organizing offensive on the part of AFL-CIO affilated unions. While viewed as a particularly tough challenge, union organizers hope it will be a spring-board for new union inroads into the expanding sunbelt area.

Another multi-union organizing drive in the South, started in late 1981, is based in Atlanta, Georgia. This campaign, coordinated by the AFL-CIO Industrial Union Department, is aimed particularly at white-collar workers and at hotel and restaurant employees. The organizing drive is being supported by religious and civil rights groups.[5]

---

4. Thomas Kochan, "How American Workers View Unions," *Monthly Labor Review*, April 1979, pp. 23-31. Kochan was interpreting a University of Michigan Survey Research Center 1977 Quality of Employment Survey.

5. Bureau of National Affairs, *Daily Labor Report*, November 2, 1981.

A recent report indicates that Southern employers are resisting strongly these organizing drives but concludes:

> The evidence is clear that southern unions and southern collective bargaining are beginning to prosper relative to their counterparts in other regions of the country. A decline in northern manufacturing industry, movement of employers to the Sun Belt, should enhance the potential for greater prosperity for unions and collective bargaining in the South.[6]

Successful organizing drives will strengthen the institutional power of labor in the United States and also serve to reinforce the use of collective bargaining as the worker's most effective tool to gain some control over the workplace environment.

Collective Bargaining

For contemporary union members, collective bargaining plays a vital role in meeting the challenges, opportunities and dangers of new technology. The flexibility of this institution — the American system of labor-management bargaining at the plant, company and industry level — enables workers to negotiate protection from the adverse effects of job-destroying technological innovation. Mature collective bargaining relationships provide a sound basis for special labor-management committees to deal with adjustment to new technology.

Historically, unions have responded in a number of ways to the introduction of new technology. In 1960, Sumner Slichter, James J. Healy and Robert Livernash reported that major determinants of union policies toward technological change were:

(1) the nature of the union, meaning specifically whether it is a craft or industrial union;

(2) the economic condition of the industry or the enterprise, or occupation, whether it is expanding or contracting, whether the industry is highly competitive or not;

(3) the nature of the technological change, the effect on jobs and on the bargaining unit, the effect on workers' skills and job responsibilities; and

(4) the stage of development of the technological change and the stage of development of union policy toward that change.[7]

Slichter, Healy and Livernash distinguish five principal policies that unions adopt when faced with technological change: willing acceptance, opposition, competition, encouragement, and adjustment with

---

6. Trevor Bain and Allan Spritzer, "Organizing in the South," *Labor Law Journal*, August, 1981 (Spring 1981 Meeting of the Industrial Relations Research Association) pp. 537-544.

7. Sumner Slichter, James J. Healy, and Robert Livernash, *The Impact of Collective Bargaining on Management*, (Washington, D.C.: The Brookings Institute, 1960), Chapter 12, "Union Policies Toward Technological Change."

an effort to control use of the new technology. They note:

> The most usual policy of unions toward technological change is willing acceptance. This happens in the numerous cases in which the technological change makes little difference in the kind and degree of skill required and has little immediate effect on the number of jobs. But the gain in productivity from the change may make it attractive by giving labor improved opportunity to bargain for wage increases. Unions may be led by favorable bargaining opportunities to accept willingly technological changes that involve a mixture of advantages and disadvantages. Thus, the bargaining advantages that accompany a change requiring greater skill may lead to willing acceptance even though it greatly reduces the number of jobs.

The authors point out that no national union in recent years has destroyed itself by fighting technological change.

> Nor is there record of any union in recent years being able to prevent technological change by opposing it — though many unions have retarded recent changes temporarily and locally. Union wage policies appear to have been partly responsible for stimulating technological change under some circumstances and may have affected the distribution of gains.

Using the approach developed by Slichter, Healy, and Livernash, Doris McLaughlin of the University of Michigan surveyed union officials, management, mediators and arbitrators on the impact of unions on the rate and direction of technological innovation.

The McLaughlin report found that willing acceptance was the most common response American labor unions make to the introduction of new technology.[8] The next most common response was initial opposition, but this was followed by adjustment, so that, in the long run, willing acceptance or adjustment were, by far, most common.

A negative union response to the introduction of technological change was invariably the result of the belief that acceptance would have an adverse effect on a large or important segment of the union's membership. If the employer convinced the union's leaders that their members would not be adversely affected, or that those who were adversely affected would receive some off-setting benefit, union opposition disappeared.

The three most important variables in determining union reaction, in order of importance, were: (1) the state of the economy, (2) union leaders' perception of the inevitability or necessity for the change, and (3) the nature of the industry.

McLaughlin noted that, depending on union perception of these three variables, a fourth variable — where decision-making power lay — becomes crucial. If the international union holds decision-making power, the reaction to new technology is made only on consideration of the first three variables. However, if decision-making power resides with local union leaders, three more variables become relevant: (5) how

---

8. Doris B. McLaughlin, *The Impact of Unions on the Rate and Direction of Technological Innovation*, Institute of Labor and Industrial Relations, University of Michigan-Wayne State University, February 1979 (Report to the National Science Foundation).

local union leaders perceive the impact of the new technology on the bargaining unit, (6) how local union leaders perceive the "quid pro quo" offered by the employer to the affected union members, and (7) how local union leaders perceive the impact on those union members left in the unit after the new technology is introduced.

Third-party action by mediators, arbitrators or judges does not seem to affect the outcome, according to the report, but appears to affect the process by which unions and management reached accommodation to the effects of new technology. These third-party agents, as outsiders, serve a useful function in taking the heat off local union leaders "when otherwise politically delicate decisions need to be made with regard to the introduction of new technology," the report states. McLaughlin concludes, unions are not the major stumbling block to new technology and higher productivity, but "employer representatives, particularly at the middle management level, were often cited as constituting the real barrier to the introduction and effective use of technological innovation."

In 1964, the Bureau of Labor Statistics reported that some major labor-management efforts to protect employees from the adverse effects of new technology have included: (1) guarantees against job or income loss and, in some cases, against loss of supplementary benefits for varying periods, (2) compensation for employees who lose their jobs, (3) guaranteed income for workers required to take lower-paying jobs, (4) provisions for retraining, (5) provisions for transfer to other plants and payment of relocation expenses, and (6) agreements to provide workers with notice of plant closings or other major changes.

Some agreements have established joint labor-management committees to recommend methods of providing for workers affected by automation. The report concluded that:

> These arrangements typically are combined with provisions for retention of workers with greatest seniority, but in a limited number of cases, efforts are made to spread work among larger numbers of employees or to encourage early retirement of workers with relatively high seniority.[9]

In 1966, the National Automation Commission called attention to the need for private sector efforts to facilitate adjustment to technological change including reliance on attrition, an advance notice early warning system, job counselling and job-finding assistance, training and retraining. The Commission noted the rationality of using the seniority principle in the case of layoffs and the seriousness of the need for pension and health benefits to continue during periods of unemployment. They also pointed out that technological improvements can bring more flexibility to work schedules and more leisure to employees through reduced hours of work per day, per week and per year.

---

9. U.S. Department of Labor, Bureau of Labor Statistics, *Collective Bargaining and Technological Change*, BLS Report No. 266, March 1964.

The record of collective bargaining response to change offers many examples of both success and failure, the Commission noted:

> Collective bargaining has proved to be an excellent vehicle for the effective management of change; it permits those directly affected by the change to deal with it first-hand and with a familiarity that takes into account peculiarities and problems peculiar to an enterprise. Especially in recent years, some managements and unions, occasionally but not usually with the help of outsiders, have developed, with varying degrees of ingenuity and success, plans to facilitate change.

But the Commission warned:

> Procedurally, the process of collective bargaining on basic issues has tended to stagnate during the life of the agreement and to accelerate frantically in an atmosphere of crisis immediately preceding contract renewal. Happily, employers and unions in a number of industries are abandoning this pattern in favor of more or less continuous discussion. Basic issues such as adjustment to technological change cannot be resolved, however, by a small team of negotiators working themselves into a state of physical and mental exhaustion for a few months every 2 or 3 years. These issues must be dealt with patiently, carefully, and above all, continuously, until satisfactory solutions emerge. This kind of bargaining calls for ability of the highest caliber on the part of leaders of both labor and management.[10]

In the fifteen years since the Automation Commission's report, with generally slow economic growth and recessions in 1969-70, 1973-75, 1980-81, economic conditions did not encourage easy adjustment to technological change. It must be emphasized that it is easier to deal with adverse effects of technological change in a general economic climate of full employment. National economic policies must aim at full employment for a variety of economic, social and moral reasons. Among those reasons we must recognize the need to facilitate successful and humane adjustments to job-destroying technology in both the private and public sectors.

Much progress has already been achieved through collective bargaining. For example a 1981 Bureau of Labor Statistics study, updating a similar 1966-67 report presents examples of contract language and identifies contracts which contain language on plant movement, interplant transfers, and relocation allowances, many of which relate to the effects of technological change.[11] Agreements limiting plant movement rose from 22 percent in the 1966-67 survey to 36 percent in the 1980-81 survey of some 1,600 contracts, while worker coverage rose from 38 percent to 49 percent. Interplant transfer provisions increased from 32 percent to 35 percent and worker coverage went from 47 percent to 49 percent. Agreements dealing with relocation allowances increased from 34 percent to 41 percent while worker coverage went up from 60 percent to 65 percent.

---

10. National Commission on Technology, Automation, and Economic Progress, *Technology and the American Economy*, Vol. 1 (U.S. Government Printing Office, Washington, DC: February 1966).

11. U.S. Department of Labor, Bureau of Labor Statistics, *Major Collective Bargaining Agreements: Interplant Transfer and Relocation Allowances*, Bulletin 1425-20, July 1981. The 1966-67 study was reported in U.S. Department of Labor, Bureau of Labor Statistics, *Major Collective Bargaining Agreements: Plant Movement, Transfer, and Relocation Allowance*, Bulletin 1425-10, July 1969.

On the issues of major technological change, work transfer, and plant closings, some contracts have a variety of provisions. For example, the UAW-General Motors contract provides for advance notice to the union in cases of technology-related permanent layoffs, a special union-company committee to deal with technology layoffs, and negotiation of rights related to plant closings, department closing, and company transfer of work. Workers have the right to training for a new job in cases of technology-related permanent layoff. In the case of plant closing, department closing or transfer of work, workers have the right to bump to another job in the same plant, transfer to a replacement facility or to a new plant. They receive preferential hiring at another plant, keep seniority with respect to fringe benefits, get moving expenses up to $1,355, take layoff with recall rights and get severance pay.

The United Steel Workers' contract with Kennecott Copper includes a no-layoff clause and attrition protection for workers affected by technology changes which will permanently eliminate their jobs. Under this contract, workers have the right to bump to another job in the same plant or in another plant. The Transit Workers' contract with the New York City transit system and the Newspaper Guild's contract with the New York Times also have no-layoff contract protection.

The Steel Workers' contract with American Can Company calls for a 12-month advance notice of permanent layoffs related to technological change. The United Food and Commercial Workers' contract with Armour calls for 6-month notice and the Guild-New York Times agreement calls for 4 months. There are contracts with advance notice requirements as short as seven days and contracts with advance notice requirements, but no specified time period.[12]

Major technology changes result from management decisions made long before technology is actually introduced. The shutdown of the Youngstown, Ohio steel plant involved corporate decisions made years earlier. The failure of management to institute worker safety-health and environmental protections should not be the first indication workers have of an impending shutdown. An "early warning" system of advance notice makes it possible to meet the problems of affected workers. With advance notice and labor-management cooperation, workers can look for or train for a new job, perhaps with the same employer in the same plant or at another location. Employer-paid retraining should be an important part of any program.

---

12. These contract provisions are listed in Industrial Union Department, AFL-CIO, *Comparative Survey of Major Collective Bargaining Agreements Manufacturing and Non-Manufacturing,* March, 1979, December, 1979.

There are other methods and techniques for labor-management cooperation to cushion adverse effects from changing technology. One is through "no-layoff" attrition which reduces the workforce by retirements and voluntary quits, protecting the jobs and earnings of those workers who remain with the company. Of course, attrition alone is not an adequate solution. "Red circle" earnings protection for workers downgraded through no fault of their own attaches a wage rate to an individual instead of to the job itself, and thus protects workers against loss of income which might result from innovation-induced downgrading.

Seniority is a key principle in protecting workers against layoffs and downgradings. This rewards long service, but does much more — it properly reflects the worker's investment in the job and the company's investment in the worker. Early retirement is an option that older workers should have available as a free choice, not as a requirement. Many older workers cannot afford to retire early and others prefer to continue working.

Transfer and relocation rights and mobility assistance to workers are other ways to provide job and income protection. Within-plant and inter-plant transfer, relocation assistance, severance pay, pension rights and seniority protections and supplemental unemployment benefits also help cushion adverse effects on workers and their families when industrial innovation occurs — all are solutions which may be negotiated within the conventional framework of collective bargaining. Shorter work weeks and reduced time per year on the job, including longer paid vacations and sabbatical leaves, also can ease the negative employment effects of technology.

The costs to the employer of the adjustment process, the adjustment cushions, should be viewed as a normal part of the expense of bringing in new technology. It is reasonable and proper that the cost of progress should include the human costs of such technological innovation and should compensate for them.

Collective bargaining can provide cushions to soften the adverse impact of technological change on workers by setting up adjustment procedures and programs at the workplace. In a full employment economy — linked with adequate employment services, employment and training programs, and unemployment compensation — the disruption of workers' lives and the job displacement resulting from innovation and technological change can be minimized.

Plant Closings and Public Policy

The increasing popularity of a conglomerate corporate structure has led to another form of disruption affecting workers in the 1980's. Sudden plant closings in this country are occurring with alarming frequency. They affect not only large industrial cities, but small towns, rural areas, and even the South, a region to which many plants have relocated. Decisions to close or relocate federal facilities are also increasingly a commonplace occurrence. The impact of plant closings on particular communities can be devastating in economic, social and personal terms. In urban areas, which often have high rates of joblessness, plant shutdowns serve to aggravate the unemployment problem. An estimated 900,000 jobs have been lost in the Northeast and Midwest alone in the last ten years. The local tax base is further weakened. Suppliers and retail stores may be forced to cut back their operations or go out of business.

Workers who lose their jobs because of plant closings may not be able to find new ones or may be forced to work at reduced pay. Family life is disrupted. The mental and physical health of displaced workers often declines at a rapid rate. According to the Bluestone-Harrison report, research over a 13-year period found that the suicide rate among workers displayed by plant closings is almost thirty times the national average.[13] Such workers also suffer a far higher than average incidence of heart disease, hypertension and other ailments.

Bills to deal with this grave economic and social problem have been introduced in Congress. Although these bills differ in some respects, they would do much to counteract the devastating effects of shutdowns and relocations. Unfortunately, they do not address the problems caused by the relocation of governmental facilities. Among other things, these bills would: (1) require firms to provide advance notice of their intentions to close or relocate a major facility, (2) advocate programs to support troubled businesses, including incentives to promote employee ownership, (3) call for the issuance of economic impact statements and federal investigation of the circumstances, and (4) require employers, whenever existing jobs cannot be saved, to provide minimal protections to their workers in such matters as transfer rights, relocation expenses, severance pay, pension protection, health care and job training.

Three states — Wisconsin, Maine, and Michigan — have laws relating to plant shutdowns, and some 15 states have proposals pending, with state labor organizations pressing for action on protective plant shutdown legislation. However, because of "competitive laxity" among the states in their efforts to attract new business and "runaway"

13. Barry Bluestone and Bennett Harrison, *Capital and Communities: The Causes and Consequences of Private Disinvestment,* (Washington, D.C.: The Progressive Alliance, 1980) pp. 78-82. The health-unemployment link is one of the most clearly documented social research conclusions, e.g. Harvey Brenner, *Estimating the Costs of National Economic Policy Implications for Mental and Physical Health, and Criminal Aggression,* Joint Economic Committee, U.S. Congress, October 26, 1976.

business, federal legislation with national plant closings standards is essential. Unfortunately, since reporting on plant closings is voluntary, the U.S. government does not have centralized, comprehensive information on this important social and economic issue.

For labor it is crucially important to require employers to recognize their responsibilities to their employees and their communities before they close a plant and to provide economic protection to workers and their families who suffer the consequences of hasty corporate action. There is nothing radical or unusual about national legislation requiring advance notice and other worker-community benefits. In other nations, private business firms — including affiliates and subsidiaries of many American firms — find they can live with laws requiring advance notice and other protections for workers and communities against the adverse effects of economic dislocation and plant shutdowns.

In terms of international comparisons, Sweden requires six months notice where more than 100 workers are involved, four months notice for 26 to 100 workers and two months for 5 to 25 workers. Under Swedish law, no dismissals may take place until the unions have been contacted and granted an opportunity to negotiate concerning the consequences of the dismissals. In the United Kingdom, 90-day notices must be given where 100 or more workers are involved and 30 days in plants employing 10 to 99 workers. Failure to communicate with the unions and to give the appropriate notice can make the employer liable for continuing to pay workers during the required notice period. In France, Greece and The Netherlands, prior to making large-scale dismissals, the firm must have permission from the government to lay off workers and in actual practice the advance notice period is as long as half a year to a year depending upon the specific circumstances. These examples indicate that advance notice is a practice which firms can tolerate. It must also be remembered that in most foreign countries the benefits paid workers are generally two-thirds of lost earnings for up to a year after the layoff.

Unfortunately, in the United States, there are, by contrast, a number of tax advantages provided for corporations which close down even viable, money-making plants. The Bluestone-Harrison report warns against the "myth" that plant shutdowns are most often due to business failure. The present tax system actually encourages shutdown of profitable operations in order to create a sizeable tax loss for the parent company.

This issue is difficult to document because no company will admit that it is shutting down a profitable plant, throwing workers on the scrapheap and demoralizing the local community simply to get a tax break. However, Harry Brill, a professor at the University of Massachusetts lays out "the tremendous, often irresistable incentives the

Internal Revenue Service offers to businesses to shut down plants." He writes, "U.S. Steel's closing of more than a dozen facilities entitled the company to hundreds of millions of dollars in tax write-offs," and then describes two U.S. Steel plants which were profitable and yet were closed down, "To treat these plants as if they were losing money is a violation of the intent of Federal tax laws and an affront to the workers who are paying for the rebates with their jobs." He continues:

> Tax breaks for abandonment were never intended by Congress to apply to viable, profit-making operations. Moreover, business losses for tax purposes are not intended to include losses deliberately incurred. Nothing in the tax code justifies interpreting loss as a voluntary cost that a business freely chooses to incur for its own reasons. . . . Unquestionably, IRS permissiveness toward business has encouraged the epidemic of plant closings. As a result, the nation's tax collector has participated in dotting the country with graveyards of empty lots and boarded buildings where vital business enterprises once resided. The agency claims that its abandonment policies are in strict adherence to the law's 'true meaning.' But to corporate management, they can be a tax bonanza, and to the worker, a harsh injustice.[14]

Congress should examine plant closings very carefully to determine if there is indeed an array of tax incentives encouraging businesses to close plants. Legislation must be created which will stop such incentives and will prevent tax-related plant shutdowns. Legislation must also be created to establish basic job and income protections for workers including pension and health care and other benefits, to deal in an effective and humane way with the economic and social dislocation resulting from plant closings.

Conclusion

The potential for misusing technology is great, but the possibility of human progress through its wise and humane use is equally great. The introduction of new technology will occur with minimal social disruption if workers and employers have an equal opportunity for discussion and joint decision-making on the subjects of changing technology and the quality of working life. Collective bargaining has been a fair and workable process for joint labor-management decisions on wages, working conditions and other major issues. It is therefore a logical mechanism for increasing the involvement of workers in such areas of decision-making as adjustment to new technology.

New technology and rising expectations that work should be humane for workers as well as profitable for business are forcing transformations at the workplace. In a "post-industrial" society, human and social values should be part of the production process. Greater autonomy and participation in decision-making on the shop floor, in the corporate boardroom, and in national economic policy-making will be given high priority. Improvements in the "quality of

---

14. Harry Brill, "It Pays to Go Out of Business," *The Progressive*, August, 1980, pp. 20-21.

work life" include a broad range of issues, such as better occupational safety and health, as well as work organization, long-run investment, employment and training decisions. The QWL issues are logical subjects for joint labor-management negotiation and decision.

Irving Bluestone, a former UAW vice president, has been a strong advocate of increased worker participation in corporation decisions. But, he warns:

> The joint union-management programs that are in existence have not yet proven themselves in any permanent sense. They must be subject constantly to review and change as management, the union, and the workers learn by doing. Although it is not possible to set forth a precise blueprint to ensure the successful participation of workers in the decision-making process, experience already indicates certain criteria that are basic:
>
> The programs should be voluntary. Workers must have the free opportunity to decide whether or not to participate in the program. To order compulsion is to invite resistance and failure.
>
> Workers should be assured that their participation in decision-making will not erode their job security or that of their fellow workers, that they will not be subject to 'speed up' by reason of it, and that the program will not violate their rights under the collective bargaining agreement.
>
> Workers should genuinely experience that they are not simply adjuncts to the tool, but that their bent toward being creative, innovative, and inventive plays a significant role in the production (or service) process.
>
> Job functions should be engineered to fit the worker; the current system is designed to make the worker fit the job on the theory that this is a more efficient production system and that, in any event, economic gain is the worker's only reason for working. This theory is wrong on both counts.
>
> The workers should be assured the widest possible latitude of self-management, responsibility, and opportunity for use of 'brainpower.' Gimmickry and manipulation of the worker must not be employed.
>
> The changes in job content and the added responsibility and involvement in decision making should be accompanied by an effective reward system.
>
> Workers should be able to foresee opportunities for growth in their work, and for promotion.
>
> The role of workers in the business should enable them to relate to the products being produced or the services being rendered, and to their meaning in society; in a broader sense, it should also enable them to relate constructively to their role in society. [15]

Workers and their unions have reasonable, understandable, and legitimate concerns about loss of jobs, loss of income and loss of life and health. If these concerns are met adequately and effectively, workers will be much more willing to accept and adjust to changing technology.

There are no simple solutions to the task of protecting workers against the adverse impacts of changing technology. In thousands of labor-management contracts covering millions of workers in both the public and private sector, unions and management have adopted a wide variety of protective provisions. They fall into a few general

---

15. Clark Kerr and Jerome M. Rosow, ed., *Work in America: The Decade Ahead,* (New York: Van Nostrand Reinhold, 1979) pp. 249-50.

categories — job protection, income protection, safety and health protection, retraining, and relocation assistance. The specifics include attrition or no-layoff protection, early warning of technological change, seniority protections, early retirement opportunities, "red circle" pay protection, shorter work-weeks or work-years, relocation rights to follow transferred operations, severance pay, negotiated safety-health laws and regulations, and many other specific labor-management collectively bargained responses to technology change.

Without full collective bargaining — no matter how enlightened or benevolent management may be — working men and women simply don't participate in the basic decisions which goven their jobs, their income, and their lives. Collective bargaining is essential to meet the challenge of technological change with a minimum of social and human dislocation. Trade unions, as always, accept the responsibility to organize and to respresent workers in their efforts to get better wages and working conditions; to assure workers of dignity on the job and protection against arbitrary action by management; and to work for general economic, social and political conditions which enhance human welfare, human dignity and human freedom.

Changing Corporate Structure and Technology in The Retail Food Industry

William Burns

Introduction

As the decade of the 1980's unfolds revolutionary changes are creating a new retail food industry. In the last few years, the large food chains have mapped out and launched a strategy of merger and acquisition in order to capture more control of the retail food industry. To put it simply, they are buying out the competition, and the evidence strongly indicates that they will continue this strategy. These chains now control over 40 percent of total U.S. grocery store sales, but they want and are gaining an even bigger share of the market.

For the first time, large foreign-based multinational corporations are buying up shares of the U.S. food industry. They now own about 10 percent of the industry and plan to acquire more. Together these developments are concentrating more and more economic power in the hands of fewer and fewer corporations in the industry. Both U.S. food chains and foreign corporations are shaping the future of the industry as they buy up the competition, close stores, cut jobs and try to force unions to bargain down wages.

The large corporations moved quickly to adopt technological changes such as scanners, boxed beef, construction of the super store, the box store, the warehouse store, and the limited item store. These technological changes are spreading rapidly and as they run their course thousands of workers will be affected. The chains are also increasing the number of part-time employees which, along with technological change, will enable them to run high-volume, highly automated stores using fewer full-time workers.

Changes in corporate structure and technology raise questions for workers and unions which can be addressed through innovative bargaining concepts. Should unions, for example, negotiate broader area

William Burns is Research Director for the United Food and Commerical Workers.

agreements with these major corporations and set up technological adjustment funds supported by company contributions? Should there be a shorter workweek for full-time employees in the industry? Should workers who want to remain in the industry be allowed to do so instead of being forced out by technological displacement? These are a few of the questions that illustrate the idea that unions must think in very broad terms when confronting dramatic change.

Industrial Concentration

To examine these changes we look first at market concentration and corporate power. Major food chains have increased their share of sales over the years and are still growing as a result of a new wave of mergers and acquisitions in the industry. The evidence suggests that the national chains have mapped out a policy of increasing their market share by simply buying out the competition. To understand the scope and significance of this policy it is necessary to review the history of mergers in retail food. Table 1 lists yearly acquisitions in the retail food industry during 1949-1977.

The first great wave of merger activity by the top 20 chains lasted from 1949-1964. Merger activity was heavy and the top 20 food chains dominated the action. They accounted for 70 percent of all sales acquired during this period, which increased their overall share of grocery store sales by more than 25 percent. In fact, 90 percent of this increase came as a result of mergers and acquisitions. In other words, they simply bought 25 percent more of the total market.

Merger activity continued strong after 1964 but the ratio of acquisitions on the part of the top 20 fell dramatically. In reaction against the acquisitive appetite of the big chains, the Federal Trade Commission, beginning in 1965, implemented a hard-line anti-merger policy aimed directly at them. The F.T.C. issued judgments against several major companies prohibiting acquisitions by food chains with annual sales of more than $500 million. These decrees remained in effect for ten years, with the last (Grand Union) expiring in 1978. As a result of this change in public policy, the top 20 chains accounted for only 10 percent of acquisitions from 1965-1975.

After the Federal Trade Commission decrees expired the big chains immediately reactivated their acquisition policies. For example, a consent agreement with Lucky Stores expired in late 1977; soon after Lucky announced its intention to make new acquisitions. In 1978 it bought Tampa Wholesale, a company operating 47 Kash'n Karry Stores. Grand Union's decree expired in June, 1978 and within a week it had made a tender offer to buy Colonial Stores, a $1.1 billion company. Grand Union had hardly digested this acquisition before it bought Weingarten, a $566 million chain. Altogether, since 1975 ap-

Table 1
Acquisitions of Food Retailers, 1949-1977

Year	By All Acquirers		By 20 Leading Food Chains		
	Acquisitions	Sales of Acquired	Acquisitions	Sales of Acquired	Percent of Total Acquired Sales
		(millions of dollars)			
1949 ——	5	66	1	47	71
1950 ——	5	4	2	3	75
1951 ——	12	28	6	25	89
1952 ——	10	71	5	55	77
1953 ——	13	88	4	77	88
1954 ——	24	76	7	37	49
1955 ——	55	559	23	465	83
1956 ——	69	450	32	31	69
1957 ——	52	319	20	194	61
1958 ——	74	517	41	361	70
1959 ——	63	319	34	136	43
1960 ——	44	307	25	201	65
1961 ——	50	518	30	407	79
1962 ——	53	306	24	179	58
1963 ——	51	568	27	463	82
1964 ——	41	312	16	188	60
1965 ——	28	558	5	61	11
1966 ——	40	539	6	110	20
1967 ——	33	1,350	3	21	2
1968 ——	51	1,155	11	139	12
1969 ——	45	715	14	41	6
1970 ——	36	688	9	74	11
1971 ——	27	435	2	28	6
1972 ——	59	1,069	6	242	23
1973 ——	27	206	13	29	14
1974 ——	18	1,591	4	30	2
1975 ——	37	337	10	127	38
1976 ——	23	882	7	742	84
1977 ——	17	1,218	4	728	60
Total ——	1,062	$15,251	391	$5,520	36

SOURCE: Unpublished Data, UFCW and Bruce Marion, University of Wisconsin

proximately 70 percent of the sales generated by recently acquired firms has gone to the top 20 chains, a new wave of merger activity returning to the pace set by these chains during 1949-1964.

Since 1977 the industry has become even more concentrated. The top 20 chains have acquired almost an additional 2 percent of total sales. Table 2 lists their recent acquisitions.

Table 2
Acquisitions By The 20 Largest Food Retailers, 1978-1980

Acquiring Firm	Firm Acquired (Number of Stores)	Annual Sales (Millions of Dollars)
1978		
Southland	Shop N Go of Elmira (26)	6.0
Grand Union	Colonial (8)	1069.0
	Colonial (Remainder) Food Fair (2)	11.0
Lucky	Tampa Wholesale (47)	250.0
Albertsons	Fisher (46)	289.0
Stop & Shop	Food Fair (1)	5.5
Pick N Pay	First National	700.0
Waldbaums	Food Fair (5)	27.5
1979		
A & P	Food Fair (2)	11.0
Skagg American Stores	American Stores Food Fair (8)	3737.0 44.0
Southland	Jiff-E-Mart (Shop Rite) (65)	14.0
Grand Union	Food Fair (1)	5.5
Lucky	Scolaris (12)	50.0
Supermarkets General	Food Fair (1)	5.5
Publix	Food Fair (1)	5.5
Stop & Shop	Food Fair (6)	33.0
National Tea	Applebaums (29)	139.6
1980		
American Stores	Albertsons (1)	6.0
Grand Union	Weingarten	566.1

SOURCE: Unpublished Data, UFCW and Bruce Marion, University of Wisconsin

Every five years the U.S. Department of Commerce conducts a census of the retail food industry. The latest was taken in 1977. Table 3 shows the change in the share of grocery store sales controlled by single store and multi-store operators from 1948-1977.

Table 3
Percentage of Grocery Store Sales Made By
Single and Multi-Store Operators, 1948-1977

Number of Units	1948	1954	1958	Year 1963	1967	1972	1977	Change From 1948 1977	From 1972 1977
Single Store	58.7	51.8	47.0	43.1	38.9	32.2	28.6	−30.1	−3.6
2 to 3 Stores	3.6	4.8	4.8	5.0	5.0	5.1	5.2	+ 1.6	+ .1
4 to 10 Stores	3.2	4.0	4.2	4.8	4.8	5.7	6.6	+ 3.4	+ .9
Total Independents	65.5	60.6	56.0	52.9	48.7	43.0	40.4	−25.1	−2.6
11 to 25 Stores	3.7	3.6	3.3	4.2	5.1	4.8	5.7	+ 2.0	+ .9
26 to 50 Stores	2.6	4.0	4.4	3.2	4.1	6.1	6.1	+ 3.5	No Change
51 to 100 Stores	1.6	2.4	4.0	5.2	6.0	6.5	7.1	+ 5.5	+ .6
Total 11-100 Stores	7.0	9.9	11.7	12.6	15.3	17.4	18.9	+11.9	+1.5
Over 100 Stores	27.4	29.4	32.3	34.5	31.1	39.6	40.7	+13.3	+1.1
Total Chains	34.4	39.3	44.0	47.1	51.4	57.0	59.6	+25.2	+2.1

SOURCE: U.S. Department of Commerce, Bureau of Census

These figures reveal certain trends in the industry. The retail grocery industry is moderately concentrated. Companies operating more than 100 stores — that is the top 20 chains — controlled about 41 percent of sales in 1977. These were the biggest chains, e.g. Safeway and Kroger. They steadily gained shares at the expense of other operators — from 27.4 percent in 1948 to 40.7 percent in 1977, a gain of 13.3 percent. They are the winners in the acquisitions game. (The top 20 chains accounts for more than 85 percent of sales of companies operating more than 100 stores. See Appendix I for information on sales and profits of the largest chains.)

Single store operators, by contrast, lost more of the market than any other group — 30 percent since 1948. In the five year period from 1972 to 1977 alone single store operators lost 3.6 percent. All other operator groups gained at their expense. The chains, companies operating 11 or more stores, picked up almost three quarters of this 3.6 percent; while the multi-store "independents" those operating fewer than 11 stores took the remainder. These multi-store "independents" have gained 5 percent over the past 30 years, but still control only 11.8 percent of the market. By 1977, single store operators, once the dominant force in the market, controlled only 29 percent as compared to 59 percent in 1948. They are the losers.

Foreign-based Food Companies Enter the U.S. Market.

The new wave of mergers which began in the mid 1970's and continues through the present involves not only U.S. food chains. For the first time in the history of the retail food industry, large foreign-based companies (primarily European) are thrusting themselves into the U.S. market. The list of foreign companies is extensive (See Appendix II), representing many countries — Belgium, England, France, Germany, The Netherlands. Union estimates indicate that foreign companies control about 10 percent of the total U.S. grocery store sales.

Some of these companies are food retailers in their own countries and others are multinational conglomerates. Whether they specialize in retail food or branch out into other industries, they are among the biggest food retailers in their own countries with market shares equal to, and in most cases in excess of, the share of the U.S. market controlled by the largest domestic chains. Ahold, for example, controls almost 20 percent of the retail food sales in its homeland — The Netherlands.[1] Foreign-based corporations are buying both large and medium-sized U.S. food chains. Their entry into the U.S. market increases domestic concentration. Consequently, large international, as well as American food chains will shape our market in the years ahead.

Already, we see the influence of foreign companies. Aldi-Benner, for example, a company that is hard-line anti-union, introduced merchandising changes which have caused job loss in the U.S. A&P and Grand Union, both now foreign-controlled, followed suit. All of them have closed stores and eliminated jobs.

Why this new wave of mergers and foreign acquisitions? There are several reasons:

(1) Population growth has slowed in the U.S. and, as a result, there is no longer an expanding market from which national retailers can increase sales. Confronted with this fact, the way to increase revenues is to buy out the competition. This is also one reason why foreign companies buy into the U.S. market. Population growth in Europe has been, and is projected to be, even lower than in the U.S.; some of the European companies entering this market openly cite brighter U.S. prospects as the reason.

(2) U.S. chains are increasing their share of market because during periods of steep inflation it is cheaper to buy assets than to build them in the form of new stores and plants.

(3) Acquisition is an easier way to enter a market. The buyer gets an established company with the consumer allegiance which a new store would have to create.

---

1. *Supermarket News*, June 30, 1980.

(4) Recent studies also indicate that market concentration makes economic sense. One report shows that profits are high for chains in markets controlled by a few retailers.[2]

(5) Foreign companies have been attracted to U.S. capital markets by declines in the value of the dollar in relation to other currencies. This devaluation of the dollar makes U.S. companies a relatively good buy.

(6) In addition, many European companies see less opportunity for profit maximization in their own countries. Based on figures the union has seen, the U.S. retail food industry is more profitable than the European industry.

(7) Finally, European governments impose restriction on the construction of large-volume stores and companies are required to obtain governmental approval for new stores. The lack of substantial legal regulation in the United States makes it an attractive area for economic colonization by European firms.

It appears that current trends will continue. For example, *Progressive Grocer*, probably the most widely read trade magazine in the industry, published the results of an extensive survey among supermarket executives about the future of the retail food industry in the 1980's. Almost half the retail industry executives believe that "the top 10 chains will account for 35 percent of all retail food sales by the end of the 1980's."[3] (At present, their share stands at about 28 percent.) If the current merger wave continues their share will be even larger than 35 percent. In addition, it appears that the acquisition appetite of foreign companies will continue. An executive of the largest Belgian food retailer told *Supermarket News* that:

> Euro money will continue to flow to the U.S. because it is virtually the only place where retailers are free to pursue profitable growth. There is also the element of reducing the political risk.[4]

And recently a spokesman of Ahold, a Dutch multinational, told *Supermarket News* Ahold was planning additional acquisitions in the U.S.[5] Other foreign companies have indicated the same (e.g., Tesco in England).

Multinational Firms and Labor.

Entrance of multinationals into an industry has certain immediate effects on workers. Multinationals create economic instability for workers and weaken their bargaining power. They often disguise their operations, ownership, and control, so the worker is left with no idea who his real employer is. Multinational conglomerates have earned a

---

2. Bruce W. Marion. et al. *The Food Retailing Industry: Market, Structure, and Profits.* (New York: Praeger Publishers, 1979).

3. *Grocery Retailing in the 1980's,* Progressive Grocer.

4. *Supermarket News,* April 11, 1977.

5. *Supermarket News,* June 30, 1980.

reputation of ruthlessness from their general business behavior. They are essentially money pools manipulated by ambitious management for one purpose — to maximize profits. If a company doesn't produce an immediate profit or if it has a few bad years, they sell it. Their objective is to maximize profits in the short-term and they shift capital rapidly in order to achieve this objective. These corporations even close or sell plants and stores that are profitable if they do not meet the highest profit expectations set by some far away management. Workers are often thrown out of work and important benefits, such as pensions, are left in jeopardy.

These multinational corporations sometimes drain their foreign subsidiaries of capital and dispose of them after they have served their purpose. In fact, they are conglomerates and operate in many industries to allocate capital to the profit center. If the grass is greener in another corporate pasture, they buy the greener pasture and pull their capital out of other industries to do it. This quick change in ownership and abuse of corporate assets jeopardize employees' job security which makes closing notice language, severance pay, store closing pensions for older workers, and so on, important collective bargaining issues.

The union's collective bargaining leverage is weakened because it is dealing with a global conglomerate that can take a strike in one country or one industry while it operates elsewhere. As a response, unions need to strengthen their international labor ties to counterbalance the increased power of these international corporations.

The Complexity of Multinational Companies.

Another critical problem unions have in dealing with a multinational corporation is discerning the real policies and operation of the company. They have to discover who controls what and how control is exercised. Cavenham, which closed down 100 Colonial Stores shortly after takeover, costing 1,000 workers their jobs, is a prime example of how a multinational can disguise control and ownership. Cavenham bought three U.S. companies: Grand Union, Colonial Stores and Weingarten. These were then organized under a corporation called Cavenham (U.S.A.). Cavenham (U.S.A.) is a wholly owned subsidiary of Cavenham (U.K.), an English company, but Cavenham (U.K.) is itself wholly owned by a French holding company based in Paris, Generale Occidentale (G.O.). The kingpin in this corporate camouflage is a European entrepreneur, Sir James Goldsmith. Goldsmith is a controversial financier with dual citizenship in England and France. He has built a worldwide financial empire based on acquisition. Goldsmith himself is the chairman or director of nearly a dozen companies, banks and corporations, a majority of which are interlocked with the Goldsmith holdings.

Chart 1 traces the general flow of control between Goldsmith and Grand Union, Colonial and Weingarten.

Chart 1
Ownership of Generale Occidentale and Its U.S. Subsidiaries.

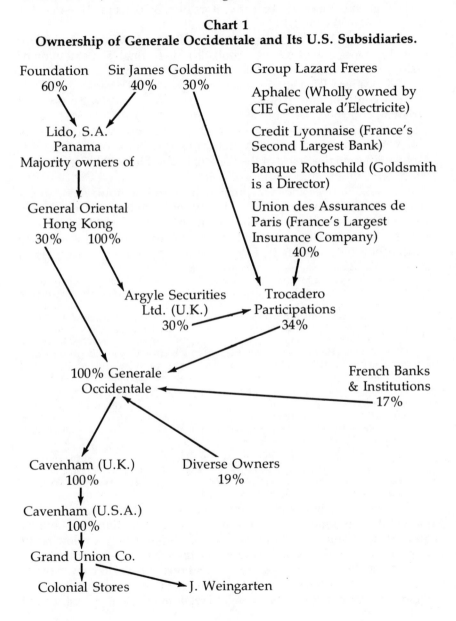

SOURCE: Wall Street Journal; Cavenham 1978-79 Annual Report

The centerpiece of Goldsmith's empire is Generale Occidentale. G.O. is owned by three financial groups but controlled by Goldsmith.

(1) French banks and other investors own 36 percent (17 percent + 19 percent on the chart).

(2) General Oriental owns 30 percent, but General Oriental is controlled by Lido, and Goldsmith controls Lido through 50 percent ownership, thereby controlling General Oriental.

(3) Trocadero Participations owns 34 percent. Trocadero is: (a) 30 percent controlled by Argyle; (Argyle is wholly owned by General Oriental, controlled by Goldsmith through Lido.); (b) 30 percent controlled by Goldsmith personally and; (c) 40 percent controlled by various French institutions, including the Bank of Rothschild. Goldsmith is on the Board of the Bank of Rothschild and is President of Trocadero, giving him additional control.

In this rather circuitous way, one man controls a multi-billion dollar financial empire and exercises a significant influence over the 20,000 union workers employed by Grand Union, Colonial and Weingarten. Goldsmith has even greater ambitions. He has indicated he wants to concentrate his interests in food retailing. According to a report in *Business Week:*

> Goldsmith is taking his Paris-based Generale Occidentale holding company out of food manufacturing and putting it even more firmly into food retailing. On April 18, he sold a string of French and British subsidiaries for about $155 million cash and stock of their companies. But his action was only the prelude to a complete exit from the food processing sector a move that Goldsmith expects to net him $250 million in cash and stock — bringing G.O.'s war chest to $400 million by midyear. He will use the fund to develop retail stores in the U.S. and to invade Argentina with modern supermarkets and he will still have plenty of spare money for acquisitions of companies or stock through is Paris-based Banque-Occidentale pour L'Industrie.

> While unloading food makers in Europe, Goldsmith is speeding G.O.'s continued drive into U.S. supermarket retailing. Goldsmith is also preparing to join the rush to narrow-range no-frills, food merchandising under his newly created Basic Food Warehouses banner. He claims the new formula stores will. . . raise G.O.'s retailing division sales by an extra $1 billion.

> Goldsmith is already eyeing several new acquisitions and Paris financial analysts are convinced he is preparing a major coup. "What he has done so far is just window dressing," says one. "His real plans are hidden and I am expecting him to do something more exotic and adventurous."[6]

This short case study illustrates the behavior of multinational conglomerates. In a global search to maximize profits, they quickly buy and sell into and out of industries, they immediately exploit profit opportunities and disguise as much of their business as possible.

Why do they camouflage their operations? What do they have to hide? In Goldsmith's own words, it is to insure his freedom. The *Wall Street Journal* quoted him as saying: "Freedom of action is vital. I want

---

6. *Business Week,* May 5, 1980, p. 58.

to act without asking people.'"[7] And in *Forbes:* "I don't owe money to the banks. I'm not running for office. I'm not a public company. I don't give a damn what anybody says. I'm going to do what I think is right. Not many people have that luxury."[8] Goldsmith has, by design, situated his financial power base in France because business regulation and surveillance there are lenient. His actions typify the behavior of multinational corporations which are not accountable to workers in either their home country or their host country.

In the face of these developments, unions must protect themselves by strengthening international labor ties and coordinating their bargaining efforts. For example, local unions that have agreements with foreign-controlled corporations and large U.S. corporate chains should meet regularly to discuss common problems and review corporate policies.

Independent Operators.

Employer representatives, in print and across the bargaining table, argue that the "independents", those companies that operate less than 11 stores, are taking business away from the big chains and for this reason the union should give the chains a break in wage rates to match the lower rates in the "independents".

The "independents" operating more than one store are growing but at the expense of the single store companies rather than large national chains. Furthermore, growth of multi-store "independents" has not been that large. Today they have about 12 percent of the market compared with 10 percent in 1967. Medium-size chains (those operating 11-50 stores) are also growing, but their growth, likewise, has been at the expense of single store operators.

Nevertheless "independents" are fierce competitors of the chains. "Independents" as a group are more profitable than both large national chains and the industry as a whole. In 1978, for example, "independents" earned a before-tax profit on sales of 2.2 percent, compared with 1.8 percent for the big chains (more than 100 stores) and 1.7 percent for the industry as a whole. Before-tax profits are more meaningful for comparison because "independent" owners often derive personal and family tax advantages from their business operations. "Independents" earn a higher return than chains in spite of the fact that their gross margin is lower. In other words, the spread between the price an "independent" pays for its groceries and the price it charges is actually less than that of the chains, but the profit the "independent" retains out of the smaller margin is higher.

Most "independents" draw competitive strength from their affiliation with large national food wholesalers. About 85 percent of all food

---

7. *Wall Street Journal,* May 16, 1980.
8. *Forbes,* September 17, 1979, p. 41.

sales by the "independents" are made by retailers who are affiliated with wholesalers. In this affiliation the wholesaler provides the support services which national or regional chains offer their stores. For example, Super Valu, one of the nation's biggest wholesalers, makes the following services available: computerized site selection; retail accounting; store engineering and design; consumer research; market analysis; advertising and promotion; field rep counseling; financing; group insurance; electronic data processing and computerized inventory control; tax counseling and estate planning; financial and budget planning; a labor relations advisory service and merchandising assistance in such areas as general merchandise, bakery, deli, meat, produce, dairy, grocery and frozen food. And, of course, the wholesalers pass along the economy-of-scale that big chains enjoy. We have to understand that when we refer to the "independent" we are not thinking about a lone operator who survives only by his wits and resourcefulness. We are really considering a large corporate power which keeps that retailer in business. The wholesaler is, in effect, a banker for the "independents". The wholesaler buys up stores, finds operators to lease them and then sells groceries to these operators.

Major wholesalers are, in fact, big corporations and they are very profitable — more so than the retailers they support. In 1978, for example, the five largest wholesalers earned a before-tax return on net worth of 39 percent compared with 36.3 percent for all independent retailers. They compare in size with the largest national retail food chains.

The conclusion to be drawn from this examination of the evidence is that food industry employees' demands for decent wages and working conditions are not unreasonable assaults on marginal operations. They can be passed back to wholesalers by their "independents" or the "independents" themselves can pay pattern wages and benefits because they are among the most profitable operators in the industry.

Labor and Technology
Scanners.

Changes in corporate structure and ownership are only part of the new environment in the retail food industry. The industry is experiencing revolutionary technological change in food retailing that will affect not only workers but also consumers. The retail food industry has adopted a new motto — "In code we trust". The code to which they refer is the Universal Product Code (UPC), a code written in bars that can be read only by electronic scanner/computers. Scanners are not in operation in more than 2,200 retail food stores across the country — approximately 7 percent of the nation's 33,000 supermarkets. The pace of installations has picked up sharply; additional stores are being converted at the rate of 100 per month. Large chains such as Winn-Dixie, Publix, Kroger, and Giant have all made policy decisions to use scanners.

A survey of its members by the Food Marketing Institute indicates that by the end of 1982 approximately one-third of all supermarkets will be converted. (The results of the survey are shown in Table 4.)

Table 4
Projected Scanning Installations
(percent)

Stores with scanning installations by end of 1981	21.0
Stores with scanning installations by end of 1982	30.7

SOURCE: *The Food Marketing Industry Speaks,* 1980 Food Marketing Institute, Washington, D.C.

At this rate the entire industry will be converted before the end of the 1980's. Conversion so far would be even greater if not for shortages resulting from scanning manufacturers' inability to produce equipment fast enough to keep up with demand. But these shortages will be eliminated now that the industry has clearly indicated the experimental stage is over and it wants full-scale conversion.

Retailers are now rushing to install scanners for a number of reasons. Primary among them is the elmination of jobs to increase corporate profits sharply. Scanners will cut and reshape the work. They reduce checkers' hours because they can check out customers more quickly and they automatically order inventory, further reducing the need for labor. Scanners also eliminate clerks' work because items don't have to be individually marked or repriced. In addition to these direct applications, scanner computers can be used to reduce store hours in every department because the computer can schedule work hours to employ as few workers as possible. Also, management is able to set work standards by tapping the computer's mechanical, mathematical brain to determine how long a job should take and thereby increase management's ability to monitor worker movements on the job. The ways in which scanning operations were used in 1980 is shown in Table 5.

Table 5
Use of Scanning Data, 1980

Use	Percent
Work Schedules	65.6
Coupon Accounting	57.0
Shrink Analysis	49.2
Shelf Allocation	12.6

SOURCE: *The Food Marketing Industry Speaks,* 1980 Food Marketing Institute, Washington, D.C.

The immediate, ongoing and pressing need of the union is to determine the precise impact of this technology on jobs — how many jobs are lost, how work is reshaped. In order to do that the union must have data on employment and hours in stores being converted to scanners. In every bargaining situation where the union has asked for data, however, the companies refused to provide the information. In these instances, the union filed unfair labor charges and was upheld. The data have still not been received, however, although the union is continuing its legal pursuit. (Appendix II contains a model union bargaining demand for information regarding scanning equipment.)

Another aspect of this technology which is important for unions is that scanners will sharply increase retailers' profits. According to the Food Marketing Institute: "Based on industry results achieved to date, a well run scanning installation can generate a net return of 1 percent of sales."[9] Historically, net profit margins in the industry have averaged about 1 percent. In other words, the industry itself is predicting that profits can be doubled as a result of scanner installation. The union believes industry employees should share in these savings across the bargaining table, in addition to protecting themselves from a slash in jobs and hours. These should be the union's twin objectives as it comes face-to-face with scanner technology.

Boxed Beef.

The second technological change of importance to workers is boxed beef. In 1975 most beef reached the back door of the retail store in carcass form. Retail butchers broke down the carcass, took out the bone, removed fat and waste, prepared the consumer-ready cuts and put the beef in the meat case — just as they had always done. Today, however, most beef enters the store already cut. It's called boxed beef. Meat cutters open the box, take out a primal or subprimal piece and cut away the cry-o-vac (acrylic) seal. Because the piece of meat has already been boned or trimmed, the meat cutter makes only one or two cuts with the saw or knife and it is ready for the meat case. Nine boxes hold a whole beef carcass, and hamburger comes already rough-ground in a tube.

This change in the way fresh beef comes to market already has cost at least 10,000 meat cutting jobs and it has not yet run its full course. These 10,000-plus jobs have been lost in retail-owned central cutting plants, wholesale beef markets across the country and retail stores. The union has members in all these sectors. In 1974, for example, the union had 42 major retailer-owned central cutting plants under contract, all

9. *Guide to Scanning,* The Food Marketing Institute.

employing skilled meat cutters. By 1980 eight of these plants were closed and seven more converted to boxed beef warehouses. Skilled jobs disappeared with the plants. Meat now comes directly from packing plants where the beef is slaughtered, broken down, packaged and boxed.

The union also has thousands of meat cutter members working in wholesale markets. These "independent" wholesalers buy beef carcasses and break them down into subprimals and portion-cuts for retailers, hotels, restaurants, hospitals, and universities. Since 1974, in just the four cities of Boston, New York, Chicago, and Los Angeles, almost 4,000 jobs have been lost. Meat that used to be cut in these wholesale markets is now cut in packing plants where the beef is slaughtered.

Even before this first stage of boxed beef technology runs its course a second stage has begun. A major meat packer, MBPXL (known as Missouri Beef and owned by Cargill), reduces subprimal cuts at the packing plant into consumer-ready cuts. The retail store butcher does not open the cry-o-vac bag to cut the meat. All he does is take it out of the box and put it in the meat case and it is ready for the consumer to buy. He doesn't even price the package. In July 1980 Hi-Speed Checkweight Company unveiled a machine that represents a major breakthrough in scanning variable weight items like meat. It weighs and prints-out the price on a single label and attaches a Universal Product Code that the scanner at the checkout can read. This is the next stage of the technology that will reach stores and wholesale markets. Iowa Beef Processors, the largest beef packer in the world, is now perfecting this technology so that any cut of beef can be made consumer-ready at the packing plant. As this process is implemented, thousands of meat cutters will be affected.

The technology being described reduces skilled retail butchers to stocking the meat case which is no different from stocking cans in the grocery section of the store. As the skill is removed from the meat cutter's job, management will attempt to bargain down their wage levels. This is an important point because retail meat cutters' wages, now among the highest in the store, help raise all wage rates by setting the upper range of earnings toward which the others are aimed. Current skill requirements of the job give workers greater bargaining leverage than would otherwise be the case. Table 6 lists relative wages for retail store job classifications based on journeyman meat cutter earnings.

Table 6
Index of Wage Rates for Selected Job Classifications
Effective Jan. 1, 1980

Job Classification	As a Ratio of Journeyman Meat Cutter Wages (percent)
Journeyman Meat Cutter	100.0
Wrapper/Weigher	85.0
Head Cashier	92.0
Journeyman Clerk	85.0

Why has boxed beef technology developed so rapidly? One of the most important reasons is that a few companies, principally Iowa Beef and Missouri Beef, have virtual monopoly control over fresh beef production. These two packers alone slaughter over one-third of the "choice" fat cattle and produce close to 50 percent of the nation's boxed beef. They are so big they dictate how beef is brought to market — it reaches the marketplace as boxed beef and on their terms. They box or further process beef because there is more profit in processing than in slaughter. By controlling processing, they control the profit center of the industry. The union must deal with this new monopoly power in packing by establishing a long-term collective bargaining policy in this area and by taking immediate action to protect its presence in the meat departments, cutting plants and wholesale houses.

Store Design.
Boxed beef is an example of how new ideas in the way food is processed and merchandised significantly affect the structure of the retail food industry and particularly the employment levels and job content for workers. Current trends in store design, such as the box store, limited assortment store and the super store, further illustrate this relationship.

While the box store and super store are opposites as merchandising concepts, they have one important thing in common — they employ fewer total workers. Both methods of merchandising sharply increase store volume without increasing the number of workers or total hours needed to operate the store. Comparing the super store with a conventional supermarket illustrates the point. The average super store employs approximately 15 percent fewer workers per dollar of sales than the average conventional store. For every $20,000 worth of weekly sales there are seven employees in the super store, compared to eight employees in a conventional store. A store doing $54,000 a week business would require nine employees for every $20,000 in sales. To put it another way, one super store employs 10 fewer workers than two average size stores whose combined sales equal that of the super store.

Not only do the super stores require fewer employees, they also employ more part-time workers. Fifty-four percent of the hours worked in an average super store are part-time hours compared with 52 percent in the average conventional store. Box stores require less than half the manhours of an average store, and all the work in the box store is done by part-time personnel. Other changes related to store design are also reducing hours: for example, cut-case displays, wheel-in modules, and prebuilt palletized displays. The trend is clearly toward high-volume, low-hours, and more part-time help.

In addition to the super store and the box store, employees are confronting the closed store. Store closings also result from technological change and change in market concentration and structure. (Appendix III reports the findings of a UFCW survey of plant closings, conversions and phasedowns during 1974-1980.) High-volume stores like the super and the box are less labor intensive and more capital efficient — in other words, they are more profitable. For this reason, the industry, and specifically the big chains, want to convert to the high-volume store. Their objective, in a word, is to do more business with fewer stores. Just as major oil companies are closing gasoline stations, big food chains are closing stores. The industry estimates there are still approximately 20 percent more supermarkets than necessary to satisfy consumer demand.[10] If these stores were to close 250,000 or more workers would lose their jobs. Unions should negotiate some control over store closings as well as the changeover to scanners and boxed beef. For example, the union should retain bargaining rights when a company shuts two or three stores and opens a super store and should also negotiate job protection in the form of transfer rights and notice of closing.

Industry's Optimistic Outlook.

Across the bargaining table and in the public forum, executives of the retail food industry are engaging in a great deal of pessimistic talk about the future of the industry. They complain about slow growth, low productivity, high energy and labor costs and competition. Privately, however, they are sizing up the future of the industry in a different way. Industry executives see the 1980's as a decade of profitable growth in which the supermarket will be transformed by capital intensive innovations involving scanning and other technological changes. Their views were revealed in a 1980 *Progressive Grocer* survey of facts and opinions about the retail food industry in the new decade.

---

10. *Chain Store Age/Supermarkets*, January, 1980.

When *Progressive Grocer* asked chain store executives and independent retail food store executives how they felt about prospects of the
entire grocery retailing industry the results showed three-quarters of
all these executives were "optimistic." When asked further how they
felt about prospects for their own company, more than 90 percent of
them were "optimistic." They said:

> We are entering an era of relatively young household families in the expansive phase
> of a life cycle, the years of child bearing and rearing, home acquisition, and rising
> incomes. These people are traditionally among the supermarkets most free spend-
> ing customers.

In other words, the 1980's will be a decade in which many new families
are formed and this will increase supermarket sales. Therefore, the
survey indicates, industry executives are very optimistic that real
growth will resume perhaps at an annual rate of 4 percent.

And what do they say privately about productivity and labor costs?
Here, industry exectuvies are also confident.

> Overall, operators are looking into the future employment picture with optimism
> and confidence that productivity will improve to reflect technological advances, to
> help offset increasing labor costs somewhat.

This is because, they believe, scanning will take over the industry,
improve productivity and increase profits. The survey highlights the
opinion of one executive who analyzed:

> Quite simply any supermarket operator without scanning in the 1980's may not be
> around to see the beginning of the 1990's. Skeptics, nowadays, are few and far
> between as both hard and soft productivity gains by scanning have been repeatedly
> documented.

Productivity will also improve as a result of other important
technological changes. In addition to scanning, these executives note,
for example, that "drop shipments of prebuilt palletized special displays will be common in larger supers." These cut-case displays will
obviously elminate manual stocking. A second way they intend to
reduce labor costs is to hire more part-time workers. Almost two-thirds
of all the executives surveyed believe, "there will be more part-time
employees in supermarkets." These executives also believe that high
energy costs can be controlled. "A lot of small incremental steps are
being taken and the accumulation effects will pay off in a 25 percent or
more reduction in energy use in the 1980's," they say. They also intend
to reduce energy costs by operating fewer hours. "A trend toward
fewer hours of operation, already noticeable, will accelerate," the
survey notes. This, of course, means fewer hours of work.

There will be further concentration by the major companies in this
decade. The market strategy of the major chains apparently is to
concentrate on highly populated urban areas. The survey concludes:

> By the close of the decade, 80% of all chain outlets are apt to be in urban and highly
> populated suburban areas leaving the lightly settled sections to independents. That
> would be consistent with the chain strategy of building super stores that require
> heavy customer traffic and huge weekly volume. And it would mean that chains will

ultimately be competing mainly against other chains in the major metropolitan area while independents will be going predominantly against other independents out in the countryside.[11]

The retail executives who forecast hard times in the food industry point to failing companies like A&P, Food Fair and First National as examples of the condition of the whole industry. But, in fact, these companies are the victims of the big chains that introduced the larger, higher volume stores and the various technological changes discussed here as the standards of operating efficiency for the industry. It is they who created the competitive environment resulting in the current fierce battle over market shares. Weak companies whether they are large or small, simply fall victim to this corporate cannibalism.

A&P is the major example. In the 1970's, the company delayed too long in remodeling, enlarging and relocating small and poorly kept stores. The economies of the competition's bigger stores (i.e., the change in technology) and the consumer's preference for cleaner and newer stores that were also closer to home sent A&P into a tailspin. Observing these management blunders and seeing the increasing battle over market shares by the big U.S. chains, (resulting in the increase in concentration), Tengelmann, the West German retail grocer, moved in to salvage A&P's remaining markets. Under Tengelmann control, nearly 2,000 A&P stores have been closed and approximately 50,000 workers, the majority of them union members, have lost their jobs, victims of mismanagement. It is clear to the union that in store-closing situations like these it should not attempt to salvage these companies and the jobs they provide with wage cuts. In fact, the stores may be in the process of being sold with new buyers actually dictating the terms of the wage cuts. The union cannot be expected to save these companies from management's mistakes.

Conclusion

Retail food is not a sick or failing industry. Profits have been very respectable. The 23 largest chains, excluding A&P and Food Fair, showed a net profit on stockholders' equity (Wall Street's acid test of profitability) of 15.7 percent in 1979. This was close to the average return on equity of 15.9 percent reported by *Fortune* Magazine in 1979 for the 500 largest corporations in the nation and was better than the return on equity for the country's largest food manufacturers (14.4 percent).

The union shares the optimism of the food industry executives interviewed by *Progressive Grocer*, and expects its members to receive a fair share of the coming prosperity. Employees should not subsidize the prosoperity of the industry or allow inflation to cut real wages or

---

11. *Grocery Retailing in the 1980's*, Progressive Grocer, 1980.

technology to eliminate and downgrade jobs. Nor should they allow themselves to fall victim to the cutthroat investment strategies of powerful and profitable multinational corporations. Vital issues such as plant closings and the introduction of new technology should be negotiated by both labor and management. By engaging in aggressive and creative collective bargaining with its new adversaries, the union will be able to protect its members and shape the changes sweeping across the retail food industry so that they benefit rather than harm workers.

Appendix I
Sales and Profits of 23 of the Top 25 Retail
Food Chains, 1976-1979[1]

Year/Chains[2]	Sales (a)	Net Income (b)	Net Worth (c)	Return on Equity (b÷c)
	(thousands of dollars)			
1979	$78,781,071	$637,392	$5,663,659	11.25%
Excluding A&P and Food Fair	70,604,669	852,278	5,431,276	15.69%
1978	71,852,216	607,790	5,397,469	11.26%
Excluding A&P and Food Fair	61,960,637	752,229	4,952,862	15.25%
1977	63,802,087	584,285	5,033,890	11.61%
Excluding A&P and Food Fair	54,076,808	577,848	4,442,108	13.01%
1976	59,207,597	511,602	4,693,713	10.90%
Excluding A&P and Food Fair	49,464,703	493,993	4,104,465	12.04%

1. Excludes Von's Grocery Company and Ralph's Grocery Company, two of the largest 25 chains, but for which figures are unavailable.
2. Table excludes net worth on Pick'n'Pay Supermarkets, which was merged into First National Supermarkets, and therefore overstates the return on equity figures for 1976-77 by approximately 0.05 percent.

SOURCE: Moody's Industrial Manual, Standard and Poor's Corporation Records; individual company reports.

Appendix II
U.S. Companies Acquired by Foreign Buyers

U.S. Company Acquired	Foreign Buyer	1979 Sales of Acquired Firm	Number of Employees of Acquired U.S. Firm
Grand Union	Cavenham Limited-Subsidiary of Generale Occidentale (U.K. & France)	3,137,612,000	33,000
Colonial Stores	Same as Above	N/A	N/A
J. Weingarten	Same As Above	566,188,000	6,500
Alterman Foods	Delhaize Freres et cie de Lion (Belgium)	435,999,000	3,600
Foodtown (N.C.)	Same as Above	415,973,000	2,450
Bi-Lo (S.C.)	Ahold (The Netherlands)	604,800,000	5,500
Red Foods Chattanooga, TN	Promodes (France)	239,000,000	2,400
Furr's	Rene Leibrand (West Germany)	616,000	8,000
Fed-Mart San Diego, CA	Hugo Mann Enterprise (West Germany)	460,000,000	9,215
Kohl's Milwaukee, WI	Brown and Williamson-Subsidiary of B.A.T. Industries Limited (United Kingdom)	492,000,000	4,000
A & P	Tengelmann (West Germany)	6,684,179,000	72,000
Aldi-Benner	Albrecht (West Germany)	N/A	N/A

Appendix III
Model Union Bargaining Demand
for Information Regarding Scanning Equipment

The union requests the following information in connection with the installation of scanning equipment in your stores. In addition to that information, we are requesting the following data:

(1) We will need a complete list of all stores in the bargaining unit which are equipped with front-end scanners and a list of scanner stores where item prices have been removed either partially or completely.

(2) In order to objectively determine the impact of scanners and prices-off, it will be necessary to review the hours of operation before installation of the scanners and/or removal of item prices. For this reason, we are asking for information on the attached sheet marked Attachment No. 1. We need this information *broken out separately for each store in the bargaining unit*. To minimize the demand for data, we are requesting this information for each store for the *third full week* in the months of January, April, July and October; for the last three years and for each of these weeks through the duration of our current collective bargaining agreement.

(3) We need information outlined on Attachment No. 2. Project this data over whatever phase-in periods for the scanners and/or removal of item prices, are planned and when the changes are fully operational. In other words, if you plan to phase in the new program over a six month period, project the data during this period. If you plan to be fully operational after six months, project the data at that time.

In addition to this information, we would like to know specifically what additional work would be created as a result of the changes contemplated. For example, will work be created which involves checking shelf-marked prices and remaining items individually priced against prices in the computer files? Also, specifically what retraining opportunities will be made available to the bargaining unit employees?

Our collective bargaining agreement with your company clearly obligates you to bargain with the union with respect to the proposed changes. All of the information we are requesting is highly relevant and material to effects on our members and we are requesting that this information be provided immediately so that we can begin bargaining.

Appendix IV
Plant Closings, Conversions and Phasedowns, 1974-1980

The UFCW has completed an analysis of operations in retail-owned central meat cutting plants under contract with the union. We examined: (1) total plant employment; (2) volume of beef carcasses being fabricated and (3) the volume of boxed beef moving through the plants. Where it was known, we also identified the packer(s) supplying the central cutting plant.

This survey is a repeat of one the union did of the same cutting plants in 1974. The purpose of the 1980 survey is to determine the impact of boxed beef technology on the operations of these cutting plants over the six-year period. A comparison of the two surveys shows the following:

(1) By 1980, eight of the 42 plants in operation in 1974 were closed: 19 percent of the original number. Seven companies operated the eight closed plants; most of the closings occurred in the two years up to 1980.

Retail Central Cutting Plants Closed Since 1974

Company	Location	Date of Closing
Safeway	Phoenix, AZ	6-80
Safeway	Washington, D.C.	5-80
National Tea	Denver, CO	12-74
Grand Union	Washington, D.C.	7-78
Giant	Washington, D.C.	7-78
Shop Rite	Dallas, TX	1-79
Liberal	Dayton, OH	6-80
A&P	New Orleans, LA	11-79

(2) Seven other plants were converted from carcass beef fabrication to boxed beef warehouses. As a result, many skilled meat cutters' jobs and those related to carcass fabrication were eliminated. Most conversions took place in 1979-1980. These seven closed plants have been converted to warehouses with boxed beef coming in one door and being shipped out to retail stores through another.

Retail Central Cutting Plants Converted to Boxed Beef Warehouses

Company	Location
Allied	Detroit, MI
Chatham	Detroit, MI
A&P	Charlotte, NC
Safeway	Richmond, CA
Safeway	Portland, OR
Pathmark	Little Falls, NJ
Wakefern	Little Falls, NJ

(3) The union lost 1,313 jobs as a result of these eight plant closings and seven plant conversions — 766 from the closings; 547 in the conversions. In 1974 there were 4,671 workers employed in the 42 central cutting plants operating at that time. The union lost 28 percent of the 1974 work force.

(4) Certain retail chains have sharply reduced their central cutting operations. For example, in 1974 Safeway operated nine plants employing 1,366 workers processing 16,255 head of cattle per week. By 1980 the company had closed two plants (Washington, D.C. and Phoenix, AZ) and converted two others to warehouses (Richmond, CA and Portland, OR). This left only five plants which employed 37 percent fewer workers producing 42 percent less fabricated beef than in 1974.

Safeway Cutting Plant Operations, 1980-1974

	1980	1974	Difference 1980/1974
Number of Plants	5	9	-4 (44%)
Number of Production Workers Employed	858	1,366	-508 (37%)
Number of Head of Cattle Fabricated Weekly	9,460	16,255	-6,795 (42%)

Of the 20 companies operating in 1974 only three increased carcass fabrication production (Kroger, Lucky's and King Sooper). The remaining 17 had either reduced or stopped production.

Impact of Boxed Beef on Wholesale Beef Fabrication

U.F.C.W.'s 1980 study analyzed the impact of boxed beef on central cutting plant operations and also reviewed U.F.C.W. employment in four major wholesale beef centers across the country: New York, Boston, Chicago and Los Angeles. Although there are many other wholesale markets in the country, these are the major ones and therefore representative of what is taking place in the others.

In 1974, 8,230 U.F.C.W. members were employed in these four wholesaling centers. By 1980 we had only 4,505 members. We had lost 3,725, or 45 percent, of our membership. This loss resulted from companies going out of business and plants being shut down.

In addition, jobs have been lost at retail stores. We don't have exact survey figures for 1974 and 1980 as we do for cutting plants and wholesale houses. But we know jobs are disappearing based on our daily observation of meat department operations. We estimate a loss of at least 5,000 retail store jobs during 1974-1980, and this is probably a conservative figure. The combined loss of membership in these three areas is therefore at least 10,000.

In addition, we also examined 29 current cutting plant agreements on file in the U.F.C.W. Research Office. Less than half of them provide severence pay, notice of closing or transfer rights in the event of plant closing or reduction.

Changing Competitive and Technology Environments in Telecommunications

George Kohl

Introduction

The telephone sits on top of a complex set of technical and social relationships. It is a technological wonder which allows us and millions of others to talk simultaneously via electronic signals over copper wires. As we talk, electronic waves move from our home telephones through two wires out into the street, from there to bigger cables, to central switching locations, (and then perhaps to a microwave tower or a satellite and back to earth to another central office) to wires in the street again and into the home of our choice. Complex machinery and electronic codes direct our call to its proper destination.

The technological complexity on which telephone service is based is not the only invisible dimension of the telecommunications network. The lives and work of the million plus employees who keep the system functioning are hidden from general view as well. Their work, and how they relate to the machines making up the system, to the public they provide with service and to the company which employs them constitute an equally complex social system.

There are a number of reasons to examine these systems more closely. First, the telecommunications industry provides a good case study of the general impact of technology. As technological change rapidly transforms the industry, it shatters old work patterns and creates new industrial possibilities. Telephone is a classic example of what happens when there is a wholesale introduction of new chip technology and management reorganizes the production process to

George Kohl is an economist in the Research Department, Communications Workers of America

utilize it. As this technology is brought on line in many other industries, the experiences of telecommunications workers provide important insights for labor in general.

Second, the convergence of data processing and telecommunications makes new production methods possible in other industries which will have a profound effect on the workforce. Numerical control programs can be written in Houston and flashed daily over telecommunications systems to Brazil to control machine tools building goods for the U.S. market. Similarly, design programs for an auto manufacturer on strike were sent to another facility so that production could continue with minimal interruption.[1] With the development of new chip equipment capable of calculating and communication, NCR claims to have reduced its manufacturing workforce dramatically and permanently because fewer parts are required in the more sophisticated machines.[2] These industrial possibilities exist because of new developments in technology — much of it in the telecommunications industry.

These current technical changes will lead to fundamental shifts in society, as did the automobile and the assembly line. These inventions and innovations spawned a whole different way of life — suburbs and shopping centers — and a new set of labor relations — mass production and industrial unions. The potential for social and industrial change inherent in today's technology is just as great.

Recent Developments in Telecommunications

Data processing and telecommunications' paths first crossed soon after the computer was invented. Data processing originally occurred in huge machines having less computing power than today's home computers. It was an unregulated industry that processed information via digital (on-off) signals controlled electronically. Its connection to telecommunications was the occasional use of phone lines as a conduit for its electrical messages. The basic telephone system was a regulated utility carrying voices which were coded as electrical waves. Transmission of phone signals was controlled electromechanically. Switches clicked on and off directing electrical waves through a maze of devices in order to make the proper connections.

Almost as soon as the computer was invented it was put to work in the telephone industry. First, computers were slowly integrated into

---

1. Harley Shaiken, "Brave New World of Work in Auto," *In These Times,* September 16-25, 1979.

2. Colin Norman, "Microelectronics at Work: Productivity and Jobs in the World Economy," World Watch Paper #39.

the operations of the telephone network: computer controlled switches directed traffic to insure correct connections; customer bills were calculated and printed by computers and eventually network tests and repairs were also computerized.

Second, as the data processing industry grew, large corporate users wanted to send messages from one computer to another. Originally this was accomplished by modulating computer digital signals or disguising them so that they seemed to be a voice to the phone company's analog equipment. This system isn't ideal for computer communications, being slower and less accurate than direct transmission of digital signals. As the frequency of computer transmission increased, new specialized equipment or data networks were developd to handle the special digital signals of computers more economically.

With the development of the transistor at Bell Labs, the potentially close relationship between data processing and telephone became evident. Government regulators and the infant data processing industry feared the competitive impact of the vast resources of the telephone company. A government anti-trust suit against AT&T was settled in 1956 with the company's agreement to stay out of the budding data processing business in order to maintain its monopoly status in telephone.

In the late 1960s, with computer use of (and in) telecommunications systems growing, the FCC examined both telecommunications and data processing to determine if government regulation was needed. In its first computer inquiry, the Commission concluded that data processing per se was distinct from the data processing equipment used to control message switching in the telecommunications network. It ruled therefore that the latter need not be regulated. Unregulated data processing activities could be pursued by regulated telephone companies as long as this was done by an arms-length subsidiary of the regulated parent firm. But, the FCC added, the Bell System was prohibited from such activities by the 1956 Consent Decree.[3]

The logic of the FCC was that communications systems simply provided the conduit for data processing, which was the actual manipulation of data. But, as the conduit became more complex and sophisticated, it was able to, and eventually had to, manipulate data in order to transmit it. The conduit-processor distinction gradually became blurred. So blurred in fact that 15 years later in a second inquiry, the FCC declared it could no longer distinquish between data proces-

---

3. Final Order Civil Action No. 17-49, *U.S. vs. Western Electric and AT&T*, January 24, 1956.

sing and common telephone service utilizing computers. In a sweeping ruling, the Commission concluded that the entire industry should be deregulated.[4]

AT&T and Competition in Telecommunications

AT&T is the dominant telephone company in the U.S. Any discussion of the industry must deal with this unique monopoly, which is governmentally-regulated but has also been the target of several antitrust suits initiated by the government. The 1956 Consent Decree was designed to limit Bell's competitive impact, but clients and customers still accused the company of obstructing the development of new telecommunications products. AT&T, critics charged, acted like a traditional monopoly: no longer innovative or inventive, but protecting its turf and fighting other firms who tried to invade its domain. The Hush-a-phone story is often used to make this point. In 1955, the FCC licensed Hush-a-phone, a gadget that slipped over the telephone mouthpiece to quiet background noise and prevent others from hearing conversations. AT&T fought this attachment as a violation of its monopoly rights. No one, it claimed, could attach a foreign gadget to Bell lines. AT&T appealed the FCC ruling and won, protecting its proprietary right to attach equipment to phone lines and thereby preserving the network in the "national interest."

Despite this zealous guarding of the telephone network, technological changes made new services possible, and big business customers demanded new equipment. Pressures for change increased and challenges to the Bell System continued.

The year 1968 marked the dawn of the competitive era in telecommunications signaled by the Federal Communications Commission's Carterphone decision. Carterphone is a piece of equipment which allows a caller from a mobile radio phone to talk to a party over Bell lines. The question again was who could attach equipment to the nation's phone system. In this order the Commission ruled that Bell could not prevent customers from attaching non-Bell equipment to its phone lines. The implications of the ruling were clearly greater than the Carterphone product. Now any company could manufacture and market equipment to attach to the nation's phone system. But the ability to attach equipment to the telephone network didn't change the industry overnight. The floodgates were opened but competition was still only a possibility, not yet a reality. Business pressures for fundamental changes in the system increased and AT&T's critics continued to chastise Bell for its lack of innovation and suppression of various forms of technological change.

---

4. Federal Communications Commission, 47CFK Part 64 Docket 20828 FCC80-189, Federal Register Vol. 45, No. 94, 51380, p. 31319.

As data processing became a part of everyday life in America, large corporate data users wanted to transmit digital signals over the telephone lines to take advantage of higher transmission speeds and cleaner signals. In response to this demand a new company, Datatran, proposed to the FCC that it operate a nationwide microwave digital communications network specifically designed to carry only data signals. The Datatran challenge triggered a Herculean response by AT&T. It rushed to market its own version of a specialized data transmission network priced at 40 percent less than the service offered by Datatran. Although AT&T was accused of predatory pricing, its service took hold and drove Datatran out of business.

The Datatran story generally serves two purposes: to show how Bell ignores the demands of customers because it is a monopoly; and to show how AT&T's resources can be mobilized against smaller, more innovative competitors in order to protect its monopoly position. However, there is a more basic lesson here than who wins the high stakes race to build a data network. More important is the insight it provides into the dynamics of technological change. In this case, changes in big business operations created a new demand, forcing the reallocation of resources into new technology to meet that demand.

The Collins Radio story is also used to describe Bell's indifferent attitude towards innovation. Again, it illustrates how technology is developed. In 1966 the Airline Coordinating Committee for Telecommunications Services (ACCTS) was formed to create industry specifications for telephone service. All businesses, including airline reservation offices, which have a large number of incoming calls need an automatic call director to queue and distribute the calls. Internal airline projections showed that the then-present generation of call directors would be overloaded and a new one needed. A call director is basically a small computer programmed to store and direct calls. It constantly polls sales agents' phone lines and automatically connects the next waiting call as soon as a line is free. According to the recently settled Justice Department anti-trust suit, ACCTS discussed its telecommunications needs with AT&T in 1968.[7] The phone company indicated a new call director system could be in place by 1975, but would not promise it. Later, in 1972, AT&T told ACCTS it would not make a final decision on the matter until 1976 and, even then, the new system would not be ready until 1980.

Meanwhile, Continental Airlines, a member of ACCTS, approached Collins Radio in August, 1971 to see if Collins could solve the industry's problem. Indeed it could. Several months later Collins personnel demonstrated the new machine to Continental and in July, 1973 Continental agreed to buy one for its Houston office. Three years after the initial discussions a Collins Radio call director was cut-in to the Bell lines at the Houston location.

The parallels in these two stories are striking. In each case changing communication needs of big business forced the develoment of new technology. In each, Bell's monopoly position explains its initial reluctance to deliver the new products or services. Each innovation was delivered by a lean and hungry competitor of Bell, while the Bell system did not respond. In each instance also, the new equipment was based on computer, microchip technology.

In one example an increasing use of computers resulted in a new telecommunications market in data transmission that Datatran rushed to fill. Datatran anticipated a demand and created a new technology to meet it. In the other case, Collins Radio developed an important technology at the request of users with increasing traffic loads. This development of new technology and exploitation of new markets have been far from orderly. In some cases the potential uses of the new technology far outstrip the actual consumer demand and firms must try to create new markets for the new services.[5] At the same time there is a consensus that a potential market exists for products that are not yet developed, a potential market so large and lucrative that whichever firm develops, introduces and markets the hardware will become a giant.[6]

Demand by big business for expanded services has also increased the rate of technological change. A limited offering of a computer transmission network may be attractive to a large company. But if it cannot reach every isolated unit of the firm, it has no value. This is particularly important for multinational corporations which have special needs to coordinate, plan and control their scattered operations. The effect then is for the needs of business to push the development of networks even more rapidly than before.

---

5. For instance, while electronic mail is technically feasible, because office equipment and transmission networks are in place, its use is far from universal. Similarly the potential profits in data communications spawned new transmission networks like MCI and SBS which have been forced to branch into long distance voice offering simply to stay in business while the data communications market "matures." In an attempt to stimulate consumer demand, telecommunications and data processing firms are currently testing new ideas such as Viewdata in Florida, the Telenet project in electronic mail, new intra-office communications experiments (i.e., the Collins, Telenet, Aetna SF-NY) SBS tele-conferencing, etc. In these cases, the information industry firms are trying to force technological change by making new advanced services available and entice a market to develop around them.

6. These products fall into two classes — first a product able to perform many functions now performed by several different and expensive pieces of hardware and second, technology able to handle new comprehensive functions — such as a controller for digital voice and data.

New chip technology expands the inherent potential of products in traditionally discrete markets: telephones become data processors, computers can communicate like telephones and typewriters become word processors and can do both. Companies which dominate their respective sectors now compete with one another as their once distinct products collapse into one new market. The size of the converging sectors is awesome. Current revenues of these companies top $159 billion. They employ 2½ million people and include some of America's biggest and best-known firms: AT&T, IBM, Xerox and the television networks. Each would like to emerge as the major telecommunications company of the 1980s, sitting on top of a $200 billion information industry market. The corporate battle will be intense and its fallout will affect workers and consumers.[7] Table 1 describes the current sector divisions.

Table 1
Statistical Portrait of
the Converging Sectors

Sector	Revenues $ Millions	Employment 000's People	Number of Businesses More Than 20 Employees	1975-80 Revenue Growth %	1975-80 Profit Growth %
Broadcasting	13,940	—	—	—	—
Telephone & Telegraph	61,453	1,106	—*	10.8	2.3
Telephone & Telegraph Equipment	10,453	141	154	13.8	3.4
Computers	26,000	306	434	24.7	13.4
Electronic Equipment	22,100	415	973	14.9	5.6
Electronic Components (Semi-conductors 35%)	24,607	520	1,672	18.2	11.5
TOTAL	158,553	2,488			

SOURCE: U.S. Industrial Outlook, U.S. Department of Commerce, Bureau of Industrial Economics.

* Total: 1,475

New Communications Technology

The new information industry can be divided into four segments: 1) semi-conductors, the industry's basic building blocks; 2) expanded communication networks, which include voice communication, data

---

7. For example see Herbert Schiller, *Who Knows: Information in the Age of the Fortune 500* (Norwood, NJ: Ablex Publishing Corp., 1980); Simon Nora and Alain Minc, *The Computerzation of Society: A Report to the President of France* (Cambridge, MA: MIT Press; 1980).

transmission, national and international networks, intra- and inter-office networks and local distribution networks; 3) computer hardware, which includes mainframe computers, mini-computers, communication devices and office equipment; and 4) new services built onto these systems ranging from home entertainment to business information systems. Although changes are taking place in all four segments, the most important areas for telephone workers are communication networks and computer hardware.

Communication Networks

To compute is not enough, there is also a need to transmit data, analysis and other signals. Today's communication system for both residential and business locations can be divided between the long distance or toll market and the local exchange. While AT&T dominates both markets, there are more than 1600 local telephone companies and a growing number of long distance carriers. Several of these long distance carriers were organized to transport the expected increases in data traffic which the information industry was to generate. When these markets failed to develop as quickly as expected, the specialized long distance carriers, including MCI, Satellite Business Systems, and SPCC carried voice messages in order to survive. In doing so, they threatened to cut into Bell's lucrative long distance revenues.

Bell's competitors presently have a relatively small share of the long distance market. For example, when private line revenues reached $1.5 billion in 1975, MCI's share was $728,000. That was its first year in the industry. MCI has since grown to $200 million in 1980 sales and is projected to total $1.43 billion by 1985. By contrast, Bell's 1979 business toll was also $15 billion. Private lines added another $2 billion. Bell's competitors have made but a small dent in its revenues with their microwave and satellite long distance networks. In the future, however, they may become more substantial rivals.

Long distance generates more than 50 percent of phone company revenues for AT&T and has been used to subsidize local service. With increasing competition in long distance markets, the Bell System will eventually be forced to lower long distance rates and subsequently raise local rates. As the company argued throughout the deregulation process: competition forces prices towards costs.

Long distance competitors are dependent on the 1600 local regulated telephone systems to provide the necessary hook-up capability. A company subscriber can buy a "private line" to interconnect all of its plants, but to talk with or transmit data to people not on the private network it is necessary to have access to local telephone lines. The remaining "natural monopoly" in telephone is the "local loop" which is able to provide universal service to any party with the flip of a switch.

However, even this area may become subject to competition. An alternative provider of local loop service is the cable TV industry. It performs the same basic function as the telephone, bringing into residential locations two or more wires that transmit electronic signals — computer, telephone or television. This creates the prospect for what has been called a "war of the wires."

Corporate telecommunications users have special network needs related to their size. The growth of multisite firms and proliferation of high-powered computers have spawned new companies to transmit the computer signals they need. These firms want service in every unit and area. The result is a growing market for computer-to-computer data transmission which presently travels over the voice network of the telephone system. The system works, but it is a slow and costly way for computers to communicate with each other. This is the reason for the push towards digital switching and the use of packet switching which allow for quicker bulk transmission.[8]

Satellite Business Systems (SBS), one of the newcomers, is developing a satellite network to permit teleconferencing and high speed data transmission. However, due to the slow emergence of the data market, SBS has decided to transmit voice to survive today while building for the future. SBS enjoyed about $11 million in 1981 revenues, while projecting 1984 revenues of $193 million. The company says that when its satellite is in orbit and its transmission capacity is sufficient, three high speed data users will become customers, as well as one other firm primarily interested in teleconferencing. The competitive importance of SBS is, first, that its marketing approach is aimed at the nation's largest companies and primarily focuses on teleconferencing. Second, it provides IBM (which is part owner of SBS) with access to a transmission network should IBM wish to compete with AT&T.

Tymnet, formed in 1972, is a data transmission and computer time-sharing company that has now developed a computer transmission network. It also offers computer software and, in some instances, the necessary hardware to allow computers to interface. Tymnet's recent electronic mail experiment with Shell Oil proved successful and it is now offering intra-organization electronic mail services in 30 cities. Its fee for bulk mailings is below that of the U.S. postal service. Tymnet

---

8. Residential telephone users primarily have shouldered the costs of upgrading telephone equipment to handle business computer needs. While existing equipment is designed to handle voice phone calls, and performs admirably, new digital equipment is needed to most efficiently transmit data. There is no accounting method which would allocate the costs of new equipment to different user groups so that the expense of upgrading equipment has been borne by all — including residential customers and telephone workers — while the benefits accrue business.

has also teamed up with SBS, Xerox and MACOM Manufacturing to experiment with coast-to-coast transmission over an alternate network using existing or potential radio, cable TV and microwave capabilities. These companies are attempting to bypass the existing telephone local network and still provide coast-to-coast communications.

The users of computer communication systems may themselves enter the data transmission business. They can develop specialized equipment and services and integrated supplier networks for their industries. For example, Citibank is developing a special system for banks by adding a mini-computer to the Bell transmission network to provide unique formats, data bases and terminals. Already it has established a time-sharing corporate subsidiary, Citishare, and in the future could conceivably service the entire industry. Special formats provide easy credit verification for banks and time-sharing permits common access to a data base of corporate information. Like Citibank, other users and user groups could develop the necessary special services and transmission networks to become carriers themselves. The result would be to further fragment the transmission network.

This proliferation of specialized carriers symbolizes the developing revolution in telecommunications. The problem for AT&T is that beyond a certain volume of transmission it becomes profitable for large users to build or buy independent network facilities rather than continuing to lease services from Bell. These future competitors of AT&T will be able to utilize many different transmission network technologies: satellite or microwave signals, analog or digital electrical signals and light waves. To recombine these new systems into one comprehensive network would require yet a new round of technological development.

Computer Hardware

Computerization of the telephone network makes the telephone itself a potential master controller of the information flow. As increased computing power is built into smaller and smaller units, it is possible for the private branch exchange (PBX) to control electronically not only the direction and completion of telephone calls, but also data processing and transmission. While Bell and Western Electric presently dominate manufacture of this equipment, they have been joined by other firms, substantial and growing ones including Harris, Rockwell, General Dynamics (Stromberg Carlson), Northern Telecom, Rolm, General Datacom, and RCA Motorola.

The advanced PBX, or "super controller," may become the center of all automated communication and data processing functions that control the rest of the computerized office. Whoever develops this centerpiece first will have unique marketing advantages for the sale of related equipment. For that reason the largest companies in telecommunications, Bell, IBM, EXXON, and the smaller tier, (those companies with less than $100 million in annual sales), are all vying to develop the dominant PBX, capable of handling both voice and data transmissions.

Western Electric's current market strength is in central office switching equipment. Eighty percent of Western Electric's production is geared for traditional telephone communications systems. Significantly, each of its products is made in at least two locations, in case Western Electric is ever divided into regulated and non-regulated components. Its greatest weakness is in PBX equipment, closely followed by customer station equipment. The leading PBX competitors are Rolm and Mytel. Rolm sells more than 1700 PBXs with an average of 300 lines; Mytel sells 10,000, averaging more than 100 lines. The Yankee Group, a communications consultant firm, estimates that more than half the PBXs having more than 500 lines are from non-Bell companies. Other major competitors of the regulated telephone companies for sales of PBX and other data processing and automated office equipment include such well-financed and experienced companies as EXXON and IBM.

Important innovations are taking place in transmission technology too. The copper wire pair may slowly become a relic of a bygone era. A variety of replacements are being developed. On land, clear glass wire strands (fiber optics) with vast transmission capacity will slowly take the place of copper wire. Fiber optic links are already being cut-in to the U.S. telephone system.[9] Through the air, microwave towers and broadband radio appear to be growing transmission media. After three years of testing in Chicago, AT&T is ready to expand its cellular radio telephone system to the nation's other urban areas. Satellite communications are also becoming commonplace. While Western Electric and AT&T dominate the U.S. fiber optic industry, they have been slower than other firms in leaving their wires behind and taking flight.

To summarize, the competitive era in telecommunications has been brought about both by the inherent potential of and demand for new techonology. The rapid technical change in all aspects of communications has led to new forms of industrial organization which in turn quicken the pace of change. The blurring of boundaries between traditionally discrete industries prompts battles for market control which range along several fronts and involve further competition to develop and market new technologies, efforts for and against regulatory re-

---

9. *Optical Fibre Technology* (London: Post Office Engineering Union, 1980) Study commissioned by Committee B; Michael Dimmler, *Technological Trends and Implications for Jobs and Employment in the Bell System* (Washingtion, D.C.: CWA Research and Development Department, 1979).

form, and multiple lawsuits. The fallout from these battles is an important element shaping the future. Indeed, as management determines market strategies, research priorities and production techniques based on a drive for profits, they are also making other, equally important, decisions for society. Fundamental social choices about the nature of work, lives of working people, and the shape of the future are quietly being made by a few. In fact, management is attempting to restructure the workplace and social system of the future without any social debate.

Labor and Telecommunications Today

The Impact of Competition on Telephone Workers

A fundamental change accompanying the competitive era in telecommunications is that telephone workers, who had organized most of their industry, suddenly find themselves working in a predominantly non-union sector. Many of the high tech companies, such as IBM and Texas Instruments, are non-union. This is a threatening development because unorganized workers retard progress on job security, working conditions, wages and benefits for the unionized workers. In addition, workers will be unable to control the adverse impact of technology in one firm if they can't control it in all firms.

Phenomenal expansion of the industry and a widespread paternalism in labor relations have kept the technical and engineering staffs unorganized. In addition, much of the production work is done by unskilled labor forces that are paid virtual minimum wage. The runaway plant threat also keeps production wages low. Offshore manufacturing by U.S. Electronics companies already accounts for $2.5 billion per year of semi-conductors which are shipped into the U.S. With a potential of one million workers, labor's most important goal — to organize the unorganized — takes on an increasing urgency.

Competition forces the regulated telephone company, typified by the Bell System, to rethink its management style. Old ways of operating under regulated monopoly no longer suffice. With deregulation, management must reconsider basic operating procedures including the role of their asset base. Return on investment for the regulated telephone company is fixed by the regulatory agency. Since the rate of return is fixed, the phone company can increase its profits only by increasing its asset base. Thus, for example, it is more profitable to lease telephones than to sell them, because leased telephones are still carried as assets and therefore continue to earn profits. If sold, they would be recorded as one-time revenues, at prices limited by the regulated rate of return.

Because of this operating mandate, it made sense for the telephone company to replace labor with capital, even if no increases in productivity or efficiency occurred. Labor was carried as a cost, but machines were carried as assets. Since the phone company could earn the regulated rate of return from assets, but not from costs, the increased asset base lifted potential earnings. An econometric study prepared for CWA by a productivity specialist shows how important this aspect of regulation has been over the past 20 years. While productivity growth generally is associated with new investment, this study indicates that the net effect of investment in new technology on productivity growth has been minimal. Measured by itself, mechanization sometimes decreased and sometimes increased operating costs. CWA's conclusion then is that the telephone company tended to overcapitalize its operations.[10] Contrary to popular belief, new investment alone did not cause rapid productivity growth in telecommunications. Instead it came about by increasing economies of scale, which resulted from the new technology, and through increased labor contributions. Deregulation may shift the company focus away from fixed rates of return toward variable return and should act as a brake upon overcapitalization.[11]

The second area of change brought on by competition involves management decisions affecting bargaining unit personnel and their jobs. For example, one management response to competition has been to increase supervisory "spans of control" and cut back middle management personnel. This reduces some of the burdensome oversupervision which characterized the telephone system. While this program will likely result in increased productivity, it will also benefit employees with better working conditions.

On the other hand, competition may increase the push for labor cost savings through minute division of labor — the dissection and splitting of craft jobs into less skilled and lower paid postions. This is now occurring in the highest paid telephone craft positions. An example is the test desk technician (TDT) whose job it was to diagnose and solve

10. Peter Chinloy, "Implications for the Communications Workers of America of Technological Change at the Bell System," *Sources of Productivity Growth at the Firm Level: The Bell System 1947-1978.* (Washington, D.C.: Communications Workers of America, 1981).

11. Tax policy also affects these corporate decisions. The current accelerated depreciation allowance, incorporated in the 1981 tax revision, creates incentives to replace people with machines even when it makes no economic sense. For example, this policy would create *negative* effective tax rates on new investment ranging from -196% on computing equipment, -76% on service industry equipment and -53% on electrical equipment by 1986. *Tax Policy Guide: The Reagan Tax Shift: A Report on the Economic Implications of the Tax Act of 1981, Part II: How It Will Affect the Economy.* (Washington, D.C.: Citizens for Tax Justice, 1982).

network problems inside the labyrinth of equipment, switches, and wires. A software program now diagnoses many system problems, replacing much of the craft work. Management has also used this technology to introduce a new job title, the description of which is to monitor computerized testing of circuits and perform a part of the original top rated work — at lower pay rates. In this instance, a skilled job was fragmented and deskilled, allowing the company to save wages and exert greater control over the work processes. A "side effect" was to make the work less interesting and challenging for the employee. Competition, with the resulting need to lower costs, generally hastens this process of job simplification, fragmentation and de-skilling which is at the heart of technological change today in telecommunications.[12]

The Impact of Technology on Telephone Workers

As this trend towards technologically-induced job simplification continues, it is important to recognize it as being a long run, far-reaching process which is already in its middle stages. Management's attack began with the reduction of operator and directory assistance jobs. Operators were once needed to assign all phone calls to the proper trunklines to reach their destination. But with automation this function was bypassed and performed by stored computer programs. Operator assistance was needed for fewer calls. Conventionally measured productivity of operators shot up as computers were utilized to direct work automatically to individual operators as soon as their lines were free. The increased work load meant more intense working hours and exertion, even though the number of hours and ostensible conditions of work did not change. Work speed-ups, along with machine control over the operator and management's childish work rules, were the main causes of job stress. This stress increased as the computer was manipulated to measure average work time on a daily basis and to schedule operator work breaks automatically according to business needs not worker needs — for some workers breaks were scheduled within 15 minutes of their arriving at work because to the computer that was a slack business time. Computerization of the operator's job had three effects: it reduced the demand for labor, intensified the work

---

12. For a general discussion of these issues see: Robert Howard, "Brave New Workplace," *Working Papers for a New Society* Nov.-Dec., 1980, p. 21; Larry Hirschorn, "The Soul of a New Worker," *Working Papers for a New Society*, Jan.-Feb., 1982, p. 42; Michael Cooley, *Architect or Bee: The Human Technological Relationship* (London: John Goodwin & Sons, 1980); Harry Braverman, *Labor and Monoploy Capital: The Degradation of Work in the Twentieth Century*, (New York: Monthly Review Press, 1974); David Montgomery, *Workers' Control in America* (Cambridge, MA: Cambridge University Press, 1979).

which remained and gave management more control over jobs.[13]

Computerization was also used to attack the work of directory assistance (DA) operators. Previously, they used paper records at decentralized sites to respond to customer requests for information. Record keeping forms then evolved from paper to microfiche to computer stored data. It is questionable, however, whether customer service improved during this evolution and whether the changes were cost effective. In addition, DA operators experienced the same stress-related health problems as did service operators. Management also used the new technology to centralize the directory assistance office. This consolidation reduces available jobs and either causes layoffs or requires transfers to the new centralized locations or does both. Yet job loss through centralization is not a necessary result of computerization. The technology that makes centralization possible also holds the potential for decentralized assistance reporting locations. Nothing inherent in the system requires centralization, but management's decision has been to deploy the system in that manner.

Telephone system management next aimed at more complicated, higher skilled craft jobs. Switching technicians have been recent victims. In the past, switching technicians located, diagnosed and repaired problems and temporarily redirected traffic. They had a significant degree of autonomy in the performance of their work and generally were assigned to a single office. With the computerized system in place, however, mobile repair groups of technicians are directed to problems by a centralized command center. The latter is staffed by a few technicians who monitor each of the different offices using video display terminals plugged into the computerized system. Technicians now work on a single aspect of switching problems. Some spend their work day monitoring a computer which reports problems and temporarily redirects traffic; others spend time repairing problems.

Since the central office is now computer controlled, the old diagnostic and mechanical skills required to do the jobs are no longer necessary. Repairs today are mostly a matter of recognizing which component the computer identifies as being faulty, pulling it out and plugging in a new one. The same process occurs here as with other job classifications. The work is centralized to require fewer workers; it is simplified to require fewer skills; it is fragmented into component parts to pave the way for automation. This process inevitably results in management attempts to lower wage rates for what are now consi-

---

13. William L. O'Neill, ed., *Women at Work* (New York: New York Times Books, 1972).

dered less demanding jobs. Thus, the final battle between management and labor is fought after the basic technical changes have taken place.

During the process of job fragmentation, management also tries to remove part of the job from the bargaining unit by describing it as a management control function. In doing so, management monopolizes knowledge of and control over the new machine and refuses to train members of the bargaining unit, thus robbing the unit of both knowledge and work. For example, after the equipment is brought on line, bargaining unit switching technicians are not trained in the total operation of the new system; that is reserved for management personnel. Using computerization technology, management simply continues the program set out in 1920 by Frederick Taylor, the father of scientific management. The technology used to remove control of work and knowledge from bargaining unit members could instead be used, with enhanced training, to utilize and develop workers' skills and knowledge.[14]

In sum, management has used the selection of new technology to attack bargaining unit jobs. This is a long term process which affects every type of job. Displacement of workers by machines is the end product of a system which begins with management simplifying work by fragmenting existing jobs. Once jobs have become sufficiently simplified, they become targets for automation. During the automation process management increases its power in the workplace by removing both knowledge and control functions from members of the bargaining unit. Automation of the telephone system also allows for greater centralization of work sites; this, in turn, increases the opportunities for further job simplification and fragmentation, thus laying the ground for another round of automation at a higher level.

The union won a set of arbitration cases preserving bargaining unit work from management takeover. After several incidents of computerization of a job function, supervisors tried to appropriate job funtions traditionally belonging to the bargaining unit. But in each instance an arbitrator ruled that what had been bargaining unit work prior to mechanization remained bargaining unit work after mechanization.

---

14. For example see: Michael Cooley, "Computerization; Taylor's Latest Disguise," *Economic and Industrial Democracy,* (1980) p. 523; Dennis Chamot and Michael Dymmel, *Cooperation or Conflict: European Experience with Technological Change at the Workplace.* (Washington, D.C.: AFL-CIO Dept. for Professional Employees, 1981); *Planning Work: Resources on Technology and Investment for Labor Education* (San Francisco, CA: California Newsreel, 1981); "The Impact of Microelectronics on Employment in Western Europe in the 1980s," European Trade Union Institute, February, 1980; "Employment and Working Conditions in the '80s: Perspective on the Significance of Technology and Economic Development for Employment and Working Conditions," Norwegian NOU, #33, 1980.

CWA also went to arbitration to prevent established job titles from being downgraded by the introduction computerized tools. In the test desk technician case discussed earlier, the union grieved both the unilateral introduction of a new piece of technology and the new job title that was proposed for it. In this case the arbitrator ruled that the management rights clause entitled the company to introduce the machine and to assign a lower paying job title to the new equipment, but provided that the job title should remain inside the bargaining unit. His ruling was based on the relatively narrow grounds of a specific management rights clause in a single contract. But it is alarming because it sanctions the downgrading of work through the introduction of new machinery.[15]

Over time the union has also negotiated a series of worker protection benefits which lessen the impact of technology on employees. Primarily these contract clauses provide income protection for workers whose jobs are downgraded or eliminated by the introduction of new technology. In addition, the union has negotiated letters of agreement with AT&T concerning monitoring and contracting out of work.

In the 1980 Bell negotiations, CWA and AT&T reached agreement to establish three joint committees on technology, job evaluation, and the quality of work life. The QWL committee, formally named the Joint CWA/AT&T Working Conditions and Service Quality Improvement Committee was established to address job pressures and other worksite problems.

After much deliberation, the union decided to participate in a Joint Job Evaluation Committee to insure members are properly compensated for their work. Joint development of a plan to document work and compensable factors and development of a mutually acceptable system of scoring jobs should better insure that workers' pay is fair in cases where technology has drastically affected the traditional hierarchy of jobs.

In addition, the 1980 contract established Technology Change Committees in every Bell operating company. The technology contract provision requires at least six months notice of any "major technological changes (including changes in equipment, organization of methods of operation) which affect employees represented by the union." Since this prior notification clause gives the union lead time to analyze proposed changes, it is the first step toward developing the real capacity to assess the impact of technology and recommend alternatives. These programs were discussed by Ronnie J. Straw, CWA Director of

---

15. The arbitration cases referred to above were filed by the Communications Workers of America against New York Telephone and involved the impact of computerization on bargaining unit work.

Development and Research, in recent Congressional testimony, part of which is reproduced as Appendix A.

CWA has also committed itself to a new organizing program. The changing nature of the telecommunications industry makes organizng the unorganized a critical element in preserving the rights and benefits won in the telephone industry. CWA has initiated a training program to upgrade job skills and add union members from the new telephone interconnect industry. The union has also begun a process of analysis by the rank and file Committee on the Future. The Committee's mandate is to consider the impact of current industrial change on the union and its members. Recommendations are expected on union structure, programs and priorities to better meet the membership's needs posed by today's problems.

Conclusion

Business demand for services which increase data processing and communications potential is one of the forces behind technological innovation. Fierce corporate competition to produce and sell for this market drives technological change. Since the objective of this technology is profitability in the competitive corporate market, the general public will not be the direct beneficiaries of the new products and services developed. At the same time, they will be asked to shoulder many of the start-up costs of dat handling and new services through increases in the regulated rate base. As prices are driven towards costs, local phone bills will rise and long distance and computer charges may fall. Service which the general public has come to expect will become more costly and less efficient. These are the conditions which are breeding new generations of technology.

The selection and production of new technology are the result of choices made by management. There are neither technological imperatives nor inherent limitations of selection in the process. Technological development has no internal logic which dictates how it will be designed, built, installed or operated. As David Noble of MIT phrased it, technology

> does not develop in a unilinear fashion; there is always a range of possibilities or alternatives that are delimited over time — as some are selected and others denied — by the social choices of those with the power to choose.[16]

Someone decides which technology to implement and in the U.S., traditionally, this power to choose has always been left in the hands of

---

16. David Noble, "Social Choice in Machine Tool Design," in *Case Studies on the Labor Process*, Andrew Zimbalist, ed. (New York: Monthly Review Press, 1979).

management which makes its choice using profitability as the main criterion with which the judge the potential of a new system. Technology put into production is therefore far from neutral.

An additional criterion used in the selection of technology is the increase of management control over workers and the work process. This translates into two ways management can increase profits. First, automation creates a factory or office in which fewer workers can produce the same product as before. The displaced workers have to look elsewhere, often in lower paid sectors. The resulting pool of unemployed or low-wage workers suppresses wage levels for all workers.

Secondly, new technology reduces skill requirements, leading to lower paid jobs. The company that is automating reduces skill levels, pays out lower wages and, depending on product prices, may increase its profits proportionately. Moreover, with increased worksite control, management extracts more "useful" work than before. Automated production processes make the work more intensive and stressful and less interesting and fulfilling than before, but also more productive.

It is important to put management's choice of the redesign of work and new technology into an historical framework which recognizes them as tools that management can use against organized labor. In other periods of history, technological change has been one of industry's chief weapons in its battle with labor. A more current example is the redesign of the air traffic control system in the wake of the controllers' strike. The design of the new system will include costly features to redesign the jobs, reducing the importance of the controllers' skills.

New technology and the redesign of work, particularly in today's virulent anti-labor climate, should be included in a list of the current corporate battles against labor. In general, labor's political and social programs are under attack by business and conservative groups. At the bargaining table, management is demanding concessions. These different angles of attack on labor cannot be isolated from one another.

Historical examples and our experience today tell us that the unilateral introduction of the microprocessor into factories and offices favors management at the expense of labor. Technology should be jointly designed and brought on line. But technology and technological choices are not well understood in this country. Nor have they been sufficiently politicized. Economic concepts like "productivity" confuse and hide what is really happening inside workplaces. Therefore, while it appears that society marches under the banner of technological progress, in fact, new technology brought on line in offices and factories is loaded with social choices — management's choices on how to create greater profitability, not how to fulfill human potential.

Appendix I

Ronnie Straw Testimony (September 19, 1981) to the House Subcommittee on Science, Research and Technology of the Committee on Science and Technology.

CWA has consistently made excellent gains for its members through collective bargaining. But we found that signing a national agreement every three years with the Bell System was not always the best way to address issues of technology that occur on the shop floor. As a result, in our 1980 negotiations, CWA and AT&T agreed to set up three joint programs to deal with day to day issues of the workplace. The three joint projects were technology change committees, a national quality of work life committee and a national job evaluation committee. I will describe each of these shortly.

We also negotiated several other benefits and ways for our members to deal with the human impact of technological change. They are:

1. Supplemental Income Protection Plan (SIPP) — These benefits are made available to eligible workers declared surplus by the Company because of technology, to a maximum of $18,000 per year.
2. Monitoring — We negotiated a Letter of Agreement with the Company eliminating diagnostic remote monitoring.
3. Technological Displacement — This clause gave workers the alternative to accept a termination allowance instead of being transferred to a lower-rated position because of technological change.
4. Reassignment Pay Protection Plan (RPPP) — This ensures that long-term employees who are downgraded because of technological change will suffer no reduction in pay.
5. Upgrades — We upgraded the operator's job in 1980 and the service representative's job in 1977. Both jobs had become underrated as technology added to the pressures and demands of the jobs.
6. Contracting Out Work — In a Letter of Understanding with the Company we ensured that telephone work would not be contracted out.
7. Time Off — We secured additional holiday and vacation time for our members to help them deal with the pressures of their jobs.

We are also getting underway several studies on technology and stress in the public sector.

Now let me return to the three joint committees I mentioned. First, I will describe to you our efforts to deal with technological change.

Our 1980 contract with the Bell System set up a Technology Change Committee in each of the Bell System Operating Companies, Western Electric and Long Lines. Each committee consists of not more than three Union and three Company representatives. Usually an Assistant Vice President from the Company and the Bargaining Committee Chairman from the Union are on the committee. The committees talk about employment and training for workers affected by technology and discuss possible applicatioons of existing programs such as SIPP, RPPP or transfers.

The technology change provision requires the company to provide the Union with at least 6 months notice of any ". . . major technological changes (including changes in equipment, organization, or methods of operation) which may affect employees represented by the Union." This may not sound like a major advance and in fact, some operating companies were providing such notice before 1981. But the reason that we are so pleased with this development is that it provides our district officers with the same data used by officers of the operating company, and it provides the leadership with the lead time necessary to analyze the changes, assess the impact, and recommend alternate methods of implementation in this forum, or others established under the contract.

Because the program is so new, it is too early to make any judgments of its effectiveness. But early reports are very encouraging. Right now, the committees are learning to work together to solve problems and build up confidence.

At present, we are also trying to build up a network through our stewards to channel information to the committee. We feel that this is the best way to harness the knowledge of the true experts on the effects of technological change: the workers. This approach does not only increase participation by the workers, but is likely to create practical solutions to the problems new technology creates.

It is our hope that the committees will mature and expand their scope of responsibility. After the parties have learned to acknowledge and respect the concerns of the other, it may be time to introduce a "vertical slice" approach to the introduction of new technology. This would mean that a group of employees from all levels of the Company, down to the shop floor, would meet to decide how the technology would be introduced. A truly cooperative effort could be quite successful in reducing the hostility and apprehension that often arises from new equipment and in contributing to its most efficient use.

This strategy, however, places a heavy burden on both the Union and the Company. If we are to be involved in the decision-making process in the introduction of new systems, we will have to do more than just react to those parts that are onerous to our membership. In the future, CWA hopes to have complete and effective Union involvement in all aspects of technological change, including veto power over the introduction of new equipment. Through negotiations, we hope the Company will allocate part of its budget to CWA to conduct studies, either jointly or separately, on the human impact of technological change.

Now let me discuss briefly with you our second joint project, worker participation. The joint national CWA/AT&T Working Conditions and Service Quality Improvement Committee set up by our 1980 contract is developing a process to help our members deal with issues of job pressures and technological change at the workplace.

We negotiated the formation of this quality of work life committee after we completed a study in 1980 for which we interviewed over 100 Union officers and staff. The study concluded that job pressures caused by oversupervision and technological changes could be handled through increased participation. And even more important from our point of view, it concluded that union involvement would make a significant *difference* in the process.

There were three reasons for this. One was that workers were more willing to trust the process if they felt their rights were clearly protected. The second was that programs with unions stressed human values, broadening the narrow productivity focus of most management programs. And the third was that union involvement tended to stabilize the efforts: it meant that they were no longer dependent, as in many other cases, on the backing of a single manager who might soon move on to another job or change his mind. It gave participation a second leg to stand on. So on those bases we decided it was worthwhile for us to take up the issue actively.

The first step of the national committee was to reach agreement on a statement of principles which is to be the framework for all worker participation activities within the Union at AT&T. In brief, these guidelines are:

— First, that workers' rights are explicitly protected. This means no layoffs or speedups will occur as a result of QWL activities; and that participation in them is voluntary.
— Second, that the activities not intrude on collective bargaining. Workers always retain the right to pursue complaints through the grievance procedure. And any changes which affect contract provisions must pass through normal bargaining channels.
— Third, there should be an explicit commitment to human goals in addition to economic ones. We have no objection to increasing productivity — we want AT&T to be an efficient and profitable company. But the values of safety, dignity and human development at work should be equal in importance.
— Fourth, the union should be involved on an equal basis in all phases of the process, from planning to implementation.
— Fifth, all decisions about work changes should come primarily from discussions by the workers themselves.

The next step must be to provide training and education about worker participation to the lower levels of the union — and, of course, the company. The National Committee has agreed on a two-day training program on QWL. We expect that in the next year or so every CWA official, down to the steward level, will have participated in at least the first day of this training. We have already trained over 150 of our Union staff and over 100 Local officers.

As for starting the process of actual participation on the shop floor, we plan to move carefully. Once the local programs begin, they will be quite independent and work out their own way of approaching QWL process. But they cannot succeed if a strong climate of support has not been created at the higher levels first.

But there are already a few exceptional cases of local projects, undertaken jointly by Union and Management, which have been going for a year or more. These programs in Illinois and Michigan have already taught us a great deal which will help in the further development of QWL efforts.

For management, worker participation requires a basic change of style. When I studied at a University Management School, and after spending a considerable amount of money, I asked what did they teach me. I concluded that they taught me to "control, control, control." No one ever said to me, be a leader-provide leadership, lead, lead.

We believe that the controlling approach to management is counter-productive. In the long run, human values support economic ones. All the evidence shows that workers that are treated fairly and given the chance to contribute fully to their work are highly productive. But managers don't always see it. The reason is that they tend to focus more on the short run, and you can always get more immediate production out of workers by pushing them and increasing control. The costs in terms of worker dissatisfaction often don't show up until the manager responsible has moved on to another position.

Given this, the Union's role in the QWL process is crucial: to stick consistently to the long-term goal, guided by the human values which we have always advocated. We see worker participation as a tremendous opportunity, as well as a challenge. The results will be a strengthened Union and hopefully all parties in the industry will benefit.

Finally, I will explain to you our third way of dealing with the effects of technology, the joint CWA/AT&T Occupational Job Evaluation Committee. This is a joint national committee of three Union and three management representatives. I am the Chairman of the Union portion of this committee.

We are charged with developing a job evaluation plan for the Bell System that produces a hierarchy of jobs acceptable to both parties. We have met monthly for the past year and are close to reaching agreement on a plan. We have decided on a methodology for documenting work and are close to agreement on a set of compensable factors and a system of scoring jobs. We plan to test out our job evaluation plan in one Company over the next year. When that is accomplished, we will be ready to recommend a plan to the CWA and AT&T national bargainers in time for 1983 negotiations.

Despite initial skepticism about job evaluation, CWA entered into this project because of a need to make sure our members were being properly compensated for their work. Technology has drastically changed jobs across the country. A job evaluation plan jointly developed and implemented by CWA will help us identify and adjust compensation where technology has rendered traditional wage relationships meaningless. Only with Union involvement can we be sure that our members are being paid for the increased skill, responsibility and adverse working conditions that result from technological change.

Response to: Changing Competitive and Technology Environments in Telecommunications

I.C. Glendenning

Technological change is not new to the telecommunications industry. The difference today is the pace of change, as well as its extent. Having observed and participated in these changes for more than four decades, I have concluded that regardless of the smoke, trauma, and anxiety that accompany each technological era, when everything is finally assimilated the advantages outweigh the disadvantages.

Telecommunications, unlike many other industries, is almost human. The heart is the central switching system; the veins and arteries are the various two-way transmission facilities serving even the most remote outposts; the brain provides the computer-software analogy; while the appendages, hands, fingers and legs, are the input/output. In fact, AT&T's familiar Yellow Pages slogan, "Let your fingers do the walking," is more than a coincidence: It conveys some subliminal connotations. Telecommunications long ago grew out of being merely a convenience and become a necessity like electricity, gas and water. Now it is an essential tool in every industry, every activity. To put the size and scope of the subject in perspective — by the end of the decade, the information-telecommunications sector is expected to be, by far, the nation's largest in economic value, taking over from food processing, which is currently the leader.

Traditionally, telecommunications was simply a matter of transmission, meaning that one wire-using sector, such as Western Union, handled the written word while Bell, the other wire-using company, took care of voice communications. Originally only people spoke to or telegraphed each other. Then we invented computers and it became clear that efficiency would be maximized if computers could talk to computers. Thus, data storage/processing and data transmission merged. It has been said, before long we will have more computers

---

I.C. Glendenning is President of the Federation of Telephone Workers in Pennsylvania.

talking to computers than people talking to people. The competitor who first markets a system that enables computers, regardless of their language, make or origin, to relate to each other, will have an advantage over all others. The transistor, silicon chip, microwave, and now laser waves through glass fibers have removed all of the previous impediments limiting information use, flow and development. These are the dimensions of the telecommunications/information age now rocketing upon us.

Before tackling the effects of these changes, it is advisable to consider the history of regulation and the impact of deregulation on the industry. Since the U.S. Justice Department's 1956 Consent Decree, AT&T, the largest telecommunications company, has been prohibited from storing or processing data and allowed only to transmit. Storage/processing was the province of IBM, the giant in the computer field. Legislation is pending in Congress and Federal Communications Commission edicts are slowly but surely guiding public policy towards permitting established telecommunications entities, as well as newcomers, to transmit, store and process data competitively.

Another factor, possibly the most important, is the historical pattern of rate setting under the regulation mode. Universal service under user rates that all could afford was basic policy. Telephone toll rates were equalized so that users in low-density calling areas paid the same rates as those in the high-density areas where the company delivered the service at a lower actual cost. Increased competition introduces delivery of services — local, toll, data, radio, TV, or whatever — at rates which reflect actual costs rather than regulated cost subsidization. The following chart graphically illustrates the difference between AT&T's costs in delivering toll call services and the rates it charges for them. It is clear that if rates reflected actual costs companies like MCI, Bell's major long-distance telephone competitor, would lose their present advantage.

Toll charges have subsidized local service by about 50 percent. That is, the mark-ups above were used to pay 50 percent of local costs as well as to equalize toll charges in low calling regions, for example, a high-density toll call for the 100 miles from Philadelphia to New York might be 10¢ in actual cost, whereas a similar 100 call in rural Pennsylvania would cost $1.50. Averaged nationally, a 100 mile call will cost about 60¢. With competition, these equalizations and subsidizations disappear. Each customer or each region will pay a rate for respective services which is more closely related to actual costs. Business will no longer be called upon, involuntarily by regulation, to bear some of the cost of residential service. Data transmission will have very favorable rates because companies and methods will compete — cable, microwave, satellite, and light wave transmission.

AT&T Toll Call Costs and Rates, Evening Rates

Rate Band	Initial Minute of Toll Call			Additional Minute of Toll Call		
	Cost	Rate	Mark-up (percent)	Cost	Rate	Mark-up (percent)
1	3.9¢	12.35¢	216.7	1.0¢	5.2¢	420.0
2	4.0¢	14.95¢	273.7	1.1¢	7.15¢	550.0
3	3.9¢	17.55¢	350.0	1.0¢	8.45¢	745.0
4	3.9¢	20.15¢	416.7	1.0¢	11.05¢	1005.0
5	3.8¢	22.75¢	483.3	1.0¢	13.00¢	1200.0
6	3.9¢	25.35¢	550.0	1.1¢	15.6¢	1318.2
7	4.2¢	26.65¢	534.5	1.2¢	16.9¢	1308.3
8	4.8¢	27.95¢	482.3	1.4¢	18.2¢	1200.0
9	4.9¢	28.60¢	483.7	1.7¢	18.85¢	1008.8
10	5.4¢	29.90¢	453.7	2.0¢	20.15¢	895.5
11	6.5¢	31.20¢	380.0	2.8¢	21.45¢	666.1

Data storage/processing will explode as chips and bubble memories improve in quality and decrease in cost exponentially. In 1981, 46 percent of the U.S. Gross National Product is communications-based, almost all of that computer-dependent. It used to be that software (the program) was given away to sell hardware (the computer). Today that is being reversed, software is now the valuable commodity. In the near future, computers may be practically given away in order to sell software. At Bell Labs today, 40 percent of the scientists are working on software programming. Western Electric is building a center outside Chicago to house 2,500 programmers developing software that can be sold to Bell System customers using data transmission, storage and processing for use when Bell is deregulated. Those are the parameters of manmade controls over the direction the information age might take.

Nearly every transmission or equipment competitor of Bell has built upon Bell Lab inventions which, under the 1956 Consent Decree, had to be given to anyone who requested the information, both at home and abroad. To illustrate, assume Bell alone had had the transistor. What other technology-centered companies would even exist today? Under deregulated competition, Bell will be able legally to keep and patent new inventions. Therefore, competitors besieged with the double necessity of furnishing service and equipment at cost plus a profit, and in the position of having to invent their own technologies or pay royalties, will have to deal with new economic pressures. The next generation of technology and capital requirements will favor the large corporations — AT&T, IBM, Exxon, GE, Westinghouse, Aetna, RCA, Cable CATV. Others will be reduced to sub-contractors and suppliers.

All this portends immense change, growth and different employee requirements within the telephone industry. However, this is not a new circumstance. We've already gone through several major shifts in employment demands:

— From 1900-1915 the lineman was highly valued because simply getting telephone wires strung was essential to the industry.

— From 1915-1930 cable splicing was the best trade. The cable splicer needed special skills for wiping hot lead sleeves, splicing small wires, making lead cables waterproof and testing wires that are now hidden under a sheath. Telephone poles could carry no more open wires, so cables containing 100-1,000 wires in a smaller space had to be used.

— From 1930-1955 electro-mechanical switchmen took over top place and top wage. Maximum training was required to maintain and adjust fine electrical relays to 1/1000th of an inch tolerance with expensive circuitry.

— Since 1955 Electronic Switching System (ESS) technicians and Private Branch Exchange (PBX) technicians have commanded the top classification and pay.

— In the future, with competition, all that will change. Top salaries, probably with built-in incentives, will go to the white-collar salesperson.

New technology and new competition will promote growth. There will be downward pressure on jobs and pay, but the vectors will come from a different direction. These new competitors, such as IBM, are non-union. The work rules, pay practices and fringe benefits of today's union employees will be severely challenged by non-union competition. Even now, employees experience stresses, strains and insecurities peculiar to the telephone industry. As the industry moves into "a dog-eat-dog" competitive mode, the productivity pressures on the individual employee will increase.

Our contracts contain certain remedial mechanisms for these problems but unions will have to introduce more preventive processes. We will have to do more to help our members with drug problems, alcoholism, mental health and stress. The Quality of Work Life concept is being heavily touted by both unions and employers as the device of tomorrow to ameliorate traditional work pressures. AT&T Chairman Charles Brown said, "We must start to work with people instead of on them." Limited QWL plans in telecommunications have already proven successful and are being promoted by both sides as deserving wide implementation. Yet, union participants in QWL must insist on:

(1) Commitment from the top of the company and the union;
(2) Joint ownership, implementation, and evaluation of the QWL plan;
(3) Right of either party to exit with proper notice.

In summary, the United States has the best telecommunications system in the world at a cost, comparably speaking, that is also the lowest in the world. My contention is that competition will spur innovation and more efforts to reduce costs. On the other hand, duplication and removal of universal service and rates may prove costly, impacting employees by changing work opportunities and working conditions. However, there will be many new jobs in the area of research, development, manufacture, installation-repair, and sale of telecommunications in the expanding information age.

We have been dangerously embarked on a policy of giving to foreign competitors the one industry in which America is now the leader. Mandated bidding requirements and foreign protection of home telecommunications industries work against us. Unrestrained, foreign intrusion into the information age will result in a repetition of what happened to the U.S. auto industry and also to cameras, television, steel, rubber, electrical parts, textiles, and on and on.

As a unionist, I am confident of the future and look forward to it. If we can only stop foreign competition from gaining access to another free ride, we can take the domestic competition in stride, adjust to the new problems and intelligently negotiate solutions. The issue today for labor unions is *how* to respond to these changing conditions. Can the labor movement acknowledge its status as a counter-institution and draw on its own rich traditions to redefine its functions and posture in a new environment? To survive these challenges, labor must clearly revitalize from within, expand and consolidate, establish vigorous public relations and greatly increase its political action.

Technological Change in the Office Workplace and Implications for Organizing

Judith Gregory

Introduction

"We are on the brink of a second industrial revolution which will eliminate drudgery and boredom once and for all," business periodicals proclaim. The technological revolution "is creating more stimulating careers for office workers," a writer rejoiced in a special feature of U.S. News and World Report.[1] Examined more closely, however, American management's idea of the "office of the future" means little more than a recreation of the factory of the past. Today's office workers find themselves threatened with many of the same processes of job degradation which undermined the skills and dignity of an earlier generation of industrial workers. Without the pressure of clerical workers organized in their own behalf, the alienation of the assembly line may well be extended to the "electronic office."

Clerical workers account for almost one in five of all U.S. workers and are among the least unionized and lowest paid members of the workforce. They are also on the front lines of office automation. The office jobs which are especially targeted for automation are dominated by women, who comprise 80 percent of clericals, 99 percent of secretaries, 93 percent of bank tellers and 95 percent of typists and keypunchers.

New office technologies, because they are extremely versatile, offer a great potential to upgrade jobs, skills and earnings, and to raise overall standards of living. Yet the opposite is occurring: jobs are being deskilled and devalued; working conditions are degraded; promotional opportunities are declining; health risks increasing; and large-scale job

Judith Gregory is Research Director, 9 to 5, National Association of Working Women. The author wishes to thank the organizers of District 925/Service Employees International Union for sharing their experiences for this article.

1. *U.S. News and World Report*, September 18, 1978.

loss is possible in the not-so-distant future. Office automation is described in futuristic terms, yet the goals and methods underlying the current wave of automation are shaped by management ideas and techniques that date back to the days of Charles Babbage and Frederick Winslow Taylor. British trade unionist and design engineer Michael Cooley calls the computer "the Trojan Horse of Taylorism" because it is used to spirit into offices the techniques of the assembly line.[2]

There are significant differences between the present surge in office computerization and those forms which were introduced before the 1970s. We are entering a second industrial revolution that has microchip technology as its base. The goal of office automation today is to automate office procedures — the flow of work — not merely to mechanize jobs by giving workers machines that allow them to perform particular tasks more quickly. Because of this we are seeing a revival of work rationalization. Taking office automation to a higher stage requires breaking down jobs as they now exist and extracting from workers the decision-making they perform, so that this knowledge can be translated into a computer program. "It's this removal of decision-making from us to the management and to computer processing which makes us first of all more expendable and secondly easier to control," economist Joan Greenbaum points out.[3] Again and again, this process reduces workers to extensions of machines linked to the computer system.

Challenges for Office Workers

Clerical work is characterized by low paying, dead-end jobs; discriminatory employment practices; and low levels of unionization. Secretaries and clerks have been undervalued and underpaid, their skills and contributions unrecognized, ever since their work was "feminized" around the turn of the century, a process which coincided with the early phases of office rationalization and mechanization. Now, computerization and related work reorganization perpetuate and intensify these long standing problems, while posing new difficulties as well.

The Problems of Deskilling

When new computer systems are introduced, certain skills may be made obsolete, while new skills are often belittled and unrewarded, and variety is lost from the work. Although this office automation improves jobs for some, the majority of office workers' jobs are more closely supervised and increasingly specialized — meaning that each

---

2. Michael Cooley, "Computerization — Taylor's Latest Disguise," *Economic and Industrial Democracy*, 1 (1980), pp. 523-539.
3. N.Y.C.O.S.H. Conference on "Health Protection for Operators of VDTs/CRTs" (January, 1980).

person performs ever smaller fractions of the larger task. When this happens, each job requires less training and offers less chance for advancement.

Deskilling can occur in a variety of ways. In the midwest headquarters of a multinational corporation, secretarial jobs were broken down into component parts when word-processing equipment was brought into the department. As a result, one woman does electronic filing all day, another extracts data all day, one answers phones all day, another handles correspondence all day, and so on. The company requires that each woman complete a "tour of duty" of several months in each subtask in order to be considered for promotion. In other words, each woman must be promoted four times to get back where she started. This is one example of how companies use new office technology as an excuse to wipe the slate clean and start over with new rules.

A recent study of Wall Street legal secretaries' jobs illustrates another way that skills are stripped away when technology is brought in and combined with new levels of job specialization and centralized administrative controls. Legal secretaries' jobs have been among the most prestigious and highly skilled of clerical occupations. But Mary Murphree of Columbia University and City University of New York (CUNY) found that

> while early forms of office computerization served to upgrade and assist secretarial worklives . . . current innovations are striking at the heart of the traditional legal secretarial craft and creating a number of serious problems. The most challenging and responsible tasks traditionally in the legal secretarial domain are gradually being transferred away from the secretaries to *cadres* of professional and para-professional workers such as para-legal assistant, librarians, accountants, personnel specialists and word-processing proof-readers, thereby reducing the secretarial function to one of merely 'telephone gatekeeper.'[4]

In the newly technologized firms, job responsibilities were split up and down. Desirable work and new skills were assigned to other workers, as well as new means of performing tedious tasks. Specialized departments were created, with the work flow centrally monitored and coordinated. Murphree noted a "growing fear of robotization" among the secretaries. Many resented the sophisticated dictating equipment and centralized transcribing pools increasingly present in large firms. Together, these technologies made many prized and hard earned skills, such as speed stenography, irrelevant. Secretaries were left in a tenuous position — still holding high status jobs but no longer using many of their skills and fearful for their future as the law firms continued their effort to phase out traditional secretaries, using the administrative cluster as a "compromise" or "interim" solution.

---

4. Mary Murphree, "Rationalization and Satisfaction in Clerical Work: A Case Study of Wall Street Legal Secretaries" (unpublished Ph.D. dissertation, Columbia University, 1981).

Devaluing Jobs

Women clericals now find themselves doing more work for less pay, working faster and for more people at once. A 1979 management survey found that fulltime video-display terminal (VDT or CRT) operators earned only seven dollars more per week on average than conventional typists. Yet consultants estimate productivity gains ranging from 50 to 500 percent when VDTs are used, depending on the type of document production involved. In some sunbelt cities, where office automation is likely to be installed at the outset, VDT typists actually earned less than conventional typists in 1979.[5]

Office reorganization plans which put clericals into clusters or pools increase the workload and also break down work relations between clericals and managers. "When they set up the administrative services center, they said it was more democratic," one woman explained. "We wouldn't have 'bosses' anymore, just 'clients.' But they were just trying to save money. A clerk gets $150 a week while a secretary gets $185 for serving just one person."[6]

Managers are using production quotas and computerized monitoring of work performance to carry out speed-ups of awesome proportions in large clerical operations. An 8 year employee of the data entry department in a utility company describes the work speed-up which took place at her office following work reorganization:

> Everything seemed just fine at work until last summer, when the company hired a mangement consulting firm, supposedly to study how *management* could work better. But instead of improving management's operation, the consultant began to carefully measure and time *our* production speed! We used to have to process a maximum of 4,000 checks a day. Now 4,000 has become the *minimum* — that's one check every 6 seconds — and the average they require is between 5,000 and 6,000 — about 4 seconds a check. They're treating us just like machines, expecting that everyone can do exactly the same amount every day, no matter how hard or easy a check is to process.[7]

Employers may even impose a "floating" rate of pay which works like a treadmill. Rose re-entered the workforce after 20 years away. Her excellent typing skills quickly landed her a job as one of twelve CRT operators in a downtown Cleveland publishing company. She found that office work had changed while she was out of the workforce. She explains:

> The chairs were good and the machines adjustable, too. But I have never been confined to one place doing key entry at such a pace. The computer at one end of the room keeps track of the keystrokes you do. The more keystrokes, the more money

5. *Office Salaries Directory, 1979-80* (Willow Grove, Pa.: Administrative Management Society, 1980).

6. Evelyn N. Glenn & Roslyn L. Feldberg, "Degraded and Deskilled: The Proletarianization of Clerical Work," *Social Problems*, 25 (October, 1977).

7. Interview from *Warning: Health Hazards for Office Workers* (Cleveland: Working Women Education Fund, 1981).

you *might* get. At the end of the day, the figures for all of us are posted. You look at your speed, you look at everyone else's and you say, 'Tomorrow I'm going to do better.' They get you thinking just like they want to, you're really pushing hard.[8]

Rose's experience may sound extreme, but the basic principles of the pay system described above are quite common. Constant computerized monitoring of individual workers' speed and volume of work is used to establish a median quota or average for the output required of each employee. The workload demanded is then continuously revised upward. Typically, workers in the lower third by speed or volume are pressured to meet the average. Once they've done so, the average then becomes the minimum acceptable level and the pressure to increase speed and workload begins again. Failure to meet the quota or average can result in disciplinary action or loss of one's job; other workers may leave voluntarily if the pace is unbearable. The use of bonus schemes which place office workers in competition for increased productivity figures is divisive and isolating but can be appealing to very fast workers. Such systems, if unchallenged, make speed-ups a way of life in the office.

Monotonous, deskilled data entry and information processing jobs will abound in the office of the future but the skilled and varied office jobs traditionally held by women may disappear. Trained, long-term employees are now threatened with job loss or with employment in downgraded jobs. In order to use expensive new office machines most efficiently, shiftwork and nightwork are being introduced more widely. In addition, piece-rate work — pay-per-line-of-information processed — is spreading, and there is even a clamor for "office homework," which suggests a return to the "cottage industry" concept of old. There is nothing new about speed-ups, piece-rate pay, or shiftwork. And there is nothing new about the drive to reduce labor costs while increasing management control over the workforce.

Consequences of Office Automation

What are the consequences if these trends continue? Several effects are evident: the potential for job loss, polarization of the workforce and increased health risk to workers. "Office homework" and the likelihood of "runaway" offices are new and threatening developments. These issues need to be addressed in both workplace organizing and public policy.

Potential for Job Loss

The dynamic of computer technology is against job creation in any sector where it is applied — it is a labor-reducing technology. Euro-

---

8. Interview in *Warnings: Health Hazards for Office Workers,* Women Working Education Fund, April, 1981.

pean studies predict enormous office displacement estimating, for example, that by 1990 there will be up to 30 percent reductions among clericals in the finance industries in France.[9] In the U.S. clerical work is still the fastest-growing occupation in the 1980s. The U.S. Department of Labor estimates that there will be 4.6 million new jobs for clerical workers, nearly one in four of all new jobs anticipated in this decade. The continued need for clerical workers appears to be masking the probable job-displacing effect of automation in office industries such as insurance and banking. It already takes fewer people to do the same or greater volume of work in many banking operations. While employment in banking is still expanding, the rate of job growth slowed from 4.5% annually from 1960-73, to 3.2% a year from 1973-76, while the volume of transactions continued to increase steadily. The finance industries are growth industries while other sectors lack similar advantage. The International Federation of Commercial, Clerical and Technical Employees (FIET) predicts that for white collar employment, "there is likely to be a cumulative employment impact hitting one sector at a time, but building up over a ten year period."[10] The effects of office automation on employment may be occurring more slowly in the U.S. than in other countries, but a dramatic loss in jobs is possible in the next 10 to 15 years. Public policy addressing these issues should be developed now.

One reason for this urgency is the historical role of the service sector as an area of new employment, particularly since World War II. In 1948, manufacturing employment accounted for approximately one in three U.S. workers. Today, fewer than one in four workers are employed in goods-production and clericals have supplanted factory workers as the largest occupational group. But microprocessor technology will affect both blue and white collar work. A 1978 study for the Organization for Economic Cooperation and Development, reported in the *New York Times*, warned "the evidence we have now is suggesting increasingly that the employment displacement effects of automation anticipated in the 1950s are now beginning to arrive."[11] In the past, as employment in manufacturing began to decline, clerical and service employment continued to grow rapidly. But if employment in key service industries is slowed as a result of automation, where will new jobs be created?

---

9. Simon Nora, *Computerization of Society* (Cambridge, MA: MIT Press, 1980).

10. *FIET Conference on Computers and Work* (Geneva: Federation of Commercial, Clerical and Technical Employees/FIET, 1979).

11. As reported by Paul Lewis in " 'Jobless Growth' for 1980s, West Warned About Impact of Automation," *New York Times*, July 5, 1978.

Polarization of Office Employment

There is increasing concern over the danger of polarization of the office employment structure, with a small number of highly technical jobs at the uppermost level and a large number of deskilled jobs at the base, and between them a skills gap that is virtually impossible to bridge.[12] Writer Barbara Garson quotes a manager who describes this pattern succinctly:

> We are moving from the pyramid shape to the Mae West. The employment chart of the future will still show those swellings on the top and we'll never completely get rid of those big bulges of clerks on the bottom. What we're trying to do right now is pull in that waistline (expensive middle management and skilled secretaries).[13]

Office workers' worries about short career paths leading to dead-end jobs are justified.

Office automation relies on a base of data entry jobs which involve repetitive, standardized, fast-paced and accurate work. Jobs become more interchangeable as many different clerical functions are homogenized into information-processing at computer terminals. The characteristics of a secondary labor market — low-wage, low benefits, high turnover, non-union, insecure and semi-skilled jobs — are extended to the office. Companies often permit or encourage deliberately high turnover rates in certain clerical operations. This practice gives them tremendous flexibility to reorganize office work as new technology is phased in. When jobs are made highly interchangeable and minimum wage clerks are hired to do them, the benefits of high turnover — avoidance of wage increases and retirement payments, and an unstable workforce less likely to unionize — outweigh any lost investment in job training.

Sex and race discrimination continue and are often intensified as office hierarchies are revamped. Minority women are especially concentrated in "back office" data processing jobs, often working on late-night or swing shifts. Again, this contrasts with the promised opportunity of technology which was supposed to allow women to move up to fill new computer-related technical and professional jobs. Clerical workers complain that only a pre-selected few are chosen for training programs in new skills, and affordable community-based programs which teach appropriate courses are few and far between. This situation is compounded by employers' complaints that computer vendors are cutting back on their training services and support which were already minimal.

---

12. Heather Menzies, *Women and the Chip* (Montreal: Institute for Research on Public Policy, 1981); James W. Driscoll, "Office Automation: The Dynamics of a Technology Boondoggle," paper, Sloan School of Management, M.I.T., March, 1981.

13. Barbara Garson, "The Electronic Sweatshop: Scanning the Office of the Future," *Mother Jones*, July, 1981.

Increased Stress and Health Problems

Increased stress and job-related health problems are a third consequence of office automation. Many health problems result from poorly designed equipment, work environments and jobs. Research also points to a relationship between lack of control in the workplace and damage to physical and psychological health. Whether workers have some control over their jobs — how fast they work, how much they do in a given time, and how they do it — is a critical factor in the incidence of health strains. Through automation, the enjoyable aspects of clerical employment — variety in work, contact with other people, natural rest breaks and changes in routine — are threatened with elimination, while the most stressful aspects — monotonous tasks, constant sitting, a relentlessly fast work pace, lack of upward job mobility — are on the rise. VDT operators report higher rates of health problems ranging from eyestrain, migraines or insomnia, to severe muscular pain in the neck, back and shoulders, to increased irritability, anxiety, depression and decline in self-esteem and sociability.

In interviews with office workers about the stress in their jobs, 9 to 5, National Association of Working Women, found that inability or reluctance to express anger or frustration is related to the arbitrary environments in which clericals work — situations characterized by lack of grievance procedures (or ineffective procedures if they do exist), unfair supervisors, discrimination and/or favoritism in promotions. Because clerical workers are overwhelmingly unorganized, it is difficult to challenge management to correct these problems.

Results from 9 to 5's Office Workers' Health Safety Survey show the leading sources of job stress cited by 960 respondents to be: (1) lack of promotions or raises, (2) low pay, (3) monotonous or repetitive work, and (4) no input into decision-making. Table 1 shows the rank order for thirteen common sources of job stress discussed in the literature.

An eight year study on "Women, Work and Coronary Heart Disease," carried out as part of the Framingham Heart Study, and released in 1980, found that women clericals developed coronary heart disease (CHD) at almost twice the rate of other women workers. The major predictors of CHD among clerical women were (1) unsupportive boss; (2) lack of job changes over a ten year period, and (3) inability or difficulty expressing anger or frustration.[14] These problems will be exacerbated in the automated office. Dead-end jobs become even more widespread as promotional opportunities are reduced. And, the computer is the ultimate unsupportive boss.

---

14. S.G. Haynes, and Manning Feinlieb, "Women, Work and Coronary Heart Disease: Prospective Findings from the Framingham Heart Study," *American Journal of Public Health,* 70 (February 1980).

Table 1
Office Worker Health and Safety
Survey[1]

Rank Order	Sources of Stress on the Job	Adjusted Frequency Response[2]
1	Lack of promotions or raises	51.7%
2	Low pay	49.0%
3	Monotonous, repetitive work	40.0%
4	No input into decision-making	35.1%
5	Heavy workload/overtime	31.5%
6	Supervision problems	30.6%
7	Unclear job descriptions	30.2%
8	Unsupportive boss	28.1%
9	Inability or reluctance to express frustration or anger	22.8%
10	Production quotas	22.4%
11	Difficulty juggling home/family responsibilities	12.8%
12	Inadequate breaks	12.6%
13	Sexual harassment	5.6%

SOURCE: *Warning: Health Hazards for the Office Worker*, (Cleveland: Working Women Education Fund, 1981).

NOTES: 1. The survey was distributed in Cleveland and Boston in the fall of 1980.

2. Adjusted frequencies are based on 915 respondents answering the questions on stress, (95.3% of the total 960 survey respondents).

The New Office Mobility

The combination of telecommunications and microprocessor technology makes it possible for office work to be geographically dispersed and reorganized. Managers will seek to use this new "office mobility" to reduce labor costs, to resist unionization, and, where there are unions, to undermine the traditional power of organized workers.

Office Homework

Electronic office homework — work done at a computer terminal in one location and transmitted to another location via phone lines — is being heavily promoted in the press and management trade journals. One business writer proclaimed that "portable terminals will be a special aid to homebound workers, such as mothers with small children," and then showed a photograph of a commodities investor lying on a Florida beach with his computer terminal beside the blanket.[15] Still in an experimental stage, it is unclear how big a trend "telecommuting" might become, however the implications of electronic homework vary depending on a worker's position of power and pres-

15. *U.S. News and World Report,* September 18, 1978.

tige. For professionals and executives having a computer at home will be very convenient, giving them a greater flexibility, whereas for clericals, such as data-entry workers, the work will be more rigidly monitored and will be paid by piece rates.

Office homework is often touted as an easy solution for the critical shortage of child care for working parents. In fact, those who could benefit most from this system — lower income mothers of small children, particularly single parents — are not necessarily the workers management will consider for this employment first, or even at all. In addition, work in the home is not the answer to the lack of child care facilities — women still desire and need daycare centers to care for children while they work, whether they are at home or in an office, and they need the wages which enable them to pay for these services.

Runaway Office Work

Restructuring of service industries is accelerated by new technological capabilities such as the electronic fund transfer system. Financial institutions are now making plans in anticipation of national banking. Some finance industry jobs are moving to lower wage states which offer a "better business climate". For example, Citibank relocated its credit operations to South Dakota because the state has no ceiling on the maximum interest rate which can be charged for credit transactions. Delaware loosened its banking laws in 1981, thus attracting credit and lending offices of ten of the nation's biggest banks including Chase Manhattan, Citibank, Chemical and Morgan Guaranty. Other states (and banks) are expected to follow suit. This may trigger a competitive chain reaction similar to that which has developed over tax incentives to business in the manufacturing sector.

The "offshore office" provides another parallel to factory experiences in which operations are moved overseas or to the sunbelt. A certain amount of bulk information processing has been performed outside of the country for some time. In the past, this work was shipped to and from offshore locations by plane, but the advent of satellite communications links makes the practice more attractive. One entrepreneur, George R. Simpson, Chairman of the New York based Satellite Data Corp., relays printed materials by satellite to Barbados where the work is done by data entry clerks whose pay averages about $1.50 per hour. In Simpson's words, "We can do the work in Barbados for less than it costs in New York to pay for floor space. . . The economics are so compelling," he told *Business Week*, "that a company could take a whole building in Hartford, Connecticut and transfer the whole function to India or Pakistan."[16]

---

16. "The Instant Off-Shore Office," *Business Week*, March 15, 1982.

Another spin-off effect of the new mobility of office work is increased subcontracting to firms specializing in "business services" such as data and word processing or computerized payrolls. In fact the rapid growth in business service employment in the 1970s may be deceptive, because it reflects the movement of work from the central offices of companies to these new specialized firms. As Michael Urquhart explains:

> The recent growth of business services is largely caused by a change in how firms handle business office functions. Employees are classified by industry based upon the major activity of the establishment employing them. Thus, for example, clerical workers who prepare financial records in a manufacturing firm are counted as employed in manufacturing. In contrast, if the establishment contracts with an outside accounting firm to prepare their records, those employees are counted as part of the services division. To the extent that firms will replace their clerical workers with agency services, a "shift" in employment from manufacturing to services occurs.[17]

Blue Shield: A Case Study

In 1976 Blue Shield introduced a new VDT system into its San Francisco office and, at the same time, set a new production quota which nearly tripled the previous figure. Each examiner was now expected to handle a minimum of 383 claims per 7½ hour shift. Blue Shield based this increase on a Methods-Time-Measurement (MTM) study, carried out by the Electronic Data Systems Corp. (EDS), in which factory time-motion techniques were applied to the office.

The traditional MTM method measures only physical movements — the fraction of a second required to hit a key, move an elbow, swivel in a chair. It doesn't measure how long it takes a claims examiner to decide whether or not a claim is valid or how much should be paid for the treatment received. In other words, the consultant's calculation of production rates did not allow the worker time to think.

The 1100 Blue Shield workers were represented by Local 3, Office and Professional Employees International Union (OPEIU) which challenged the new quota, by filing a grievance that was eventually settled in arbitration. The union argued that Blue Shield's extraordinary production quota had a harmful effect on workers' health and pointed out that error rates had skyrocketed. But, according to an occupational health specialist who consulted with the union for this hearing, the arbitrator saw the union's arguments as efforts to "humanize the workplace" and therefore "social science"; by contrast, he accepted the company's methods as "scientific management" with which he was familiar from numerous factory cases. He sustained the company's right to maintain the extraordinary production rate.

---

17. Michael Urquhart, "The Service Industry — Is It Recession Proof?", *Monthly Labor Review*, Vol. 104, No. 10, October, 1981.

Local 3's workers went out on strike in the winter of 1980-81 for 4½ months. Health protection for VDT operators and an attempt to gain some control over production quotas were major issues in the strike. When the strike was settled, the union had won two important goals which were contained in letters of understanding from Blue Shield. The first concerned health and safety protection for VDT operators. Blue Shield agreed to redesign the desk height, lighting and positioning in VDT work areas. The second letter of understanding assured that production rates would be monitored monthly rather than weekly, thereby giving workers more breathing space in dealing with supervisors.

During the strike Blue Shield took a number of actions which are part of an emerging pattern of technological strike-breaking.[18] They brought in between 350-375 temporary employees to do part of the strikers' work. Because they had introduced a rigid, standardized VDT system, the company could train these replacements quickly. In addition, the company permanently shifted 448 of the claims handling jobs out of San Francisco to two non-union offices in smaller cities. Advances in telecommunications technology allowed the company to coordinate the work performed at these more remote locations. Blue Shield has shared this knowledge gained from this strike with other industry employers — for example, a corporate representative described Blue Shield's strike preparations at a health industry conference in 1981. This employer exchange of anti-union strategies has become a common occurrence. Clearly, unions need to respond by sharing their experiences in dealing with runaway work threats in all industries.

Implications for Organizing

Observers from C. Wright Mills onward have predicted massive unionization of office workers as white collar work becomes more "proletarianized" as a result of automation. While the level of white collar unionization has increased, the workforce has grown at such a rapid rate that the proportion of unionized clericals has remained fairly steady. About one in five of all clericals in the public and private sectors are unionized. Unionized clericals are particularly concentrated in the public sector; estimates are that less than one in ten private sector clericals have union representations. In the finance industry, which employs one in four clerical workers, the level of unionization is less than 3%.[19]

---

18. For a fuller discussion, see Harley Shaiken, "Computers as Strike-Breakers," *Technology Review*, April 1982.

19. Bureau of Labor Statistics, *Characteristics of Organized Workers* (Washington, DC: Government Printing Office, 1981).

However the office technologies of the 1970s and 80s represent a qualitative leap over previous forms of mechanization. Jobs in the office of the future will be radically altered. Workers suffering from the abuses of new technologies are therefore more likely to seek union protection. The experience of District 925/Service Employees International Union (SEIU) bears this out, but the relationship between technology and unionism is more complicated than one might predict.[20] The experiences of District 925/SEIU organizers, discussed below, indicate the complex effects of new office technologies on union organizing. Two general points should be kept in mind: (1) new technology rarely is an issue in and of itself, but is integrally related to other problems which have long characterized office work; and (2) the rate of introduction of office technologies varies among industries and companies. This is to say that the methods used by employers to change from the "social" to the "electronic" office are still in flux — and vary greatly in degrees of subtlety.

An organizer in the Midwest has described the reaction of university employees where computerized systems are being considered, but have not yet been purchased.

> Generally, people are dying to get a chance to work on a VDT or CRT. They see it as a step up, as a new skill. They're not considering the health consequences, at least not yet. A few employees are worried about the longer-term effects; they're usually the most aware ones, but not necessarily the ones who are having the most health problems.

Another organizer explains that workers who have just started on VDTs or word processors often hesitate to express the doubts or difficulties they are having with a new system because they fear losing their jobs.

A District 925/SEIU organizer on the East Coast comments on the ways word-processors are brought into law firms: (1) the company hires new people at the minimum wage to work in word-processing pools, sometimes in large centers, other times in small departmental pools or "clusters" of two or more word-processing specialists, or (2) several legal secretaries are trained on the new equipment and get raises for their new skills which are integrated into their overall job duties, or (3) secretaries are trained in word-processing as an added part of their jobs without any additional pay, or (4) the firm's secretaries are redefined as word-processing specialists and moved laterally into word-processing pools or clusters. "The drift is towards the first one," the organizer says. "because there's tremendous logic for

---

20. In March of 1981 Working Women (now 9-to-5) joined with the Service Employees International Union (SEIU) to create District 925/SEIU, a new union for clerical workers. District 925/SEIU combines the strength of the women's movement with the strength of the trade union movement.

management to move as quickly as they can towards having minimum wage clerks doing these new specialized jobs in a full-time way."

In insurance companies the work is both "clerical-intensive," and "computer-intensive." At one small office, some 90 claims processors work full-time at terminals. They have flextime, but they also have mandatory overtime — they are often scheduled for five or six consecutive 10-hour days. They get no rest breaks during eight hours at the terminals. They are mostly women under 35 who have children or are starting families. Their full-time pay averages $9,500 a year, and many hold second jobs to make ends meet.

Their work exacts a toll on their health. Many who never wore glasses now do, and some have changed prescriptions more than once within a year. One woman, 24-years old, has developed heart disease which she and her doctor believe is related to the stress of her working conditions. Many of the women who are pregnant or are planning to become pregnant are afriad of low level radiation from the terminals.

The procedures and methods for handling claims change constantly — five times in one six-month period — but one factor is constant: all production quotas always go up. At this company, the organizer believes that the VDT work has had an important influence on how examiners see themselves as workers in need of a union: "They're all in one room, no one has a specialty, and they're very interchangeable. It's a national company — there's no union anywhere. These women see the need to fight organization with organization. They know they cannot make it on their own."

Some tentative conclusions can be drawn from the organizing experiences of District 925/SEIU. First, there are important differences among industries in how systems are brought in and how clerical workers perceive resultant changes. Organizers should identify a company's current level of computerization (or mechanization) and research its local and national plans for both the short and long-term. Extensive office automation requires major financial investments and usually involves years of planning. "Showcase" pilot projects may precede changes which will occur throughout a company or a department. National or multinational companies may develop a "prototype" system for certain operations such as letters-of-credit, claims examination and customer billing. This is done in a headquarters or research center, however the model system can then be implemented very quickly in other locations or operations. Sometimes it is possible to find out about plans in the public sector by examining budget documents to identify major purchases of computer systems and the uses for which they are intended (which may include displacing staff).

Secondly, in discussing the issues raised by automation with clerical workers, it is important to distinguish between short term gains and long term problems. Learning to work on a new computer system often means an increase in pay and any step up is an important one when the average annual pay for clericals is less than $11,000. Nearly one in seven women office workers who headed families in 1980 earned income below the official poverty level of $8,450 for a family of four.[21] It is useful for workers to understand that new technology may allow an employer to raise salaries slightly while still maintaining low wage ceilings overall. Furthermore, VDT training frequently means training into another narrow, monotonous job. Once the skill is learned, the job becomes routine. Finally, employers may try to downgrade jobs at a later date, claiming they have re-assessed the value and skills of the job after computerization has taken place.

Office automation opens up several new avenues for discussion with workers. Clearly the potential effect of such computerization on employees' health and well-being is a compelling issue. In addition, there is some question as to whether new forms of work reorganization actually achieve the stated goal of increased productivity. This becomes a strategic point of discussion for both workers and consumers as new systems in some cases decrease service quality.

Occupational Health

As noted previously, stress research and surveys conducted by 9-to-5 show that lack of control, low pay, the absence of grievance procedures, and dead-end jobs all contribute to the epidemic of stress-related diseases among office workers. In a field study conducted by the National Institute of Occupational Safety and Health in 1979-80, researchers found higher levels of job stress among VDT operators in strictly clerical jobs than they had found among workers in any other occupation studied, including many air traffic controllers.[22] In the same study, VDT operators reported feelings of being "constantly watched" by the computer and through it by their supervisors. A majority of the clerical VDT users also said they feared their jobs would be replaced by a computer at some time in the near future. This job stress could well increase as office automation proceeds, and as jobs are further rationalized and routinized, speed-ups become more widespread, jobs become more insecure and technological advances allow management to extend absolute control over the workplace.

Steve Sauter of the Department of Preventive Medicine at the University of Wisconsin-Madison, proposes a number of reasons why

---

21. *Office Work in America* (Cleveland: 9-to-5/National Association of Working Women, 1982); these figures are drawn from Department of Labor and Bureau of the Census figures.

22. U.S. Department of Health and Human Services, "Potential Health Hazards of Video Display Terminals," DHHS (NIOSH) Publication No. 81-129 (Cincinnati, 1981).

tightly controlled work with a VDT can be even more stressful than assembly line work.[23] Some assembly line workers can "work ahead" or "accumulate" (delay) work or "spell" one another briefly. But with VDTs, individual performance can be constantly monitored, so it becomes impossible to either work ahead or accumulate work. In the phone company and in many customer service jobs, automatic call distributors connect operators to a second call as soon as they complete the first. In many insurance companies, prompters installed in the terminals mean that four new claims pop onto the screen as soon as the operator punches the last key of the previous four. The faster you work, the sooner you get more work. If a VDT operator pauses for a moment, the fact that the machine is not in use is noted on a computer printout for the supervisor's use. The operator cannot be "spelled" by another operator because she is trapped in a one-to-one interaction with the machine. Therefore, this electronic equivalent of the moving assembly line eliminates the possibility of even minimal worker control over the system.

Effects of Productivity and Service Quality

These factory-like speed-ups are conducted in the name of productivity. But studies of automation, machine-pacing and stress show that error rates increase from 40 to 400 percent when control over the pace of work is taken away from people and transferred to a machine system.[24] Though the new office technologies do improve the speed of document production, this emphasis on speed above accuracy, common in piece-rate and machine-paced settings, is likely to have a detrimental effect on real productivity. The number of key strokes per hour or lines processed per day are typically used to assess performance, but increased errors are not deducted from this figure which means that those measurements are misleading. More importantly, the motivation to produce perfect work is diminished.

In an ongoing study of office work being conducted by Shoshonah Zuboff of the Harvard Business School, one clerical worker is quoted as saying, "when a person makes a mistake with a computer, to try and get that mistake corrected is so much red tape. So you tend to let it go. Maybe when they see how bad the information is, they'll give us back our jobs."

---

23. S.L. Sauter, G.P. Harding, M.F. Gottlieb, J.J. Quackenboss, "VDT-Computer Automation of Work Practices as a Stressor in Information Processing Jobs: Some Methodological Considerations," in *Machine Facing and Occupational* Stress; Proceedings of the International Conference, Purdue University, March, 1981, pp. 353-360.

24. B.H. Beith, "Work Repetition and Pacing as a Source of Occupational Stress," presented to the International Conference on Machine Pacing and Occupational Stress, NIOSH and Purdue University, March, 1981.

In another situation, workers in the bill collection department of a large store were under such pressure to meet production demands that from time to time they would invent customers. As Zuboff reports:

Collections workers who lost control over the work process could only retrieve some sense of mastery by keying fictitious data into the system of accounts files. Their managers were confronted with high productivity figures that were not matched by the size of the monthly revenues. As one collector put it: "People get so discouraged because the work keeps flowing into your terminal, no matter how much you finish. The only way to deal with it is to fake some work. How else can we keep our heads above water?"[25]

Efficiency may be eroded in subtler ways. One firm which reorganized and automated its offices according to the rigid plan which was then being promoted by IBM, cut back their secretarial staff by 30 percent, but found that "much was lost in the human factors area." The managers complained about decreased efficiency which resulted from the loss of one-to-one relationships between managers and secretaries.[26] Other managers complain about the higher level of tension in the workplace and, in some cases, the lack of real dollar savings in the switchover to the "office of the future."

Consumers, as well as workers will be affected by work reorganization and computer technology. Many bankers predict that by 1990, 50 percent of all transactions will be done by automatic teller machines rather than "human tellers." A film shown at the American Bankers Association convention in 1981 suggested "if people insist on seeing a human being, just charge them extra."

In a study of computerization carried out in the Swedish State Social Insurance offices, employees became worried after VDTs were introduced because they felt their knowledge was shifting from a concrete understanding of their work situation, their co-workers and the insurance business, to an abstract processing of information and an understanding of the machine's functions instead. Nine thousand of the 19,000 union members participated in study groups to discuss the effects of new technology on their work. They commented on their work:

Today our knowledge consists largely of how the machine works — how we can feed in the input data . . . the risk involved in the new forms of knowledge is that our knowledge of insurance is pushed into the background. The chances of being able to provide adequate and correct information about insurance and its aims may be reduced. It becomes difficult to give exact and detailed explanations of the decisions and other materials sent out by the computer.[27]

25. Shoshonah Zuboff, "Psychological and Organizational Implications of Computer-mediated Work," CISR #71, Sloan Working Paper #1224-81, MIT, Sloan School of Management, Cambridge, MA, June, 1981.

26. Datapro Research Corp., "Evolving Office of the Future," in *Office Automation Solutions Handbook* (Delran, NJ: Datapro, 1978).

27. Bo Göranzon & Kalle Mäkilä, *Electronic Data Processing in the Social Insurance Offices, Programme of Action for the Swedish Union of Insurance Employees* (Stockholm: Swedish Union of Insurance Employees, 1981).

The Swedish Union of Insurance Employers worked with computer specialists and researchers from the Swedish Center for Working Life and conducted intensive education among its membership on how computers could be used to improve working conditions and service delivery. Among other provisions, the union asked that:

— the work be arranged in a way that gives the personnel an understanding of the insured and enables them to provide information about insurance in a simple and easily understandable way;

— that personal contact with the insured is increased;

— that rather than centralizing the work into larger offices, a number of smaller offices be created throughout the country so that the offices are more accessible to the insured;

— that workers be given more training and that the training for the workers must provide them with an overall view of the various types of insurance and a better understanding of the problems of the insured;

— that skilled jobs in social insurance shall not be computerized.

Thus, the union's proposal seeks to use the flexibility and geographical mobility provided by computer technology to the advantage of workers and the general public by improving both work and service to the consumer, a situation which would exactly reverse the experiences of the Local 3 Blue Shield workers.

Conclusion

Clerical jobs, possibly because of their identification as "women's work," have historically been undervalued in terms of pay, as well as status and respect. The restructured, automated "office of the future" will not ease this tendency. In fact, as clerical jobs are broken down and deskilled and secretaries are redefined as "word processors," the inequitable treatment will undoubtedly intensify. There will be an increasing emphasis on speed and productivity without proportionately increased wages; major reductions in the amount of employee control over work; and greatly increased stress for office workers, as well as serious potential health hazards from VDTs.

Automation is a process, the effects of which are similar wherever it is applied. As office working conditions become more monotonous, tightly controlled and economically exploitive, the necessity for collective action in the form of unions should become as apparent to clerical workers of the 1980s as it did to industrial workers of the 1930s. These new workplace conditions will be interacting with the changing attitudes of many women workers about themselves — increased assertiveness and self-reliance, as well as a realization of the necessity for economic self-dependency.

The need for unions in the office is strong and getting stronger. The conditions necessary for successful organizing are present and becoming widespread. We are indeed "on the brink of a second industrial revolution," but the most revolutionary effect of the new technology may not be enhanced speed or productivity. Instead, it may well be the long-overdue introduction of organized labor on a wide scale into the "office of the future."

Unions and Technology in the Office

Ruth Fister Mathews

Introduction

While researching this paper I spoke with a number of union representatives involved in organizing clerical workers for the Office and Professional Employees International Union (OPEIU), the United Food and Commercial Workers (UFCW), District 65 of the United Auto Workers (UAW) and the Communications Workers of America (CWA). I posed this question. "Is technology the organizing issue of the 1980s?" They all said that although computers and other electronic communication devices affect the way office workers perform their jobs, workers generally do not respond to organizing strategies directed to other than economic issues. Most felt that an organizing campaign could be derailed if it focussed mainly on the effects of new technology.

As a one-time clerical worker and union organizer, now labor educator, I understood the importance of economic issues, but it was difficult for me to believe that such a radical change in work as automatic electronic equipment would not serve as a catalyst for union organization. Surely new technology visibly and dramatically alters the organization of office work so that clericals will see the need for collective responses.

Historically workers formed unions in response to dehumanizing work and deteriorating working conditions brought on by technological development. Craft and textile workers were among the first to feel the effects of the industrialization process in the 1800s. They were also among the first to unite and demonstrate against those conditions.

Ruth Fister Mathews is Associate Dean, Center for Labor Studies, Empire State College (SUNY).

Industrial workers of the 1930s responded to the dehumanizing aspects of factory technology by joining unions. That office workers appear more hesitant to organize, even though similar objective industrial conditions may exist in their workplaces, raises questions for which both unionists and educators continually seek answers. For unions to be successful in organizing clerical workers they will need to understand women's historical role in the labor process, since the vast majority of clericals are women. Unions must also challenge certain prevailing assumptions about women as paid workers. To understand the complexity of these issues, we need to examine how feminization of the office workforce occurred and then discuss innovative union responses to the special needs of women workers.

Women and Office Work

There are numerous histories and analytical accounts of clerical work.[1] Others specifically record women's struggles as clericals.[2] A comprehensive examination requires uniting these two issues so that a broader perspective is gained. From the historical struggle between labor and management it is clear that management pursues two goals: the economic purpose of reducing labor costs and the social objective of regulating worker behavior in order to dilute resistance. But to regulate the clerical labor process, where women make up 80 percent of the labor force, management must control women.

The Historical Role of Women in the Office

Anyone reading Charles Dickens' *Christmas Carol* gets a sense of what the 19th century British office was like. Dickens may have exaggerated his rendition to tell a story but offices, in fact, were small, poorly lit and ventilated, and had few employees. The handful of workers were young men serving apprenticeships in anticipation of someday taking over the business. A little time off the job and, of course, the traditional Christmas goose came their way through the personal benevolence of the employers, but their deference and loyalty were required in return. Yet wages were good — they surpassed production earnings during 1850-60.[3] In the United States the situation

---

1. David Lockwood, *The Blackcoated Workers* (London: Allen & Unwin, 1958); C. Wright Mills, *White Collar* (New York, Oxford University Press, 1956); and Michael Crozier, *The World of the Office Worker* (New York: Schocken Books, 1971).
2. Louise Kapp Howe, *Pink Collar Workers* (New York: G.P. Putnam & Sons, 1977); Barbara Garson. *All the Livelong Day* (New York: Doubleday, 1975); Jean Tepperman. *Not Servants, Not Machines* (Boston; Beacon Press, 1976). Other books contain specific chapters about women clericals: Barbara Mayer Wertheimer. *We Were There* (New York: Pantheon Books, 1977); Elizabeth Faulkner Baker. *Technology and Women's Work* (New York & London: Columbia University Press, 1964).
3. Lockwood, *Blackcoated Workers*, p. 6.

was much the same as in England. At the turn of the century average clerical wages were double those of production and transportation workers.[4]

While men held office jobs, employed women worked in manufacturing. In 1850, 28 out of every 1000 women over the age of 10 were employed in manufacturing (by 1900 the ratio had risen to 46).[5] The 1850 census showed women working in 174 out of 261 recorded occupations — including such manufacturing industries as textiles, apparel, bookbinding, brushes, buttons, hardware, gloves, rubber wear, umbrellas, and cabinetware.[6] Nineteenth century factories and early 20th century sweat shops were inhospitable places to work for both men and women. For women, in addition to these poor conditions, wage rates were lower than those for men, even though women represented a larger proportion of the workforce.[7]

Women eventually moved into clerical work in much the same way as they had moved into textile work. Their paid jobs mirrored their home functions. They had domesticated the home and wilderness by transforming raw materials into useful goods. When the textile industry became commercially profitable and in need of external labor, women were expected to respond. Those who refused the call were chastized for "eating the bread of idleness."[8] Thus, when the paper explosion occurred in the early 1900s women again were urged to supply the needed labor force. The same manual dexterity which made her valuable for loom work this time equipped her for the typewriter. As an office mother-wife, she was a natural. Said one manager:

> I expect from my stenographer the same service that I get from the sun, with this exception: the sun often goes on a strike and it is necessary for me to use artificial light, but I pay my stenographers to work six days out of every seven, and I expect her all the while to radiate my office with sunshine and sympathetic interest in all the things I am trying to do.[9]

---

4. Harry Braverman. Labor and Monopoly Capital: *The Degradation of Work in the Twentieth Century* (New York: Monthly Review Press, 1974).

5. Edith Abbott, *Women in Industry* (New York: Arno & The New York Times, 1969) p. 83. (Originally published in 1910 by D. Appleton & Co.) Abbott cautions the use of early statistics due to the manner and methods by which these statistics were generated. See Appendix B, pgs. 352-362 for that discussion.

6. Frieda Miller, "Women at Work Then and Now," *The American Federationist*, AFL-CIO, 58(1951).

7. U.S. Bureau of Labor. *Conditions of Women and Child Wage Earners in the United States* (Washington, DC: Government Printing Office, 1915); Edith Abbott, *Women in Industry*; and "The History of Industrial Employment of Women in the United States," *Journal of Political Economy* (October, 1906).

8. Edith Abbott, *Women in Industry*, p. 323.

9. Harry C. Spillman, "The Stenographer Plus," *Ladies Home Journal*, February, 1916, cited in Margery Davies, "Women's Place is at the Typewriter: The Feminization of Clerical Work," *Radical America* 8(July-Aug 1974) p. 16.

A business writer at the time explained:

Their (women's) conscious or subconscious intention someday to marry, and their conscious or subconscious willingness to be directed by men, render them amendable and obedient and relieve them of the ambition which makes it difficult for men to put their devotion into secretarial work.[10]

Most of the early office workers were women with high school educations.[11] Rarely did working class women move from the loom to the typewriter. They were allowed into the office only after scientific management principles had segmented and departmentalized clerical work, separating "mental" and "manual" occupations. By the late 1930s and early 1940s, commercial courses at public high schools were filling America's offices with trained working class women. On the eve of World War II, 93 percent of the nation's stenographers, typists and secretaries were women.[12] Moreover, they were women who had been socialized to accept authority and provide loyalty and confidentiality.

Office work has a clear "service" aspect. General job duties such as shorthand, typing, duplicating, and bookkeeping are performed at the behest and for the use of others. Clericals are rarely allowed to compose and sign communications, design and give reports, alter and revamp procedures, instead they service and care for those who do — tasks presumed to be more natural for women. Promotional ladders for women clericals usually end at the executive secretary rung, a position in which they do more and more of their boss's work, but with no more personal credit. Some women, including the secretary interviewed by Studs Terkel, learn to find comfort in their subordinate positions.

I feel like I'm sharing somewhat of the business life of the men. So I think I'm much happier as the secretary to an executive than I would be in some woman's field where I could perhaps make more money. But it wouldn't be an extension of a successful executive. I'm perfectly happy in my status.[13]

This work hierarchy in which many women perform services for male bosses on a one-to-one basis encourages isolated, individualized and privatized relationships on the job rather than collective worker responses.

Women in the Contemporary Office

Today the office is clearly a woman's domain. In 1979 there were 18 million clerical workers, 16 million of whom, or 80 percent, were women. The Department of Labor projects that by 1990 there will be 20 million additional white collar jobs, about 4.8 million of them clerical. If the historic ratio holds, 3.8 million of these jobs will be filled by

10. "Women in Business: I," *Fortune*, 12 (July 1935), cited in Davies, "Women's Place."

11. Baker, *Technology and Women's Work*, p. 215.

12. Davies, "Women's Place," pgs. 22-23.

13. Interview with Annie Bogan in Studs Terkel, *Working* (New York: Pantheon Books, 1972) p. 56.

women, for a total female clerical workforce of nearly 20 million, one of the largest occupational groups in the labor force.[14]

The statistics are clear. Women work for economic reasons. In March, 1978, 47.6 percent of all U.S. wives worked or were looking for work. Half the working wives had children under 18 years of age. Median income for the 18.2 million families having female heads of households was $7,765, only half as much as the $14,538 for families headed by males.[15]

Women workers in 1981 were paid an average of $224 a week as compared to $347 for men. Thus, for every $100 a man earns, a woman earns $64.70. "Worse yet," according to a 1980 report, "the poorest people in the United States were women. They have, in fact, become our 'nouveau poor.'" The report shows that 90 percent of those receiving minimum Social Security benefits in this country were women; 60 percent of all Medicare enrollees were women; 69 percent of food stamps were issued to households headed by women; and 80 percent of households receiving money from Aid to Families with Dependent Children were headed by women. Three out of every four Americans living in poverty were women.[16] These are startling figures. Clearly women in the labor force must be taken seriously because they represent a vulnerable class of workers who could help themselves through collective action.

In 1981, the National Commission of Working Women conducted a series of regional dialogues in order to call attention to the plight of women workers who are concentrated in low-paying, low-status jobs and do not enjoy institutional and organizational protection against competitive labor markets. They found that "as a group, women in the 1980s are isolated and underrepresented. They are in no particular network to which they can turn for help, nor are they in touch with policy-makers."[17] This finding reveals the need for an organizational response to technological revolution in offices.

Women and Unions

Women clerical workers are increasingly vocal and resistant. Women bank employees held a public forum in New York City on Women's Equality Day in August, 1981. The forum was sponsored by two organizations, Working Women and Women Office Workers, and,

14. *Race Against Time: An Overview of Office Automation* (Cleveland: Working Women Education Fund, 1981) p. 5.

15. U.S. Dept. of Labor, Bureau of Labor Statistics, *Marital and Family Characteristics of Workers: 1970-1978*, Special Labor Force Repot 219 (Washington, DC: Government Printing Office, 1979).

16. Lloyd Shearer, "Intelligence Report," *Parade Magazine*, April 8, 1982.

17. "Albany, New York Conference Material," National Commission on Working Women (April, 1979).

by design, offered an opportunity to speak openly about working conditions in the banking industry. One woman testified that after fourteen years working at one New York bank, she earned only $11,000 annually; another woman told of earning minimum wages as a bank teller.

In addition, two recent films depict office workers' resistance. *The Wilmar Eight* shows how eight bank clericals refused to continue to train their male supervisors.[18] And, of course, the commercially successful *Nine to Five* humorously portrays women organizing to reorganize their office.

The Coalition of Labor Union Women (CLUW), organized in 1974, represents some 6,000 union women and speaks out in support of increased clerical organizing. Working Women joined with the Service Employees International Union in 1981 to form District 925/SEIU for the purpose of organizing women clericals. Other unions, such as UFCW, have had recent organizing success with bank employees and CWA continues to represent large numbers of women workers in telecommunications. District 65/UAW and the American Federation of State, County and Municipal Employees (AFSCME) also organize and represent women in the public sector. However, organization of clericals is still very low — in the finance industry, less than 3 percent.[19]

Office Technology

The technological revolution now sweeping offices demands the attention of both the women's movement and organized labor. Typewriters, file cabinets and copiers, the familiar office equipment of the past, are absent from the "office of the future." Computers, word processors and telecommunications equipment are reorganizing the office, restructuring tasks and redefining clerical jobs. Typists have become word processor operators, file clerks are now data-entry clerks and secretaries are administrative support staff. Word processing centers, which are generally isolated from the rest of the work force, contain women who sit in cockpit-like stations and operate video display terminals (VDTs) for eight hours a day, five days a week. Not only are their jobs deadeningly routine, they are also supervised electronically. A 3M Corporation executive writes that "business can finally monitor and measure the productivity of the clerical function."[20]

Machine rationalization breaks down meaningful jobs into discrete tasks and automatic processes. It deskills work and makes employers

---

18. *The Wilmar Eight*, directed by Lee Grant, produced by Julie Thompson and Mary Beth Yarrow, is available through California Newsreel.

19. U.S. Dept. of Labor, Bureau of Labor Statistics, *The Characteristics of Organized Workers* (Washington, DC: Government Printing Office, 1981).

20. "Word Processing and the Work Process," *Dollars and Sense* 69(September 1981).

less dependent on any unique group of workers. As job skills are destroyed, previously identifiable groups of workers disappear and join the ranks of interchangeable labor units. Typing skills, for example, are no longer a prerequisite for working in a modern office. Estimated training time for a VDT operator is three to four days. Easily trained workers are also easily removed. Worker leverage is reduced when skills are decreased and any organized resistance must take other forms. Pay is often lowered also. Such deskilling therefore accomplishes both of management's objectives — reducing labor costs and reducing worker control.

Why is clerical work now being industrialized? Many argue that the second industrial revolution is occurring. Expanding markets, increasing population and improving transportation generated the first industrial revolution, but none of these accounts for the current radical change in clerical labor. Others argue that women, whether or not they are declared feminists, have been affected by the women's movement both at home and at work. Office women no longer serve their bosses as "the sun serves the earth." Rather, women have become more assertive about their rights as workers and therefore less easily manageable. In many offices, women resist doing the old office housekeeping chores, such as making coffee, delivering lunches, and running personal errands for the boss.

Whatever the reasons for increasing resistance by clerical workers, we know from historical studies that employers use technology to remove power from workers. One researcher found that industrialists in 1920 were willing to move the labor force back in technological time in order to regain control of the labor process and diminish worker militance.[21] Another study illustrates how Western Union introduced the already developed telegraph machine in the early 1900s, precisely when the company's skilled workers began to effectively act in concert.[22] And, currently, economist Joan Greenbaum argues that capital recruits, educates and perpetuates a pool of managers who are trained to talk about boosting the efficiency of labor, but who actually control worker reactions. This control is accomplished through specialized personnel recruitment practices and a centralized organizational information system.[23]

---

21. Philip McLewin, "Labor Conflict and Technological Change: The Family Shop in Paterson, New Jersey" (unpublished paper); Dr. McLewin based his research on the silk industry after a militant 1913 silk strike. Requests for information can be directed to him at Ramapo College of New Jersey, in Mahwah, New Jersey.

22. Charles Craypo, "The Impact of Changing Corporate Structure and Technology on Telegraph Labor: 1870-1978," *Labor Studies Journal* 3(Winter 1979).

23. Joan M. Greenbaum, *In the Name of Efficiency* (Philadelphia: Temple University Press, 1979).

A number of conclusions can be drawn about technology and clerical work. A majority of the clerical workforce is female and, for the most part, is becoming more assertive. Second, management uses technology not only for labor saving reasons, but also to control worker behavior. Third, the labor/management struggle that started in the 1800s favors managers because they own and control the technology used to deprive workers and their unions of power.

Union Response to Office Technology

Unions can affect the unilateral use of technology against worker interests by arguing for advance notification of technological change and by insisting on determination of its use and follow up procedures for its implementation. To do so, however, they must have strength. But unions don't have strength unless they organize new workers. Organizing clericals presents particular challenges to existing union structures because 16½ of the 18 million clerical workers are women.

Unions will need to recognize at the outset, not only that clericals are women, but that there is a patriarchal social structure within which women workers function. (Patriarchy is a set of power exchanges between men who either consciously or subsconsciously oppress women by stereotypical behavior). The social institutions led by men are structured in such a way that women are denied equal access to them. Women come into office work and stay there. Office work is low-paid and low-status. These two conditions exist because of a social power structure which supports the process. Employers profit from an ideology which suggests that women are passive, mindless, unfocussed, non-creative creatures. Unionists, male and female, are products of the society in which this idea dominates, therefore they often share this stereotype of women. But, unions cannot afford to buy this ideology because if they do, they simply serve management's objective. True, it is not easy to cut through generations of socialization. But both men and women in the trade union movement must find ways to overcome these images and instead achieve organizational solidarity.

To organize women at their wage jobs, it is necessary to understand the importance of their unpaid jobs. A woman's position in the family is central to the society's health and growth. A woman is therefore expected to

(1) socialize young people to adopt and adapt to social norms and regulations;

(2) provide emotional support to parents, children, husbands and, in many cases, also act as arbitrator and peace maker;

(3) serve a family constituency from whom she is separated for hours at a time;

(4) clean and care for the home environment, for which she is physically responsible and

(5) purchase materials which sustain and maintain family members.

These functions are mainly supportive ones. Women do not normally object to performing them, however, even though they do so without monetary compensation. Yet in a society which measures status by money earnings, unpaid positions are not legitimate. Housewives' labor is not included in national product accounting which is used to calculate the GNP. Is it any wonder then that women enter the paid labor market believing that they lack work experience, leadership skills, financial sophistication or collective behavior expertise? Unions must provide leadership in changing that negative consciousness.

Women workers need to organize in order to protect themselves. Equally important, unions need the strength that large numbers of women workers can provide. The following insights and suggestions are intended to help women and unions support each other and achieve their mutual goals.

1. *Role Models*

Unions should be places where favorable female role models can be found — competent women visible as organizers and officers. It is not that men cannot organize women, or that men cannot effectively represent women, or even that men do not know the issues which affect women. But if unions reflect the same power structure that exists in management, they send two negative messages to women: this "union stuff" is not going to be any different than it is at home or at work, and women who act assertively, take charge, or make responsible decisions will be perceived as threatening to men.

2. *Education*

Unions should design educational programs which reveal the history of women workers and their contributions to the labor movement. For example, women wage earners in textiles were the first to experience and respond to technological change. Women today should know that. It would not only raise their consciousness but also give them an historical identity. Furthermore, wives and mothers have been central to labor's strike effectiveness. Films like *Harlan County* and *With Babies and Banners* are reminders of how women have supported union causes. Working class history has been denied to all working people, but women's history has especially been denied to them.

Educational programs should also define male/female discrimination as a union issue, not as just a "women's" issue. Women's issues are not, as a rule, taken seriously.

3. Social Services

Unions must provide social services to women so that they have equal access to collective action. Specifically, this means that a child care plan should be argued both in the union hall and at the negotiating table. Women who cannot attend union meetings cannot assume leadership positions or actively participate in other union activities and, therefore, cannot be counted upon to support the union. Other crucial services are economic benefits such as personal leave to allow women time to take care of family responsibilities and educational leave to encourage women to prepare for leadership.

4. Coalitions

Unions should reach out to local or regional women's groups to form organizational linkages. There is a natural alliance between the women's movement and the trade union movement. Local women's groups can help organizing drives, for instance, with information on child care, legal services, counseling services and so on. A frequent inability of labor and women's groups to form coalitions in the past needs to be openly discussed so that the two may reach a plateau whereby cooperation provides support for working women.

Innovative ideas, including new structural approaches for organizing women workers, should be attempted. CLUW could act as a catalyst in this process. Trade unions and women's groups might coordinate their community support activity and articulate the union/women's issues in organizing drives.

5. Technology

To organize clerical workers around technology issues unions have to implement specific strategies. Translating technological processes and effects into understandable terms is the first step. The economic benefits of union membership are still primary motives for workers to join unions. There are direct monetary costs in working with VDTs. Headaches, muscle spasms, vision defects and tension are not simply side effects to be cured by aspirin or jogging. They mean medical bills, inability to work, loss of economic opportunities and inability to function as a wife and mother. Union organizers must discuss with the rank and file methods to control the unilateral introduction of technology into their workplaces, such as requesting advance notification of technological change, right to refuse assignments, or the formation of union-management quality of work life committees.

Offering members technological education is a second step. For workers to act responsibly, they must have information. Since technological information is not readily available to them, it is up to the union to provide this education. There are two types of important information: (1) That which is necessary to have a practical understanding of the technology used at the worksite. Demystifying the computer is the key to controlling it. External technicians might be used as resource people and instructors. (2) That information which is necessary to protect workers against harmful effects of technology. This kind of knowledge gives workers the tools to diagnose worksite problems. It also suggests practical methods of action. For example, given the increasing inadequacy of the inspection and penalty procedures of the Occupational Safety and Health Administration, labor-management committees on safety and health should remain active. These groups and others like them should be seen as critical links to rank and file technology education. In addition, colleges and universities, through existing Labor Studies/Labor Education divisions, can be called upon to conduct research and to analyze the consequences of technology so that unions are armed with facts, rather than blue smoke.

These suggestions, of course, do not exhaust the list of possible union responses. Unions could also broaden the collective bargaining process to include union rights in the use of technology. However, the above strategies can be important for unions attempting to organize clerical workers. Unions like District 925/SEIU, CWA, OPEIU, UFCW and District 65/UAW are working to protect their members and enhance their working lives. The above discussion is not meant to discredit their efforts. Rather, these measures, I believe, should be integrated into any union's agenda if they are to get and keep women as union members.

Case Studies of IAM Local Experiences with the Introduction of New Technologies

Leslie E. Nulty

Introduction

The International Association of Machinists and Aerospace Workers (IAM) has a tradition of local autonomy and responsibility. At most, perhaps 20 percent of its membership is covered by national master agreements, and a large part of that minority is in the transportation sector: railroads and airlines. Thus, although its major "jurisdiction" overlaps many other industrial units, the IAM's internal form and function are somewhat different.

Because of this paucity of master agreements, the IAM has a system of industrial conferences and coordinated bargaining committees (for specific firms) in which representatives of the particular locals or districts meet to review the current state and outlook for the firm or industry and to discuss union strategy. The electronics industry conference has met annually since the 1950s; but by convention decision in 1968 it was rechristened the Electronics and New Technology Conference. It is chaired by a member of the union's International Executive Council and is the principal forum for addressing problems of technological change at the national level. Conference recommendations are transmitted throughout the union in a variety of ways: conference participants report at their regional staff meetings which are attended by, among others, elected business representatives — the first level of full-time staff; the union newspaper covers the conference; and the International Research Department uses conference recommendations in responding to requests for specific information or assistance that come in from the field.

Leslie Nulty is a Staff Assistant to the International President, International Association of Machinists and Aerospace Workers.

In addition, the Research Department prepares a manual of model contract language for all full time staff. This manual has had model language on the subject of technological change since 1960. (Current model language is discussed in Appendix A.) Although it contains no specific reference to technology, the union's Constitution has included language on the related question of work rules and the proper jurisdiction of the union since its early days. Finally, acting upon the recommendation of the 1981 Electronics and New Technology Conference, the union newspaper now carries a regular column on the issue.

In selecting and preparing the four case studies that follow an attempt was made to reflect the enormous diversity of industries and firms organized by the IAM. Unfortunately, due to time and other constraints, the aerospace industry is not included, admittedly an important omission. The cases were identified and pursued on the basis of experiences aired at our Electronics and New Technology Conference, other conferences, and from the experience of our Research Department in aiding locals which had contacted the International for support in negotiations on the issue of technological change.

This is an historical study; an attempt to determine how Machinist locals have coped with technological changes occurring in the past ten years. For the members of these locals a fully automated plant or machine shop is still something they read about in magazines or hear about from experts at union conferences. Their own experiences are largely incremental.[1] As indicated in these studies, specific contract language governing the introduction of new methods or machines was not available to any of the locals involved. Language on training rights for bargaining unit members varies considerably. Neither transfer rights, severance pay, nor relocation allowances were relevant in any of these cases (although they have been important in other IAM experiences). Instead, these locals were able to use informal information networks, contract language defining the bargaining unit, job descriptions, their own intrinsic skills and knowledge of the work process and the grievance procedure, as levers to insure that technological change was not an unrestricted prerogative of management.

Whether these tools will be adequate for the scale of technological change that is projected for the next decade is another question. None of the stories told here is "over" — each is part of a continuous process

---

1. An aerospace study especially in plants where military production is being carried out might be different. Most of the developmental work on computerization of manufacturing and design and their integration has been carried out by the Department of Defense. This, plus a cost-plus, non-competitive market environment, has enabled defense contractors to get to go farther and faster in advanced automation than civilian industry.

of negotiation and response. New developments are constantly occurring. There is no way to predict how successful the locals will be in their determination to improve relevant contract language in upcoming rounds of negotiations.

These cases show that management is often prepared to go to extreme lengths — including cutting into its own potential profits — in order to reduce the power and influence as well as the number of manual workers. If unions and their members are to prevail in this familiar struggle, they must have a wide range of strategies and tools at their disposal, not the least of which is unionization of the draftsmen, engineers, and computer programmers with whom they otherwise will be forced to compete for work.

Case 1: The Introduction of Computer Numerical Controlled (CNC) Machine Tools in a Small Specialty Shop

Background.

The employer in question is a privately-held family-owned firm that dates back to 1865.[2] The IAM organized the workers in 1946 and since that time has remained the exclusive bargaining agent. There has never been a strike at the plant and a union shop has been a part of the agreement since the first contract.

IAM membership in 1981 was 89; the bargaining unit worked two shifts. Almost all were skilled or semi-skilled workers. Peak membership was 125, reached in early 1979. Major layoffs occurred just after the settlement of the current contract, in April and August, 1979. No new workers have been hired since the peak and laid-off workers with less than five years seniority have not been recalled. Although the union has a strong apprenticeship clause in the contract, it has been several years since new apprentices have been hired.

The 1979 layoffs appear not directly attributable to the introduction of computer numerical controlled (CNC) machine tools, which had begun in 1975. Rather, the cutbacks were a result of a decline in sales. On the other hand, the presence of higher performance CNC machines may well have contributed to the company's failure to recall low-seniority workers. By 1981 the firm had in place four CNC machine tools: a jig mill, a shaft lathe, and two chuckers. An additional jig mill was expected at the time this study was conducted.

---

2. Employers and local unions in these case studies are not identified as a condition under which the research was conducted and reported.

Workers' Control over the Production Process

A contract clause designated "The Union and the Company" gives management complete discretion over the introduction of new machines. Yet members were able to obtain advance knowledge of new machine decisions because of good working relationships and informal social contact with the substantial white collar-technical workforce — consisting of approximately 30 non-bargaining unit designers, computer programmers, engineers and draftsmen. Thus the union has found ways to adjust to an equipment mix and workplace organization unilaterally designated by management.

The members' strength in this regard came from a combination of their high skill levels, the specialty nature of the product and strong contract language covering job posting, bidding rights, and company training. The agreement required management to first consider workers in the existing labor force to train for new vacancies, skills or machines. In the past this meant that helpers were able to become machine tool operators and machine tool operators with sufficient seniority learned to operate and understand virtually all the machines in the shop, which in turn enabled them to acquire knowledge and skills equivalent to those of a journeyman machinist with formal apprenticeship training. Such workers could bid for the top-rated "machinist" slots within the bargaining unit, but unlike the apprentice-trained journeymen, they were not able to walk into "machinist" positions with other firms.

Under the local contract in 1981, members who bid and were accepted to train for a new job had a 90-day qualifying period during which they could choose to return to their former job. If the worker failed to qualify on the new job, he was guaranteed his old job back. This meant the worker had the right to "try out" new machines and reject them in favor of his former job.

Indeed there was significant experimentation of this sort. As a result, it appears older workers, accustomed to manually controlled machine tools, are far less comfortable with CNC machines than younger workers. In at least one case, a journeyman machinist took a pay cut in order to gain experience with the new generation of machine tools, only to find that the lack of operator control and much higher machine speeds were not to his liking. He returned to his higher paid classification and former job. Apparently this has happened often enough that management gave notice of its desire to change the contract so that a bidder on a new job would have to hold that job for a year before being allowed either to bid another job or return to their former position.

Union concession on this issue would limit the worker's ability to choose among jobs according to personal preferences. Because of the greater mental stress associated with CNC operations, it is not clear such a change would actually benefit management. The high speeds of CNC machines (three to four times that of standard machines) require enormous operator concentration in a specialty operation like this, where expensive alloy castings are machined to fine specifications. Forcing workers who are not comfortable with that kind of work to do it for a year is likely to result in both potentially expensive errors and employee discontent.

The additional CNC jig mill raises another issue. Workers learned through informal conversation with foremen and engineers that this machine does two jobs simultaneously. While a worker sets-up one job, the other is being machined. Since the current contract has no specific language on manning requirements, it is not clear how workers will respond to this speed-up.

Health and Safety.

CNC machines were introduced when delivery times for orders had backed-up two to three years and excess demand for pumps brought new competitors into the industry. Thus the firm's motive for installing CNC was to increase production rapidly in a short period of time.[3] Under pressure to get the product out, however, management performed virtually no preventive maintenance on the machines and ran them at the highest possible speed contrary to the advice of the workers. Not surprisingly this led to equipment failure and expensive downtime. Then, after two or three years, management learned that the maximum is not necessarily the optimum and its engineers reduced "standards" — the designated machine speeds given the workers for each type of material and part. But in practice the workers use their knowledge and skill to reprogram machine feeds and speeds to get the job done best as they see it, not necessarily according to the engineers' standards.

Yet there is still a lack of preventive maintenance which contributes to job stress since machines may fly apart or throw off the workpiece without warning. Nevertheless, worker suggestions that better maintenance might lead to better production have been shrugged off by management despite the fact these are $350,000 machines purchased with loans at 18-to-20 percent interest rates. The members have an explanation, in their words: "You know — workers are the lowest form of animal life." Although the potential safety risk to the workers seems greater with CNC machines, in fact the injury rate on standard machines in this plant is higher because virtually all the standard

---

3. Increasing the work force would probably have required building a new plant — a long-term undertaking.

machines are unguarded — a condition inviting a formal OSHA non-compliance citation. Worker complaints prompted management to begin building machine guards.[4]

Industrial safety experts are not aware of any formal, rigorous studies having been done on the comparative health and safety experiences of standard and CNC machine tools. Plant management suggests that CNC machines are probably noisier because of their higher operating speeds. This is hazardous in a shop where noise levels are already quite high. The only monitoring of noise levels of which the workers are aware has been done by the company's insurer. Workers were not informed of the readings but say that the shop always seemed to be more quiet on days the insurance company's inspector came around.

Skill Effects.

Introduction of computer controls in machining operations is not seen as skill dilution by the workers. Indeed, management concedes that it makes sense to train a worker for CNC operations only if that worker has extensive prior experience with standard or numerical control machines or both. IAM members operating CNC machines in this shop were trained by the machine manufacturer and, as mentioned above, are able to edit and change the computer program for desired speeds and feeds. But they also work closely with in-house programmers when (as often happens) the computers create errors in their own programs. Traditional machining skills are essential to identify and correct such errors.

Postscript.

As this is written in 1981, workers have learned via the grapevine and local media (only white collar employees were formally notified by management) that the family-owned firm was being acquired by a large, sophisticated multi-plant corporation. They expect there will be changes in the work patterns and relationships described here and are concerned about a loss of union leverage in future contract negotiations.

---

4. The local president's CNC lathe shattered its guard glass in his face when the machine threw off the piece on which he was working.

Case 2. Robots and Computerization: Different Implications for Toolroom Workers

Background.

Confronting a "mature" market characterizated by slow long-run growth and cyclical depression as consequences of the poor housing market, this large major appliance manufacturer, one of the strongest conglomerate multinational corporations in the world, is rapidly upgrading its manufacturing operations through robotics and computerization. At the industrial complex involved in this case study, roughly 300 IAM tool and die workers are employed. Another industrial union represents the 14,000 production and maintenance workers. Total employment in 1981 was 19,000 — down from a 1973 peak of 22,000. Six separate product lines are built in six separate buildings, each one of which has its own tool room.

The original production line robot was installed ten years ago to remove plastic parts from their molds and transfer them to a fixture on a machine which trimmed the parts. It was kept in a fenced off area and used by the company as a "show piece" operation. Five years later additional robots were brought in to do spray painting and glueing. These jobs, the most undesirable, were low-skill, high turnover positions filled by workers with the lowest seniority, who bid out of them as soon as they could. Nonetheless, production workers preferred even those "dirty" jobs to being unemployed. In 1981 there were 60 robots in use and the company expected to have 90 in place early the following year.

With the exception of replacement or repair of tools and fixtures that are part of the robots, none of the maintenance and repair work on robots is under IAM jurisdiction. Although disagreements do arise occasionally between the IAM and the union representing the maintenance workers, these are generally settled amicably and there have been no problems between the two in allocating work associated with the new machines.

Employment Impact of Robots.

Because tool and die workers' responsibilities are confined to replacement and repair of tools and fixtures, robots have had little impact on the amount or kind of work they do. The employment impact falls largely on the unskilled production workers. Indeed, in the most recent and currently projected rounds of layoffs, toolroom workers will be unaffected. In 1980, 3500 people were laid off and all were recalled within six months, but no journeymen toolmakers were furloughed, only apprentices.[5] The company has told the union that over the long-run it anticipates a permanent decline in the operation's labor force of 20 percent as a result of the market outlook for its products — no reduction was attributed specifically to the introduction of robots. In fact, 1981 production was so far ahead of demand that final inventory was stored in boxcars, the company's warehouse space having been exhausted. Obviously any acceleration of robotization will accelerate the long-term reduction in production employment. The firm expects to achieve the projected reduction in jobs through attrition and an unspecified program of retraining and placement.

Production workers have reportedly come to accept the robots despite initial fear and resentment. This is largely due to their concern that the plant would otherwise become obsolescent and noncompetitive. Unskilled production workers can and do apply for the company's apprenticeship program for training tool and die makers. If upgrading the toolroom (as described below) leads to an increase in and diversification of toolroom operations, it might provide partial compensation for the loss of unskilled jobs to robots. Nor do skilled tool and die makers see robots as a threat to their jobs — mainly because they know there is a shortage of toolmakers in the area. They believe the company is likely to avoid temporary layoffs for fear of losing skilled workers to other firms. To them, the amount of work associated with robots, as with any other type of machine, is largely a function of the size of the operation: how many machines are in use and how frequently their tools and dies have to be changed. The number of toolroom jobs relates less to *the amount of work to* be done than to the *kind* of work done.

CNC Machine Tools.

In mid-1981 the first CNC machine tool — a milling machine — was put into operation in one of the tool rooms. More are expected to be installed in the five other tool rooms in the complex. Tool room workers have two different responses to these machines. One group looks at the superior speed, quality and reliability of these machines and is concerned that there will be fewer jobs for tool makers. Another group believes that the superior performance creates the potential for staunching the subcontracting of work out of the bargaining unit.

Thirty years ago when the plant opened all new die-making, which is the heart of the tool and die makers craft, was done in-house. Within a decade, however, it began to be subcontracted to other firms. The result was that tool room operations at this plant became confined to comparatively routine replacement and repair work.

---

5. To the IAM local this was a mistake because it delayed the skill-progress of its apprentices. The company has had difficulty hiring qualified tool-makers. No toolroom employees were scheduled for layoff in the cutbacks during the last quarter of 1981.

Most of the machinery in the tool rooms is now 30 years old, encouraging even further subcontracting to more modern facilities where the work can be done more cheaply. In addition, with the current slump in the market and intense competitive pressures, subcontracting may appear even more profitable to management. Toolroom workers hope that the addition of state-of-the-art machine tools will make it more attractive to the company to retain work in-house and eventually go back to the production of original dies — work they consider far more creative, interesting and, therefore, desirable.

The current union contract gives the skilled workers a lever for exploiting this possibility. In 1979 a special "farm-out" agreement was negotiated which requires joint union-management discussion of proposed subcontracting of "work normally performed by members of the bargaining unit on existing production tooling." It specifies a managment "show cause" report and a prohibition against any subcontracting challenged by the union until that challenge is resolved. Resolution can be accomplished either through satisfactory negotiations or, failing that, accelerated grievance procedure where the case goes immediately to the step preceding arbitration. However the company does have the right to implement the proposed subcontract once the grievance procedure has been invoked.

Workers' control and skill development.

The workers have not yet experienced a problem with management attempting to restrict their knowledge or responsibilities regarding CNC machines. They are, of course, still in a training period. Workers themselves have been able to determine the system for selecting who receives training first. (Only eight people can be trained at one time.) They decided to suspend the usual seniority-based selection system because the workers with the highest seniority will retire in the next few months and their training would therefore be without purpose. Instead they held a lottery. Excluding those near retirement, all of the members participated.

Training classes last four hours and include training in computer language and programming. Training time is paid at straight time hourly rates and those participating in the training report that it is serious and challenging. Initially the members feared they would be denied programming knowledge because of reports of similar company behavior at other locations. This has not occurred at the training level, but it remains to be seen what will happen when computer programmers begin to assert their jurisdictional claims.[6] Their awareness of the possibility, however, makes the IAM membership determined to get appropriate language in their next contract to assure that they maintain control of the programming function.

6. Computer programmers already are at the plant site working on computer-aided design; they are not in the IAM bargaining unit.

Case 3: New Products and New Jobs; Protecting the Union's Jurisdiction

Background

This company, a division of a giant multinational conglomerate, signed an agreement with the IAM local in the early 1970s covering all plants in the greater metropolitan area.[7] Since then the division's revenue has more than doubled as have employment and IAM membership, and the number of plants covered by the agreement has increased from three to six. Although the contract does not contain a union shop provision, IAM membership has averaged 90-95 percent of the eligible labor force. This membership growth was achieved despite job-displacing automation in several operations: electrostatic painting, automated test equipment, automated assembly and CNC machines in the machine shop; and in spite of new product development which caused a decline in the share of total output by those jobs in which IAM membership originally was concentrated.

For the past ten years the local union leadership has been aware of the future implications of technological change and shifts in products and markets. Local officers have attended industry conferences to keep up with new developments in the field. Their diligence and persistence in policing the contract enabled the local to overcome technological barriers to membership growth that might otherwise have gone unnoticed. Repeatedly the union discovered that manufacturing operations ancillary to existing operations were being conducted by the employer in unmarked facilities, sometimes with workers hired through an intermediary source and designated "independent contractors." Through perseverance and sophisticated bargaining, the union was able to get both the contracted workers and their work brought under the contract.

Responding to new products and "new" jobs.

Within the last five years two major operating changes occurred. Work on the new product line of advanced equipment began and then new assembly procedures were introduced for both old and new products. The union was not informed of the new product line. Instead, it learned that developmental work was being done in an unmarked plant in an industrial park located far from the original manufacturing complex. When the union brought this to local management's attention, and pointed out that its contract covered all operations in the metropolitan area, management indicated that union rec-

---

7. The company did so in return for union agreement to change from an incentive pay system to measured day-work.

ognition would be granted when the work progressed from development to actual production. Indeed, one year later, when relatively simple components were brought into the main plant for assembly, the IAM did get jurisdiction over these jobs.

Soon thereafter, production of a more complex precision component was brought into the main plant. The workers assigned to this operation were a mix of low skilled "independent contractors", on the one hand, and skilled personnel, called "lab technicians" and holding two-year degrees in analog and digital circuitry with course work in microprocessing, on the other.[8] A year after the union discovered the "developmental" plant, and after it repeatedly raised the issue of bargaining unit work being done by non-unit workers, the sub-assembly jobs in question also came under the IAM contract.

Construction then began on a new facility to house the division's final assembly and staging work for the new product. "Staging" is the very technical, highly skilled part of the operation that describes the final linking together of a complex system of components. Until two years ago this work was usually done where the machinery would be used, by locally-based service staff employed by the corporation. Sometimes it was performed by workers from production who were taken to the manufacturing site. More recently, however, customers have been anxious to get these systems operating and therefore less willing to accept delays caused by insufficient field staff to do the staging. Customer pressure led to the staging function being carried out at the manufacturing site prior to shipment.

The IAM local insists staging work belongs within the bargaining unit, but so far the company has restricted it to approximately two hundred "lab technicians" who are not in the unit. Having introduced the new job task, the company argues that the work is not under the union's jurisdiction because union members have never done it before. The union maintains that when this work was done in the field union members sometimes did it and, in any case, they certainly have skills and ability equal to the task. It points out that the "lab technician" skills and other qualifications used in "staging" are virtually the same as those of workers in the top-rated bargaining unit classifications. Moreover, the pay is the same, the two groups of workers get the same work orders and have the same relationship to engineering staff. Yet "lab technician" working conditions are far superior. They do not punch time clocks, they have more independence and lighter supervi-

---

8. Young people were hired out of school and paid by the contracting firm at about $1.50 an hour below the lowest paid union workers. They have no seniority rights and are subject to termination at will. Although the local union has not been able to prove it, because the corporate chartering records on file with the state are incomplete, it suspects that the contractor may be a bogus concern set up by the parent corporation.

sion, do not meet daily production quotas and they enjoy more liberal sick leave policy. Moreover, they benefit from advanced training in the computer systems component of the final product — training the company has thus far denied IAM members.

Because it has no specific contract language governing training rights, the local uses other means to claim staging work. Although the IAM's proposal that "lab technician" work properly belongs within the bargaining unit has been rejected, continuous progress is being made. When, for example, the company failed to provide requested information on the numbers of "lab technicians," their responsibilities and job descriptions — information essential for bargaining on the issue — the union filed a "refusal to bargain" unfair labor practice charge. The company offered to compromise by bringing the "contractor" jobs into the bargaining unit and the charge was dropped. This experience convinced local leadership the company does not want the issue before the NLRB. The union believes it has a strong case if it asks the Board for a unit clarification decision in the matter. It prefers not to take that step as long as continuous progress is made towards expansion of the unit. Negotiations to that effect occur almost weekly. To date, this strategy has proved successful in maintaining membership growth and bargaining unit strength.

Case 4: Company Willingness to Incur High Costs to Reduce Worker Control: Computerization of Parts Fabrication in Aircraft Maintenance and Repair

Background.
In January 1980 a computer-controlled parts fabrication machine was brought into the aircraft service section of a major domestic airline's home base. The fabrication shop of this service section produces parts in-house for aircraft maintenance and repair. The shop is part of an enormously large complex — total IAM employment at the home base is around 5500. The union local is part of a national complex of locals in other cities that negotiate with the same employer through the IAM airlines district to which they belong. The officers and staff of the district handle all negotiations and grievance processing under a union shop agreement which has been in effect for more than 40 years. Workers there traditionally enjoyed complete responsibility for producing parts according to engineering specifications. They are highly skilled workers with generally considerable seniority. Each worker was able to handle each request, "from A to Z," according to the local union, and to operate every machine in the shop.

There have been no recent layoffs in this shop but five jobs were eliminated through attrition. Management's decisions regarding the organization of work following the introduction of the new machine has meant that work traditionally performed by union members has been transferred out of fabricating and assigned to non-union members in computer programming. This happened without any apparent technological or efficiency rationale. If anything, efficiency, profitability and other normal management criteria for decision-making point in the opposite direction, that is, towards *more* functions and responsibility being brought into the fabrication shop.

Workers' Control.

The machine in this case study is an automatic turret punch press that produces batches of parts from sheet metal. Its computerized control system can be operated from either taped programs or those introduced directly by the machine operator.

Prior to installation, shop workers bid for inclusion in a "machine crew" to be trained to run the press. When a mechanic and salesman demonstrated the machine, which is unlike any in the shop, the workers learned that the manufacturer provides purchasers a free two-week school for employees to learn to operate and program the machine. They requested to be sent for the instruction but were turned down, although the airline later sent a supervisor, an engineer, a programmer and an electrical shop foreman. Shop workers were told training was inappropriate for them and that a computer programmer would need two years to become proficient in writing programs for the machine. They interpreted this response as implying that they were incapable of acquiring the necessary skills and knowledge. They immediately filed a grievance because, in their words:

> Something is wrong with a system that sends everyone involved with the equipment to school except the four people responsible to operate and maintain it eight hours a day. . . A grievance was filed because we began to relaize that we were being deliberately kept away from the information required to do our job.

In their view, which is supported by the experience discussed below, it is impossible to separate the programming and production functions. The company's attempt to do so is seen as a violation of that section of the union contract which defines the union's jurisdiction as covering "all work involved in . . . overhauling, repairing, fabrication . . . and machine tool work in connection therewith."

Meanwhile, having been denied access to the formal training course, two members of the machine crew took the machine manuals home at night and taught themselves to program the machine manually. Not only did they become proficient programmers after six months of self-study, they discovered errors in the manufacturer's manual that the computer programmers only learned from "errata" corrections sent by the manufacturer! Four months after the machine was installed and during the period when the grievance was being processed, an on-off switch was put on the computer to stop the machine crew from working with it. Needless to say, this was a minor, easily-overcome impediment for experienced machine shop workers, but they saw it as part of a pattern of harassment and pressure designed to keep them from controlling the computer aspects of the new operation. By posting printed procedural rules the company tried to divide the work between white-collar programmers stationed at one end of the airfield and machine loaders in the fabrication shop at the other end. The latter were ordered not to do any programming but to work cooperatively with the non-union computer programmers to help *them* get the errors out of *their* programs.

Separating the two functions this way clearly violates the principles of the machine design. According to the manufacturer's manual:

> Programming is the process of analyzing an Engineering drawing, selecting an order of punching, and transferring this drawing information in the selected order to a program sheet. The program sheet becomes a basis for preparation of a program tape. . . Evaluation of the Engineering drawing, selection of a machining sequence, and preparation of the program sheet is done by a programmer. The programmer must have a *working knowledge of machine shop practices, blueprint reading, tool design, and sheet metal fabricating techniques.* A good background in mathematics, especially trigonometry and algebra, is desirable.

Such skills, abilities and educational requirements characterize shop workers, but *not* computer programmers, who lack the specified "working knowledge of machine shop practices and sheet metal fabricating techniques." In fact, the workers themselves would clearly demonstrate that management's division of labor is inefficient and imposes enormous financial cost.

Under the company's scheme a parts order that comes into the fabrication shop and requires use of the CNC turret punch is not filled until the shop requests and receives a computer tape from the programming center. When the tape has errors, or the machine introduces errors the workers are not supposed to edit it but to call in the programmers to make corrections. This method results in a turn-around time for filling parts requests of a week or more. Moreover, because programmers lack the production knowledge of shop workers, their programs are less efficient in the use of materials and lead to expensive scrappage rates. Skilled shop workers estimate they can produce a given part at a cost which is 94 percent lower than under management's method, not even counting potential savings from shorter turn-around times. They further estimate that if they had full responsibility for programming, with the computer programmers on call as specialized consultants, they could fill some parts orders in a couple of hours rather than a week. If they also had the tape printer and plotter now available only to the programmers they could further reduce costs and increase output.[9]

---

9. This would return pattern-making to machine shop workers who lost it when computer assisted design was introduced.

These workers are especially embittered because several years ago, when the company was on the verge of bankruptcy, union members voted to accept wage concessions. This was done with an understanding that they would be made whole when profits improved. True, during the first three years of that agreement union members got back more than they had conceded. But in 1980, when the computerized parts fabricating machine was brought in, and again in 1981, under the combined impact on the airline industry of deregulation, the PATCO strike and economic recession, the company has shown losses. The result was to force workers to give up a percentage of their pay. Now they see management intransigence that increases operating costs and depresses profits and they cannot understand it.

The way in which management introduced the CNC machine created friction among union workers in the shop. Those *not* on the machine crew work rough parts stamped out by the CNC punch press, a machine they have not been trained to use. They are "reduced to" bending, deburring and otherwise finishing someone else's work, rather than doing the job "A to Z" as they had prior to CNC. As for the CNC machine crew, management told them to teach other workers how to load the CNC machine with tapes, punches, dies and sheet metal and how to turn it on and off, but *not* how to program it. This contravenes the manufacturer's manual, which stresses that *safe* and economical use requires "the operator to be thoroughly familiar with the system prior to use of the system." Management's insistence means that workers conducting the training are not allowed to answer questions trainees might ask. Workers who violate direct orders in this matter can be threatened by a letter of reprimand, loss of pay or loss of employment. Although the union would not permit such discipline to be imposed, the mere potential for conflict is another source of pressure on workers.

These management decisions inject an unnecessary element of stress into daily work relationships which would not be present if the machine manufacturer's instructions were followed. To the workers involved, the situation is filled with grim irony. This firm has been vocal about labor-management cooperation and its interest in having workers make productivity-raising suggestions. Yet at every step of the grievance procedure, thus far, workers' complaints have been denied and their suggestions for improvement ignored and turned into a source of harassment.

The grievance is now (1981) at the arbitration stage. But about one thousand other cases are also at that step, mainly because the company appears to have adopted a policy of denying most grievances at each of the earlier stages. Naturally the union has to give higher priority to discharge and pay complaints. So considerable delay in the CNC case is inevitable.[10]

Conclusion

Insofar as the experiences described in these four cases of technology and labor response in IAM machine shops reflect general industry trends, a number of conclusions can be drawn.

1. Employer profitability and productivity are not necessarily the most important considerations in management decisions regarding method and timing in technological change. An explanation for this is that management uses crude and inaccurate means of evaluating technology's impact. An obsession with operating "control" encourages management to focus on direct labor costs to the exclusion of other costs.

2. Workers get training and upgrading in new production processes only when they aggressively assert a claim to that right.

3. New technology creates jobs and skills for union members only when workers intervene to make sure that happens. Passive acceptance of management-designed technological change may result in severe job loss or downgrading or both.

4. Skilled workers are better able to adjust to new technology than are the unskilled. For the labor force as a whole building upward job mobility into the entire spectrum of job structures is essential. But we must also recognize that unskilled workers cannot move into skilled categories without solid numeracy and literacy. Inadequacies have to be remedied through expansion of adult education and high school equivalency programs that focus on skill acquistion, not merely paper certification.

5. Conventional blue collar/white collar interpretation of the labor market is a management-imposed division that is no longer appropriate. Its perpetuation through restrictive job classifications unilaterally designed by employers is a major barrier to improved productivity.

---

10. One worker even wrote the company's chief executive officer, after having cornered him on a flight where he related the whole story, protesting, in his words, the "cold war over control of the machine operation." Meanwhile, worker frustration and disillusionment remains over not being allowed to develop skills and improve output.

Appendix A
IAM Model Contract Language on Technological Change

The paragraphs that follow comprise an advisory document sent out to all IAM Local Lodges after the 1981 Machnist Electronics and New Technology Conference.

The model contract language suggested below is intended to provide guidance for locals wishing to negotiate improved security language into their agreements relating to issues of technological change. The jumping off point for this effort was the already existing language recommended in the IAM Model Contract Manual. That language has been examined in detail by each of the two collective bargaining workshops of the 1981 Electronic and New Technology Conference. Changes representing improvements in protection have been incorporated in these revised recommendations.

A word of warning is necessary! *This language does not represent an integrated proposal to be submitted "as is"*. It is instead, a setting forth of options and alternative approaches. For example, a bargaining unit which negotiated the language herein recommended relative to *Reduction in Force Due to Technological Change,* which provides only for reduction by "attrition", would then have no need, or little need, for language dealing with *Rate Retention, Retraining and Transfer Rights and Relocation Expenses.*

Therefore, in extracting language from this document for proposals to employers, care must be taken to insure consistent intent, without internal conflict between the items selected. Further it is necessary to examine how the selected clauses might dove-tail with or impinge upon the meaning of existing contract language; especially language which already provides some protection (such as transfer rights of laid-off employees whether or not it was occasioned by technological change).

Finally, specific language must be tailored to the individual contract in many instances to insure that the new clauses do no violence to existing seniority and bargaining unit definition arrangements. We have tried to indicate where decisions of this type must be made by providing choices. However, since it is impossible to anticipate all variations of contract language, it is essential that each local determine the modifications necessary to maximize the effectiveness of these recommendations in each negotiating situation.

What is New Technology?

Often the new technology is in place before the union is fully aware of what is happening. Thus, the first step is to reach agreement, in advance, on what constitutes new technology so that the rest of the program can begin.

Article ___.1
Technological change shall be defined as any alteration in equipment, material, methods, and/or changes in work design. This should also include any change in product line.

Advance Notice

In the event of management's introducing new technology it is imperative that the union firmly establish the right to advance notice, the right to certain kinds of information and the obligation to bargain over necessary adjustments through clear and specific contract language. By being required to give advance notice of plans to introduce technological change, the union will have time to negotiate all of the necessary adjustment programs. Expensive automated equipment is usually ordered long before its installation. If management is required to inform the Union at the time the equipment is ordered, there would be ample opportunity for the Union and Company to negotiate in advance for the changes. Good-faith labor management planning, *before* the new equipment is installed, can eliminate hardships for workers and disruption in the plant.

Article ___.1
The company will advise the Union of any proposed technological changes prior to the time of the final decision, but not less than six months prior to institution of such change. The Company will promptly meet with the Union to negotiate regarding the effects of the proposed technological changes.

___.2
The company shall be required to provide the Union with full information regarding the proposed technological changes in order to determine the effects on the bargaining unit. Failure to reach agreement during these negotiations shall eliminate any restriction on the Union's right to strike. The Union shall, at its option, have the right to submit any dispute arising under this Article to the grievance and arbitration procedure.

Joint Consultation

Since it is impossible to predict all of the negative effects of technological changes before they are incorporated, it is necessary to establish a committee of labor-management representatives to negotiate the impact of such changes. With a joint committee the Union can require information as to the consequences involved in the changes and negotiate adequate safeguards for the workers affected.

Article ___.1
There will be established a Joint Union-Management Committee for Technological Change, comprised of equal representation from the

Union and Management, to study the problems arising from technological change in relation to the effect on the employees in the bargaining unit. The Union shall be entitled to all necessary information relevant to the proposed technological change including any new or increased health hazard associated with the new technology. The Committee shall meet at the request of either party.

Reduction In Force By Attrition
If the introduction of automated equipment is carefully planned, the Union can avoid layoffs even when fewer workers are necessary for a particular operation. Layoffs have been totally avoided by allowing any necessary reduction of force to take place gradually as a result of voluntary quits, retirement or death.

Article _____ .2
During the term of this agreement, no member of the bargaining unit shall be laid off or downgraded as either the direct or indirect result of technological change. Any reduction in the work force made necessary by technological change shall be accomplished by attrition. The term "attrition" shall be defined as the reduction of the work force by such natural means as death, voluntary quits, retirement and discharge for just cause.

New or Changed Job Classifications
As a standard rule — in all situations of changed jobs — the question of eligibility, wage rates, and effective date for new dates is paramount. This is especially true when new jobs are introduced or existing jobs are substantially altered. Ignoring important changes in job content, management has frequently insisted on maintaining the existing classification structure.

In other instances, it has sought to destroy the boundaries between existing skilled classifications.

Further, management often seeks to use technological change to downgrade existing jobs and, consequently, their rates of pay. While "red-circle" rates have always been a means of protecting present workers' pay scales, this approach takes on special meaning.

Article _____ .1
In the event the introduction of technological change results in either the establishment of new job classifications or a change in existing job classifications, employees within the (department, bargaining unit, plant), shall be given preference to such new and/or revised work resulting from these changes in order of seniority.

_____.2

All new job classifications created as the result of technological change which includes any of the work historically and/or currently performed by bargaining unit personnel shall be considered as coming under the scope of the bargaining unit. All current job classifications in the bargaining unit which are changed as the result of technological change shall remain within the bargaining unit. Any new job classification created as the result of a new product line shall be considered as falling within the scope of the existing bargaining unit.

_____.3

Rates of pay for new and/or revised job classifications shall be negotiated but, in no event, shall the negotiated earnings of the revised job be less than they were prior to the technological change. All such negotiated rates of pay shall be retroactive to the date of the introduction of such new equipment or processes.

_____.4

Employees who are displaced or downgraded from their regular job classifications as a result of technological change shall suffer no reduction in their hourly rate of pay. Such employees shall continue to receive all general wage increases, cost-of-living allowances, appropriate skill adjustments, if any, and any other increases necessary to maintain their equivalent rate of pay.

Retraining

The language that plays the most important role and gives the worker the greatest benefit to adjust to technological changes is that which affords him the opportunity to retrain for new jobs, preferably in the same plant where he is presently employed. When training is required, there are a number of details which can be translated into contract language. Every effort should be made to negotiate provisions for training employees during working hours at company expense and prevailing rates of pay with senior employees having a prior claim to training opportunities. Every effort should be made to make available to the worker the opportunity to acquire the added knowledge and skills to perform any new work introduced.

Training, however, must be examined within a larger context. There will be situations where either the new technology requires substantially fewer workers or present employees are not capable of successful retraining. In these cases, it should be the company's responsibility to train the employee for jobs not necessarily related to the new technology *per se*. These jobs may be within the existing facility or at other plants of the company or, as a last resort, in the community at large.

Article _____ .1

When, as a result of technological change, new and/or revised job classifications are introduced into the bargaining unit, the Company shall insure that employees will be given the opportunity to acquire the knowledge and skills necessary to qualify for these new and/or revised job classifications.

_____ .2

In the event, retraining for the new and/or revised job classifications is not feasible, the Company will provide the necessary training for job classifications not related to the new technologies. This will include training for jobs in other departments in the plant, and if necessary, for jobs at other Company plants.

_____ 3.

If a job with the Company is not feasible, the Company shall then initiate discussion with appropriate representatives of state and federal unemployment and job placement agencies with regard to job openings and/or skill shortages in the community. Should such openings exist, the Company will undertake to provide the necessary training so that affected employees can qualify for these jobs.

_____ .4

The Company shall establish, at its own expense and during regularly scheduled working hours, an adequate retraining program for affected employees. During the training period, the employee shall be paid at the established rate of pay for the job classification held prior to entering the training program.

Transfer Rights and Relocation Benefits

To provide senior workers with the greatest possible protection against job loss, unions have sought to establish the right to transfer to jobs in other plants.

The right to transfer to other plants may have a number of variations. For example, it may be confined to employees who are laid off because of a plant or department shutdown or extended to employees laid off for any reason at all. Also, it may be limited, on the one hand, to new plants, to situations in which existing operations have been moved to a new location, or to all plants in a given area or community; on the other hand, an employee may have the right to transfer to any plant of the company regardless of its "newness", type of operation, or location. Employees who transfer may retain full seniority rights or they may retain only those rights based on accredited service. A prime prerequisite to transferring to a different area is the ability to pay for the move. Thus, transferred employees should be given moving expenses and other allowances.

Article _____ .1

Any employee on indefinite layoff or who is subject to separation because of technological change shall have preference with respect to rehire at other Company plants where there are employment opportunities.

_____ .2

Employees laid off due to technological change shall be given preference over individuals not previously employed by the Company, in order of seniority, for job openings at other plants represented by the IAM, provided that all more senior employees from the plant experiencing technolocial change have waived their right to transfer subsequent to employee notification of the technological change producing the current reduction in force. Such more senior employees as select not to waive their right to transfer shall have preference over those on layoff or who otherwise would be displaced by the technological change.

_____ .3

For the first six months of employment, such employees will retain their seniority in the plant from which they transferred and be subject to recall in accordance with the seniority provisions of the collective bargaining agreement covering that plant. At the end of the first six months of employment, the employee shall have the option of continuing as a permanent employee at the new plant or returning to layoff status at the plant from which he transferred.

_____ .4

Employees transferred to a new plant in accordance with the above procedure shall be entitled to:
   a) Full credit for all seniority with the Company.
   b) All wages and fringe benefits as provided at the new plant.
   c) Reimbursement for all reasonable expenses incurred in relocating to the new plant.

NOTE: The effectiveness of the language will depend upon whether other plants of the Company are organized, if so, by whom and the contract language in effect at those plants. The transfer clause in the contract should spell out who can transfer and under what conditions the move to different departments, plants and locations takes place.

Transfer programs require a review of existing seniority provisions and the purposes of such provisions.

Seniority provisions which allow transfer only within an occupation or a department may not protect long-service workers when a particular department or occupation becomes obsolete or is phased out. The question becomes particularly important when an entire operation or department is seriously affected by technological change. Such problems have often led to revised seniority rules so as to provide workers greater protection in exercising job retention rights.

The question of seniority can involve difficult problems regarding the merger of departments, moving of employees to other plants of the Company or reducing the normal work force as a result of technological change.

The seniority unit is often related to the degree of interchangeability among the jobs, since seniority generally functions easiest in a unit where skills are relatively interchangeable. As specialization increases, the seniority unit often becomes smaller. The more specialized the seniority grouping, the less protection the employee has in case of technological changes in his work situation. A seniority unit that works fine for selecting persons to work overtime, or to set vacation schedules, may not meet the needs of technological changes in the work process.

The introduction of computers, tape controlled machines and other technological advances has served to aggravate the problems of erosion of bargaining unit jobs. In many instances, new technology not only has been used to eliminate many jobs, but the operation of new equipment has been assigned to out-of-unit employees further infringing on the job rights of our members. All the improved benefits provided by our contracts are of little value if the jobs of our members are improperly assigned to out-of-unit employees.

Article _____ .1

Technological changes which affect jobs in the (bargaining unit, department, plant) will not be used as a basis for changing such jobs from bargaining unit status to non-bargaining unit status. When a new job is introduced into the plant, or the content of a job is significantly changed as a result of the introduction of either new equipment, materials or methods which are normally within the scope of the bargaining unit, or they are combined with duties which are not normally within the bargaining unit, the resulting job within the plant shall be considered as clearly within the bargaining unit. The Company will furnish all information requested by the Union in order to make a determination as to whether in fact such changed job duties are within compliance of this provision.

New Plants

The preceding langauge attempts to deal with jobs created and/or affected by new technology and remain within existing company facilities. In fact, companies too often build new plants or facilities, incorporating the latest in technology, and close the older, "less-productive" operations. It is one thing to "follow our work" when it remains within the same physical site. It is something else, when the work is done at a new and distant plant.

The problems of dealing with plant closings, either due to technological change or for any other reason, can also be dealt with in the collective bargaining agreement. The first approach is to require automatic recognition. The alternative is to require neutrality on the part of the company when the new facilities are being organized.

Article _____ .1 (Automatic Recognition)

The Company agrees that, in the event any new plants are opened either to manufacture products similar to those now being produced at plants in which the IAM is currently the bargaining representative or to produce a new product line, it will automatically recognize the IAM as the representative of the workers at the new plants. This is contingent upon the union showing proof that a majority of the employees at the new plant have indicated their desire to have the IAM act as their collective bargaining agent.

Article _____ .1 (Company Neutrality)

Over the years, the Company has developed and will continue to strive to maintain and improve its constructive and harmonious relationship with the International Association of Machinists and Aerospace Workers (IAM) in locations where the IAM represents its employees. The Company places high value on the continuation and improvement of the relationship with the IAM. In situations where the IAM seeks to organize the employees in a plant who is not presently represented by a Union, the Company will neither discourage nor encourage the Union efforts to organize these employees, but will observe a posture of strict neutrality in these matters.

_____ .2

Additionally, neither the Company nor its agents will engage in dilatory tactics of any kind to delay its obligation to bargain with the IAM once the NLRB has certified the IAM as the bargaining agent of these employees and/or has ordered the Company to bargain with the IAM. The Company and Union will conduct themselves in such organizing campaigns in a constructive manner which does not misrepresent to employees the facts and circumstances surrounding their employment.

_____ .3

Should either party charge violations of this agreement, the party alleging a violation shall request that the Federal Mediation and Conciliation Service (FMCS) appoint a neutral party to investigate the allegation. Such neutral party shall be empowered to direct the offending party to make an immediate public disclaimer of the offense and state that such actions are in violation of this agreement.

_____ .4

The parties agree that the remedy contained in the paragraph above is not intended as an exclusive remedy.and that the Union wavies no rights, it has to seek other remedies either before the National Labor Relations Board or the Courts.

Article _____ .1 (Preferential Transfer to New Plant)

During the term of this agreement, current employees of the Company represented by the IAM, shall be given preference over applicants not previously employed by the Company in order by seniority to fill job openings at any new company facility. An employee shall be required to register his wish to exercise his right to transfer under this provision.

Response to: IAM Case Studies

Steven Deutsch

There is a common thread throughout the Machinists' union (IAM) case studies which have been presented; namely, it is in the best interest of unions and workers to know in advance of impending technological change which management wishes to introduce, and to know its impact on job security and the working environment as well as to obtain appropriate training and education for affected workers. The IAM understands this and has moved to develop model contract language for its members — a major step forward.

Some of the conclusions which Leslie Nulty draws are well-documented in the broad literature on the history of automation and technological change and work life in America.[1] These include the fact that management introduces new technology not merely to maximize profit but also to control workers. Another is that the job-creating potential of automation is not inherent and will be realized only through worker efforts to secure retraining. She also notes that some of the distinctions between white and blue collar workers are artificial and that the era of microelectronics will see a shared impact and need for the two to unify in terms of organizing, bargaining, and efforts to gain protection and control over technology.

Perhaps it is especially important to point out her estimate that only 7 percent of machine tools in use in American industry today are numerically controlled; which alerts us to the revolutionary potential yet to be realized. This becomes even more striking when a comparison of US and Japanese data shows that while 35 percent of robots in the US are used in spot welding, compared to 15 percent in Japan, loading machine tools comprise 50 percent of Japanese robots and only 20

Steven Deutsch is a Professor of Sociology on the faculty of the Labor Education and Research Center, The University of Oregon.

1. Indicative of this genre of writing is David F. Noble, "Social Change in Machine Design: The Case of Automatically Controlled Machine Tools," in Andrew Zimbalist (ed) *Case Studies in the Labor Process*, New York: 1979, Monthly Review Press.

percent in the US; similarly, 30 percent of Japanese robots are used in assembly compared to 10 percent here — all within a context which has 4100 robots in the US and 14,000 in use in Japan today.[2] The point of this comparison is that present planning around numerically controlled and electronically programmed machinery only touches on the introduction of potentially revolutionary changes and the likely pace of adoption in the next decade will be staggering.

Nulty's second case study involves robots. However, it is short and not really indicative of the total impact robots will have in coming years. The IAM has done some robotics analysis and training and presented this at their convention and in regional staff training seminars and shop steward training classes. It has done more in this regard than many unions. The monthly paper, *The Machinist*, now includes a regular column on new technology and the union is clearly attempting to increase member awareness of the impact of technological change and appreciation of the need to struggle in bargaining over means to protect jobs and conditions.

A few key points made in the case studies are worth stressing. It is demonstrable that piece-rate incentive systems are contrary to improving safety conditions in industry. Note in case three that management was pressured to abandon such a wage system; and in case one we see important health and safety discussion. Technology should be considered a legitimate part of the health and safety concern and taken into account by health and safety committees. As management introduces new chemicals and synthetics into industry without sufficient testing, workers are increasingly demanding the right to know what they are exposed to, what potential hazards. So, too, should workers pressure for health and safety considerations as new technology is introduced into the work site.[3]

Nulty's analysis of these case studies also supports a conclusion reached by the Machinists in another context. The IAM has been losing membership and jobs in part due to the "capital flight" or run-away shop phenomenon in the US. Multinational employers have moved plants and entire industries from the older, highly unionized northeastern part of the United States, to lower-paying, less organized sections of the US sunbelt, and ouside the United States entirely. The IAM has produced a film on this topic, "We Didn't Want It to Happen This Way," which chronicles the demise of American electronic component manufacturing, light steel manufactured parts, etc. The film's

---

2. Steve Lohr, "New in Japan: The Manless Factory," *The New York Times*, December 13, 1981.

3. This point is argued in Steven Deutsch, "Extending Workplace Democracy: Struggles to Come in Safety and Health," *Labor Studies Journal* 6(Spring 1981) pp. 124-132, and Steven Deutsch, "Work Environment Reform and Industrial Democracy," *Sociology of Work and Occupations* 8(May 1981) pp. 180-194.

message is that workers must have the right to know in advance of corporate decisions which will adversely affect them. This right can be negotiated in bargaining agreements or set into state and federal law or both.

A similar conclusion has been drawn by the IAM in the face of new technology which affects plant location, job security, work organization and job tasks, and associated concerns. The union's model contract language on technology strongly urges providing such a mechanism to allow workers to participate actively in the planning and introduction of new technology, to protect jobs and quality of working life as much as possible, and to gain training to improve their job opportunities and ability to enhance job content. The major addition I would make to Nulty's report and the fine leadership of the IAM on this issue is the need to put technology under existing safety and health laws and explore further legislative remedies to augment collective bargaining language. These case studies and the presentation of the model contract language are an important contribution.

Changing Technology, Corporate Structure and Geographical Concentration in the Printing Industry

Gregory Giebel

Introduction

Printers have long been a subject of scholarly attention. Robert Blauner in *Alienation and Freedom: The Factory Worker and His Industry* offers this description of printers and their work:

Printers do not own the shops in which they work; nor do they have any claim to the finished products. But this is virtually all they have in common with alienated modern factory workers. In some ways, the printer is an anachronism in the age of large-scale industrial organization. His relation to his work is reminiscent of pre-industrial independent craftsmen. Craft technology, favorable economic conditions, and powerful work organizations and traditions result in the highest levels of freedom and control in the work process among industrial workers today. Because printers work in relatively small plants, their work is not as subdivided as work in most industries. They are meaningfully related to the total organization of work, and are less dominated by the hierarchic authority structure characteristic of modern industrial organization. Because of the nature of their work they are not subject to the discipline that falls on the average factory worker. Their control over the work process extends into the social relations of production giving printers a unique influence over their conditions of employment.[1]

While scholars studied their worklives, printers gave evidence of considerable satisfaction with their occupation. Many researchers attribute the printers' satisfaction to the inherent nature of their work, the skill requirements of their jobs and the power of their unions. Many printers shared this view — but this left them poorly prepared for the fate which befell them beginning in the mid-1960s.

During the past two decades significant transformations have occurred in the industry's technology, corporate structure and geographic location. Comprehension of the impact of this revolution is

---

Gregory Giebel is an Associate Professor of Labor Studies at the University of the District of Columbia.

1. Robert Blauner, *Alienation and Freedom* (Chicago: University of Chicago Press, 1964), p. 56.

difficult because of the industry's size and diversity and the varying rates of change occurring in industry segments.

The factors which contributed to the revolution in printing during the last fifteen years are not dissimilar from those which have confronted workers in other American industries. Technological innovations, changes in the organization of firms, and geographic decentralization of printing centers occurred in such rapid succession that traditional union responses proved inadequate when confronting these changes. The development and installation of new systems with design features which transferred control of work to those machines created employment instability in the industry. Printing markets changed because population shifts reduced printing demand in areas of traditional union strength. Mergers and acquisitions changed industrial organization by creating chain operations and conglomerate firms which competed with the older, independently-owned single plant operations.

Each of these changes, while discussed separately in the sections which follow, occurred in concert, thereby magnifying their individual effects upon the industry's workers and its unions. Some unions have been powerless to respond to these changes while others have struggled to control the influx of new workers, changed skills, and a reduction in importance of autonomous printing centers. These mutually reinforcing revolutions created a situation in which the "invisible hand" of unrestrained competition grasped printing, threatening the traditional relationship of work and workers which is the industry's hallmark.

The Printing Industry

Prior to the recent rapid transformations in printing, the most notable period of change occurred before the turn of the century when new technology changed manual operations into mechanized processes. The introduction of mechanical typesetting, and faster presses accelerated the printing process and productivity and threatened to erode worker control of jobs, creating a massive displacement of the workforce. If this change had not been accompanied by a dramatic increase in the demand for printing there would have been an oversupply of printers, leaving unions powerless to shield their members from the consequences of deskillization and wage competition.

One author, writing of this period, estimated that the potential displacement of hand typesetters by the Linotype machine could be estimated at 36,000 but the actual displacement was relatively small because of the tremendous expansion of newspaper, book and commercial printing. The union printer, while commanding higher wages, was not without virtues because, in Baker's words, "It was soon found that almost every part of the skill of hand composition is useful in the working of the machine and that printers were far more efficient than those who had no knowledge of the trade."[2]

Following this early period of rapid mechanization, the industry continued to expand along with the national economy and local markets which it served. This long period of stability and growth was characterized by occasional economic downturns, population and market changes, gradual technological innovations, business failures, and jurisdictional rivalries among unions. During these years printers achieved higher social and economic status and began to see themselves as "elite" blue collar workers. They were considered unique, skilled craftsmen whose literacy level, democratic unions, job control, and compensation afforded them the highest rung on the working class ladder.

Historically, printing firms acceded to union demands in order to meet production commitments. The fear of losing customers of their relatively non-differentiated products and high capitalization costs associated with the purchase of new technology led to a trade-off which allowed union printers to retain their jobs and permitted them to protect work rules and regulations.

Today printing is a highly competitive industry, although characterized by a moderate level of concentration. There are 89 corporations, employing over 500 workers each, which are engaged primarily in printing and publishing. These firms account for only 1 percent of printing and publishing establishments, but 38 percent of employment. Their economic resources, multiple plant operations, and modern technology enable them to compete for the lucrative mass-market segment of the industry.

The greatest level of industry competition occurs between small and medium size firms which employ over 60 percent of printing and publishing workers. This is particularly true of the commercial segment which contains small and medium size firms competing in local or regional printing centers. The great number of these firms, which produce relatively non-differentiated industry products, creates a high level of price competition.

Labor and Printing

The printing industry unions, which were organized prior to the turn of the century, were able to bring considerable stability to this competitive industry by reducing the level of wage competition among

---

2. Elizabeth Faulkner Baker, *Printers and Technology* (New York: Columbia University Press, 1957), p. 27. See also Harry Kelber and Carl Schlesinger, *Union Printers and Controlled Automation* (New York: The Free Press, 1967).

industry workers. This was particularly true for printers who were able to establish strong bargaining positions by regulating the availability of skilled workers within their separate craft jurisdictions.

Printing unions were able to retain a strong bargaining structure by maintaining a relatively high degree of unionization within the dominant and largely autonomous printing centers. As a result of their occupational autonomy, printing unions created jurisdictional boundaries which were strengthened by their separate political institutions. Through their apprenticeship systems and contract language, printers were able to control the supply of workers within local markets thereby lessening competition for jobs.

Contracts were negotiated at the local level so that union leaders remained responsive to membership concerns, vigilant in contract enforcement, and sensitive to competition from unorganized firms. In collective bargaining negotiations few concessions were offered to weaker firms because displaced printers were able to find employment in other unionized shops. This bargaining position was in keeping with their journeyman's heritage. Strong contracts could only be maintained by reducing the competitive pressure upon printers to cheapen the value of their labor.

Seymour Martin Lipset described this contract posture as he observed it in the I.T.U. Local "Big Six" in New York:

> The union has insisted on the closed shop, guaranteed either through written contract or verbal agreement, even though the closed shop is illegal under the Taft-Hartley law. Every worker in the composing room, including the foreman, must be a member of the I.T.U. The inclusion of the foreman as a member of the union, which dates back to the nineteenth century, has meant that foremen are subject to union sanctions if they violate union laws at the behest of the employer. There have been many cases in the history of the union in which foremen were fined for violating union laws. Union laws which must be accepted by union publishers in every contract prescribe that employees must be hired or discharged under the regulations of the union's priority (seniority) system. All vacancies must be filled from among the irregularly employed men who are on the substitute list of a given plant, and the substitute who has been longest on the list must be given the first vacancy regardless of the employer's or foreman's opinion of the relative capabilities of available men. Similarly, reduction in the size of the work force must follow the priority order of employment in the shop.
>   I.T.U. laws which determine conditions of employment, maximum length of work week or work day, priority, closing shop, use of reproduced material, control over all composing-room work, and other work conditions, are non-negotiable in local contracts. All union employers must accept all provisions of the I.T.U. law.[3]

Technological Change in Printing

Technological changes have been a constant threat to printers as they are to workers in most industries. The changes which occurred

---

3. Seymour Martin Lipset, Martin Trow and James Coleman, *Union Democracy* (New York: The Free Press, 1956), pp. 24-25.

throughout the industry's history were, for the most part, gradual. This allowed printers to adjust the supply of labor in the affected industry segments and this, in turn, reduced the negative consequences of the change. Displaced workers could be retrained and transferred to areas of emerging demand. Apprenticeship programs could be reduced or redirected to supply skill training in areas which would be in relatively short supply.

The new technology which was introduced was most often a refinement of an existing process and did not eliminate the entire process because it did not affect other components with which it was integrated. This provided printers and their unions with leverage in their negotiations with employers. Employers remained dependent upon an entire process and while the refinement of a particular component reduced worker control over that portion of the process, the employers were still dependent upon the labor of printers who were not directly affected.

Robert Heilbroner has observed that technology has a geometric rate of growth as opposed to the more conventional arithmetic models found in nature.[4] The gradual changes in components of a process eventually created opportunities for an entire process to be altered with the addition of one more technological innovation. Thus, the changes in the industry and their effect upon printers were not the consequence of a single innovation but rather were the result of one more innovation combined with those which had preceded it.

A significant factor which contributes to the impact of new technology is the source of the technology's development and supply. Many industries maintain considerable control over the speed of introduction of new technology through their control over its development and their product markets. Steel and telephone are examples of industries which retain control over the implementation of new technology. Until recently the domestic automobile industry maintained similar control.

Printing, which is primarily composed of small and medium size, independently owned firms relies almost exclusively upon companies outside of the industry for technological development and supply. Those industry suppliers which include some of this nation's largest firms, such as IBM, Kodak, Xerox, DuPont, 3M and Weyerhaeuser to name but a few, are in intense competition with each other to carve out control of new markets for their products and services. The printing industry, with total sales of nearly $70 billion in 1980, represents a territory of enormous potential. The competitive pressure upon indus-

---

4. Robert Heilbroner, *The Making of an Economic Society* (Englewood Clifts, N.J.: Prentice Hall, 1972), pp. 239-241.

try suppliers has caused them to offer printing firms attractive induce-
ments to purchase a supplier's particular technological component.
This competition has occurred despite the industry having become
destabilized because of chronic overcapacity. The large industry
suppliers reason that the overcapacity is a short run phenomenon and
that their enormous resources will allow them to survive this struggle
and become the beneficiaries of the orders of those printers who, by
surviving themselves, became dependent in the process.

The technological revolution which enveloped the industry was not
a universal conversion of one process to another. Instead the new
machinery altered competitive advantages of various processes at different stages in production from the pre-press (preparatory) phase to
the post-press (finishing) phase. In general, the lithographic and gravure process became much more competitive with the letterpress process which had been dominant since the beginning of the mass production of printing.

At the preparatory stage of printing production, photocomposition
became competitive for a great deal of the work which was formerly
done by hot-metal typecasting. The application of this technology
which included the use of electronic systems was the first major advancement in composition since the introduction of hot-metal line
casting machines in the 1890s. Phototypesetting machines are faster,
allow for a greater range of type size and styles, and do not present
storage problems for large product items. The efficiency of this innovation is demonstrated by a computer-set phone directory of 75,000
entries which takes only 16 hours to phototypeset. The same job would
require 1,250 hours on a tape-operated linecaster producing at an
average of 18,000 characters per hour. A similar example is furnished
by a book, which would require six months to be typeset by hot metal.
This material can be set by photocomposition in three weeks.

The introduction of photocomposition combined with the use of
CRTs has been responsible for a breakthrough in printing technology
which some industry analysts predict will eventually rank in significance with movable type, the cylinder press, and the line-casting
machine, which it will replace.[5] Another prepress innovation which
once was thought to be exotic, but which is now commonly found in
the industry is the use of laser beams in color scanning. This method of
color separation, which replaces photographic techniques, offers better control over quality. This is an important consideration in color printing. Scanners, combined with computers, are able to produce com-

---

5. "Summary Survey of Graphic Arts Technology, 1971" prepared by Graphic Arts
Research Center (Rochester, N.Y.: Rochester Institute of Technology, 1971).

pletely color-corrected separations which may be enlarged, reduced screened or merged with copy.[6]

The pressroom, too, has undergone change, but in this area the technological changes have resulted in the conversion of letterpress into offset lithography. Electronic monitoring equipment now allows for automated control over four color, web-fed lithographic presses and tension control infeeds permit these presses to be run continuously without having to be shut down for new rolls of paper. These innovations permit lithographic printers to obtain a significant cost-per-impression advantage without sacrificing quality in reproduction. The gravure process has become increasingly competitive with lithography for work which requires longer press runs. These changes in the comparative advantage of the traditional division of labor in the pressroom have altered this industry segment's demand for printers.

The finishing phase of production has been the least affected by the technological innovations and thus remains the most labor intensive. However, the ability to add post-press operations onto the rear-end of the high speed web-fed presses is now a reality and this promises to transform the bindery and eliminate great numbers of production workers. It is now possible to fold, cut, collate, glue and staple within the press run. It is no longer mechanically necessary to perform each of these processes individually and thus the storage, movement and labor associated with these operations can be greatly reduced.

The result of these technological innovations and the many others too numerous to recite has been the elimination of some components and processes and the enhancement of others. During the 1970s, the number of production workers in the printing and publishing industry declined by over 50,000. But this is only an average of one worker for each of the industry's 50,000 firms. The transformation of work in this industry cannot be explained simply in terms of numerical layoffs or new technology. Much of the new technology has created new jobs. What the new technology changed is the type of job which the printer is required to perform. Unless older workers are retrained this change provided the employer with an opportunity to replace them with younger ones. These new workers are often less expensive than older ones and to the extent that the new work required less skill and experience, the new worker became even less expensive. The technological innovations also provided the employer with an opportunity to attempt to replace union workers with less expensive non-union labor. This became a possibility because the technological changes interacted with other changes which the industry was concurrently undergoing.

---

6. Ibid., p. 213.

Geographic Relocation in Printing

The most notable of the other changes is the relocation of printing facilities. The vast majority of printing in this country has traditionally been concentrated in printing centers. In 1963, the fifty largest printing centers accounted for over 60 percent of all commercial printing establishments in the U.S., 71 percent of the industry's total employment, and 75 percent of the total value added. Even more revealing is the fact that in 1963 nearly two-fifths of all printing establishments, 50 percent of all employment, and 50 percent of the value added by printing was concentrated in the nation's ten largest centers.[7] During the next fifteen to twenty years, a great exodus out of these centers occurred. It is always difficult to pinpoint the start or end of a trend, but 1963, 1967 and 1972 data on the fifty largest metropolitan printing and publishing centers supplied by the Census of Manufacturers clearly reveals the movement of firms out of the large traditional printing centers. The data in Table I for the industry as a whole reveal that, while the growth rate for the dollar value of printing rose by 37 percent and 41 percent during the two periods, the number of shops and employees recorded less than proportional gains.

Table I
Printing and Publishing
U.S. Total

	Year			% Change	
	1972	1967	1963	67-72	63-67
Establishments	41,585	37,898	38,090	+ 9.5	− 0.3
Employees (in thousands)	1,056	1,031	913	2.4	+12.9
Value Added Manufacture (in millions)	20,197	14,355	10,476	+40.7	+37.0

SOURCE: Printing and Publishing Quarterly, U.S. Department of Commerce Industry Reports, April 1971, Vol. 12, No. 2 and October 1975, Vol. 6, No. 4.

While some of the increased value of production was no doubt due to inflation, an analysis of productivity and profits reveals that the greater portion of this gain can be assigned to an increase in both demand and productivity. The percentage change in employment slowed considerably during the second period, while the increase in number of shops which occurred during the same period is largely attributable to an

---

7. U.S. Department of Commerce, Printing and Publishing Quarterly Industry Report, Vol. 12, No. 4, October 1971, pp. 21-23.

increase in rural, suburban, and southern plants. An analysis of the eleven largest non-southern, non-suburban metropolitan printing centers yield the data in Table II.

Table II
Analysis of Change in Eleven Largest Non-Southern
Non-Suburban Metropolitan Printing Centers

	Establishments				Employment				Value Added			
	%Change		National Rank		%Change		National Rank		%Change		National Rank	
	67-72	63-67	67-72	63-67	67-72	63-67	67-72	63-67	67-72	63-67	67-72	63-67
New York	− 4.3	− 7.6	1	1	−15.3	+ 8.9	1	1	+21.7	+29.7	1	1
Chicago	+ 8.7	− 0.9	2	2	− 2.4	+11.6	2	2	+36.1	+34.1	2	2
Philadelphia	+ 8.3	− 8.7	4	3	− 1.9	+ 3.2	4	4	+29.1	+23.1	4	3
Los Angeles	+19.6	− 2.3	3	4	+ 5.4	+14.5	3	3	+50.0	+34.9	3	4
Boston	+ 9.9	− 0.3	5	5	− 3.9	+ 7.2	5	5	+29.7	+25.9	5	5
San Francisco	+19.9	− 2.3	6	6	−10.4	− 2.1	9/10	8	+18.6	+36.3	8	6
Washington	+36.2	+12.6	8	8	+14.8	+19.6	6	6	+52.6	+48.5	6	7
Detroit	+ 5.1	− 2.3	7	7	− 3.9	+17.8	7	9	+41.7	+33.0	7	8
Cleveland	9.5	− 9.6	13	10	−18.5	+25.4	13	10	+39.9	+33.8	10	9
Baltimore	4.1	− 0.3	14	NA	1.8	+ 7.5	17	16	+37.5	35.2	18	18
Pittsburgh	− 5.1	− 4.9	12	NA	− 2.3	+11.8	22	21	32.4	+28.8	23	21

(NA) — Not available

SOURCE: U.S. Department of Commerce, Printing and Publishing Quarterly Industry Reports. April 1971, Vol. 12, No. 2 and October 1975, Vol. 6, No. 4.

These data reveal the emergence of a trend which continues to the present. In the area of employment, the eleven large printing centers, including all of the very largest, with the exception of Washington and Los Angeles, failed to perform as well as the national average for the 1967-1972 period. Most of the centers registered a net loss in employment during the same time that the value of shipments increased by over 40 percent nationally and over 30 percent in these large printing centers. Most of the large printing centers lost proportionately more shops during the 1963-1967 period than were lost nationally and many of these centers failed to come back proportionally as well as did the industry during the subsequent 1967-1972 recovery. In summary, by the end of the decade considerably more printing was being produced in the traditional printing centers by proportionately fewer employees. Also during this decade, these printing centers experienced proportionately greater losses in establishments and failed to recover as well as did the industry in general.

This trend is attributable to a number of factors which collectively supplied many firms with an adequate justification for the decision to relocate. First, traditional printing centers were the historic base of power for printing unions. A decrease in establishments followed by a decrease in employment, both of which occurred at a time of rising levels of printing production, caused labor relations to become strained. Second, printing centers located in congested industrial areas of city centers impeded the smooth transportation and storage of supplies and products. Third, center-city operations invariably meant crowded multiple-floor operations and this created production snags and bottlenecks for the newer and larger machinery. Fourth, the newer, more totally integrated printing systems made utilization of small specialty shops less necessary. Fifth, the new technology made employers less dependent upon the printer's skill supplied by printing unions. Sixth, customers were more geographically dispersed, thereby permitting other production locations. Finally, both workers and owners moved out of center city and transportation to the plant became increasingly more difficult and expensive.

The trend away from geographically concentrated printing centers becomes more apparent when reference is made to a selected group of cities or regional areas which experienced the trend in the opposite direction. In short, this is where many of the firms, jobs, and production relocated. These data reveal a distinct contrast compared with the trend witnessed in the traditional printing centers. In almost every metropolitan area included in this second group, the performance outpaced the national average in each of the three categories and for both time periods. Particularly impressive was the growth in establishments and production during the 1967-1972 period.

The relocation of firms to rural, suburban and southern areas was rapid and pronounced (see Table III.) Some of the migration can be explained simply in terms of reflecting a master trend associated with the massive population migration from the older industrialized states of the Northeast and Midwest to the "sunbelt" states of the South and Southwest. Between 1970 and 1975 the population of the "sunbelt" and mountain states grew by more than 9 percent — eight times the combined Northeast-Great Lakes growth rate of 1 percent. Employment rose 17 percent in the southern states and 25 percent in the mountain states between 1969 and 1973, but only 1.7 percent in the mid-Atlantic states. By 1975 the sunbelt states accounted for 36 percent of the U.S. population and had achieved by then a self-sustaining growth in new factories, service industries, finance, and housing.

The relocation of printing establishments can also be associated with an improved transportation system which became operational during the decade. Firms wishing to expand production could strategically locate between multiple markets. The rural locations, which were once at a disadvantage, could, with the completion of interstate highway systems, become advantageous to firms wishing multiple-market penetration.

The physical layout of new facilities also provided firms with incentives to relocate. Large single-level facilities could be obtained often at minimal expense through industrial development authorities. The physical structures could be chosen and designed so as to allow supplies to be brought into one end, produced in a single line, and emerge as finished product at the other.

Table III
Analysis of Change in Other Metropolitan Printing Centers

	Establishments			Employment				Value Added			
	%Change		National Rank		%Change		National Rank		%Change		National Rank	
	67-72	63-67	67-72	63-67	67-72	63-67	67-72	63-67	67-72	63-67	67-72	63-67
Anahem, Santa Anna	89.9	13.8			20.4	48.5	32	34	60.8	84.0	31	32
Atlanta	37.1	+3.5			13.4	26.2	20	22	55.5	54.5	21	20
Charlotte-Gastonia	79.0	NA			31.0	NA	47	NA	98.0	NA	45	NA
Dallas-Fort Worth	21.3	+9.9			19.1	24.4	11	19	64.0	50.6	13	17
Houston	32.2	14.9			31.4	10.0	23	28	92.7	38.2	24	31
Kansas City	6.8	+2.7	18/19	15	12.3	33.9	9/10	11	45.8	85.1	9	10
Miami	45.1	10.2			34.5	35.0	28	30	36.8	40.0	22	35
Nashville, Davidson	58.3	13.4			9.4	14.1	29	23	47.5	29.2	32	27
Nassau-Suffolk	46.8	NA			20.7	NA	19	NA	85.6	NA	16	NA
Oklahoma City	16.0	NA			26.9	NA	48	NA	93.4	NA	48	NA
Phoenix	27.8	+0.6			42.2	17.9	37/38	44	100.2	31.5	38	47
San Diego	43.7	12.9			18.9	32.1	40-42	42	72.8	50.0	37	40
San Jose	43.7	+5.2			28.6	35.3	35/36	39	76.2	65.2	30	33
Tampa-St. Petersburg	27.3	NA			48.3	NA	43	47	98.9	NA	42	48

SOURCE: Printing and Publishing Quarterly Industry Reports, April 1971, Vol. 12, No. 2 and October 1975, Vol. 6, No. 4.

A final feature common to most of the area chosen for relocation involves labor costs. The differences between the average weekly industrial wage rates for states is illustrated in Table IV.

Table IV
Selected Percentages and Average
Weekly Industrial Wages
(1965-1973)

States	Wage/week	%Unionized	%Increase Shops	%Increase Employees
Michigan	$248	40	− 0.2	+16.3
Ohio	223	36	− 1.9	+ 6.5
Oregon	219	31	+13.7	+35.3
Indiana	217	36	− 1.7	+18.6
Washington	216	40	+ 6.7	+28.4
New Mexico	144	15	4.0	+21.5
Mississippi	141	13	6.9	+30.3
South Carolina	140	10	19.3	+37.7
Arkansas	138	18	10.5	+29.2
North Carolina	135	8	21.9	+36.1

SOURCE: U.S. Dept. of Labor, Printing Industry Bulletin No. 1806, 1974.

While high percentages of unionization and higher wages did not discourage some firms from moving to the far West, it is interesting to note the increase in both shops and employees in low-wage, low-union states. The contrast between wages is not simply limited to the difference between organized versus unorganized workers — as the list in Table V of average union-hourly wage rates for all printing trades reveals.

Table V
1971 Union Wage Rates by Region

U.S.	$5.47
New England	5.51
Mid-Atlantic	5.78
Border States	5.20
Southeast	4.55
Great Lakes	5.54
Mid-West	5.06
South West	4.51
Mountain	4.91
Pacific	5.60

SOURCE: U.S. Department of Labor, Printing Industry, Bulletin No. 177, 1973.

As these lists reveal, the wage differentials between regions and states are considerable. Similar differentials are also found between urban and rural areas within states.

In addition to wage differentials, the areas chosen for relocation often provide employers with almost complete freedom to establish work rules. New technology allows many of the traditional rules to be redefined such that new job responsibilities and manning provisions are established without the need to negotiate agreements. This flexibility allows management to reduce labor costs even further than the wage differentials permit.

More recent data furnished by the GAIU's Research Department establishes that the trend has continued. Between 1975 and 1981, the South and West continued to grow at a rate disproportionate to that of the East and North Central. This growth is displayed in Table VI.

In states which have right-to-work-laws, the growth rate was significantly greater than those states which have afforded unions some measure of security as illustrated in Table VII.

Table VI
Regional Growth Patterns (1975-1981)

	Printing & Publishing	Commercial Printing	Lithographic Commercial
Northeast	3%	2%	32%
South	31%	33%	62%
West	39%	35%	63%
North Central	69%	9%	28%

SOURCE: GAIU Research Dept., 1981.

Table VII
Union Security vs. Right to Work States (1975-1981)

	Right to Work States	Union Security States
Printing & Publishing	31%	9%
Commercial Printing	36%	10%
Lithography	70%	35%

SOURCE: GAIU Research Dept., 1981.

Thus the relocation of printing firms brought with it a decentralization of the industry's traditional centers of production. As the migration away from the union's base of power occurred, it heightened the impact created by the new technology. Firms which moved were free to introduce technological innovations without having to negotiate the effect of conversion with unions. Those which remained in the traditional centers of production were able to negotiate more favorable terms of conversion because of the increased competition from firms outside of the union's base of power. Both of these changes were exacerbated by a third change which was also creating a revolutionary impact upon workers and their unions — chain shop operations.

Chain-Shop Operations in Printing

The third change which occurred in the industry involved the increased formation of multiple plant operations. The great number of small firms and a relatively low level of capitalization have historically led to consolidations through mergers and acquisitions. This pattern was never of great significance because these consolidations involved a small proportion of both firms and people and the industry conditions were not destabilized by new technology and geographic decentralization. However, the rapid increase in consolidations which occurred throughout the entire economy in the latter portion of the 1960s and early 1970s was strongly reflected in the printing industry. Industry

trade journals devoted great attention to the change in corporate structure. One journal, *Printing Management*, was led to report:

> With this continuing trend of mergers, there are likely to be only two sizes of
> printing companies in about five years: the very large firm with sophisticated
> management and equipment, and the very small plant with a single owner and less
> than $250,000 in sales. The plants selling and producing $350,000 to $10 million will
> most likely become part of larger companies due to increased costs of doing busi-
> ness.[8]

For the most part the mergers were initially vertical and horizontal
rather than conglomerate in form and were generally the result of a
need to reduce operating costs coupled with the need for newer,
costlier, more sophisticated equipment. Through mergers some firms
gained an ability to more completely utilize equipment and spread
overhead to operations on a two and three shift basis. Other firms
gained entry to multiple markets that often provided more balance
with which to counteract idiosyncracies of particular markets. Still
other mergers provided printing firms with an opportunity to diversify
into different market or product segments.

As a result of the period of rapid mergers and acquisitions, the
structure of the industry was transformed. The medium and small
privately-owned printing firms operating in single shops within local
or regionally autonomous markets often confronted firms which operated multiple plants in several markets. These latter firms had considerably greater access to financial, managerial, sales and other labor
resources. The structural movement toward chain operations was
given a further boost when the industry appeared to be discovered by
Wall Street financial analysts who were engineering acquisitions for
conglomerated firms. One industry expert on consolidations was
moved to comment: "the largest recent transactions in the printing and
publishing industry may categorically be placed in the class of conglomerate type consolidations."[9] Large non-printing firms such as
Litton, American Standard, GAF Corp., American Can, Republic Corporation and American Cyanimid, to name but a few, moved aggressively into the industry.

The introduction of chain operations further hastened the demise of
the printer's traditional bases of power. Chains could generate enormous   leverage   upon   local   unions   because   they   could
transfer work from one plant to another. The threat of a strike was
reduced because of the chain's ability to complete work at other operations. The threat to close less productive or troublesome operations

---

8. Harold Trimmer, "Mergers in Printing: Why and Where They Are Happening,"
Printing Management (January, 1970) p. 44.

9. Charles Sexton, "Mergers and Acquisitions," *Graphic Arts Management* (February, 1968) p. 62.

became a reality for many printers which created disquieting reverber-ations for everyone else. The decision to acquire new technology now became linked to the decision as to where to install the technology and this often left local unions in the precarious position of bidding against each other in order to provide the most favorable climate.

Chains also brought to the industry a more sophisticated and venge-ful approach to labor management relations. Industrial relations specialists replaced owners in the collective bargaining process. For-merly, the owners of single plants were apt to have been printers themselves which often contributed to a less adversarial relationship. Absentee owners, through their surrogate labor relations specialists, pursued a number of strategies to strengthen management control over the workforce. Unorganized plants were made to stay that way, while organized plants were pitted against each other in a Darwinian struggle for survival of the fittest. Cross-subsidization, the loss of cost and profit information associated with individually owned plants, and the reduction of trust and security contributed to the chain shop structure becoming a powerful new weapon in the changing industrial environment.

Conclusion

New technology, geographic location, and chain-shop operations combined to transform the printing industry and alter the traditional relations between workers and their work. Local autonomy, rigid jurisdictional boundaries between unions, provincial politics, and lim-ited economic resources combined to obstruct the emergence of a coordinated response by industry unions. In general, each union was left to its own devices when confronting the harmful effects of the new printing industry. Some were powerless to resist and lost their mem-bers through termination, attrition and buyouts.

For some printing unions merger was the most effective response to these changes. For example, the Amalgamated Lithographers of America, the International Photoengravers Union of North America, and the International Brotherhood of Bookbinders merged in the early 1970s to form the Graphic Arts International Union (GAIU). This merger was designed to unify disparate labor organizations in the graphic arts industry, to eliminate inter-union rivalries, to promote organizing and to protect the economic interests and job security of employees. It represented an attempt by printing unions to respond to the dramatic changes in technology and corporate structure which created a new graphic arts industry.

Response to: Changing Technology, Corporate Structure and Geographical Concentration in the Printing Industry

John Stagg

The Graphic Arts International Union (GAIU) has maintained as a cardinal principle that it will crest with technology. The opening statement in a paper I wrote in 1975 for the Graphic Arts Technical Foundation was:

> There does not appear to be any totally new technology that would have a severe, immediate impact upon either employment or the adjustment of the skills of our members. What seems to be the order of the day might be summed up in two words — faster and better. Most of what we have been able to identify as either process or equipment that might change the industry are refinements of technology that has been with us.

These sentiments remain true today. In fact, now more than ever printers must respond to changing technology and new corporate structures through union mergers, collective bargaining, education and training, and political action.

Printing is the sixth largest industry in the U.S.; including paper-workers, employment is well over one million. The GAIU has organized 110,000 of those; the Printing Pressmen are approximately the same size. The International Typographical Union and the American Newspaper Guild have also organized in the industry and merger with these unions is a possible response to the impact of technology. At this time, the GAIU is pursuing merger with the Printing Pressmen. At any time, merger is an extremely difficult experience. The GAIU has just spent nine years assimilating the Bookbinders, the Lithographers and the Photoengravers. As complicated as the process is, I don't think there's any way to survive in this climate without mergers. Significantly, while we're discussing merger, so are the employers. It's not unusual to find that a huge printing company is now owned by a diversified multinational, and this process of conglomeration will continue.

John Stagg is the Education Director of the Graphic Arts International Union.

Collective bargaining is an important hedge against the adverse effects of new technology, but printing is the most fragmented industry in the country, a condition which makes strong national bargaining more difficult. There are more than 45,000 individual entrepreneurs involved in printing and 65,000 in-plant shops. The GAIU represents about 4,500 contracts. Eighty percent of its membership is in shops that have twenty members or less, so bargaining becomes a difficult consideration, particularly since employers are attempting to stay away from association-wide bargaining. The union is trying to convince the employers to come together and bargain, while the employers are trying to bargain in smaller individual units. We have developed a "chain-shop" clause that addresses itself particularly to the issue of agglomeration.

Our locals unquestionably have autonomy. They are fiercely independent. Most contracts run three years and do not have common expiration dates. As part of preparation for bargaining the GAIU conducts a conference called "Coordination of Negotiations" at which approximately one-third of the locals come together for a week and discuss "standard form contracts." As a result most of the locals generate similar contract proposals. One of the Graphic Arts Union's primary principles is a "cost of living" clause that protects workers from the impact of inflation. The union also has contract clauses that address the concept of technology. A "new machines and processes" clause requires an employer who's planning on installing a new technique or machinery to meet with the union ninety days prior to the installation in order to discuss the impact on that particular shop.

Another GAIU response to the impact of changing technology is in the area of retirement and pension. Over fifteen years ago the union negotiated an "early retirement program" which required members to retire at sixty five and allowed them to retire as early as sixty two. Later, the requirement to retire at sixty five became illegal; however, many people still take the early retirement option which creates entry-level employment opportunities in the industry.

One strategy in printing has been to maintain a liaison with the industry outside of bargaining procedures. The unions meet with major employers around the country to discuss changes that impact on employers and workers. This has been effective in the past and this informal relationship is important for labor and management. However, with employers today feeling they have the upper hand, the GAIU is moving more carefully in this area.

A critical union response in order to maintain strength is to organize. In order to maintain the current membership level in the face of high turnover and job loss, the union today must organize forty two people for every one person previously organized. To protect member-

ship gains, the GAIU raised the financial resources necessary to subsidize organizing campaigns. Through a special assessment of the
membership, an organizing fund was generated. The organizing staff
expanded by about 600 percent — which means the union now
employs ten people. There are area coordinators. Sophisticated training procedures have been instituted for those coordinators. There
is an emphasis on careful targeting and utilization of the AFL-CIO and
international unions to help do a better job of organizing.

The union went after a 300 person plant in Senatobia, Mississippi
five times in five years and was successful the fifth time. A substantial
amount of money was invested in·that campaign which would not
have been successful except for a single individual who held it together. At one convention, he was introduced as a person who was
laboring in the vineyards and he spoke of the problems they had in
organizing. At the next convention, he was introduced as president of
the local and was greeted with a spontaneous standing ovation. Despite such difficult campaigns, the union continues to organize because it must in order to survive.

Another response to technology is education and training. The
GAIU went to the membership fifteen years ago and asked them to
support the concept of a fund for an international education training
and retraining program. This program — apprenticeship training,
journeyman retraining, and upgrading — has been going on for fifteen
years, dealing almost entirely with craft training, but the GAIU has
approved a fund to extend trade union education to more general
areas.

There are fifty functioning programs around the country with probably the world's largest Graphic Arts faculty — over 400 people. Every
semester 3,000 students are enrolled in programs which are locally
funded, bargained and administered. Close to $4 million per year is
generated and spent on craft education. Full-blown facilities exist in
fifteen cities with more than $6 million worth of equipment on the
floor. The GAIU will not teach tomorrow's skills with yesterday's
equipment; the newest technology is utilized. The union begs and
borrows, but rarely buys this technology. The industry cooperates in
this regard because, as with pensions, education is an area in which
employers get a return from their investment. These are very specific,
craft-oriented considerations that enable workers to confront new
technology.

Other educational and training programs have also been launched.
The union discovered around five years ago that it was possible to do
business with the government. The Department of Labor had what
they call "dump money" available at the end of a fiscal period — about
$200 thousand. These funds subsidized "Programs for Equal Progres-

sion" (PEP) which involved the upgrading of women's skills. The money was used to pay employers for the release time necessary for the women to take part in the program. Around 300 women have gone through the program in the past three years with a retention rate of 95 percent, which is very high. Women's wages were increased; in many cases 100 percent — an average of $5.50 per hour. So the GAIU used the government and its own resources and cooperated with employers to develop a training program which is the only model the Department of Labor has for upgrading women's skills.

Another governmentally funded program was "Career Equity for Workers" (CEW). The purpose of this program was to find out why women did not upgrade, then develop an educational intervention that would assist them in doing that. The program lasted two years. Women in printing were not taking the opportunity to upgrade because they did not believe they had the opportunity. The union had to convince the women that the opportunities were there.

There is an occupational safety and health program called "Safety and Health Awareness for Employees and Employers" (SHAPE) which is now in its fourth year. Two of the interesting health areas which SHAPE investigates are stress and ergonomics — how new technologies impact on workers' health. This program required government and labor cooperation to protect worker safety and health from technology and workplace hazards.

The American Vocational Association is reviewing vocational education in printing and the union has been asked to participate in writing new standards. The GAIU is on the national Board of Directors of the American Association of Junior and Community Colleges representing labor in the development of educational programs.

Unions need to become strongly involved in political action and legislative issues. The reason GAIU moved its international headquarters from New York to Washington was mainly to become more active in legislative matters. Political efforts are now coordinated with other unions. Joint legislative conferences are conducted.

The GAIU is comfortable with the fact that we are in a high technology industry because we have the tools to cope with it. The conclusion to the paper I wrote in 1975 was:

> Inevitably, though, the total industry must join together to prevent greater numbers of people who are graphic arts workers from being thrown on society's slag heap, which is a mountain of, among others, unemployed auto workers who don't buy books and unemployed printers who don't buy cars.

That fact remains true today. Unions must work together in responding to this threat through collective bargaining, educational and training programs and political action.

Auto Crisis and Union Response

Lydia Fischer

Introduction

Since 1979 the American auto industry has been in the most serious crisis of its history. Production has dropped almost one-third; employment has fallen by about as much. The crisis engulfs a number of companies and scores of thousands of workers in related industries. Faced with these critical circumstances, the United Auto Workers (UAW) has developed new approaches to both its public policy and its collective bargaining programs. For many years after the end of the Second World War, a handful of North American corporations domi-nated the U.S. auto market. This began changing in the mid-1960s with an increasing rate of deconcentration in the world-wide industry. Along with gradual intensification of competition, the share of the U.S. market taken by imports rose, although to still modest levels.

The oil crisis ushered in a shift in domestic demand toward a product substantially different from that with which domestic producers had had extensive experience. New consumer preferences were not easily met with the traditional product lines coming out of Detroit. Quite suddenly, imported vehicles were taking fully one-fourth of the American market — which continues to be by far the largest in the world. Parts importation has also become much greater. At the same time, recessionary economic policies pursued by Washington have inflicted a double-whammy on the beleaguered auto industry and its workers. These policies brought about high interest rates, increasing unemployment, low growth in real incomes, and triggering a cata-strophic drop in the demand for cars and trucks.

Lydia Fischer is Research Associate, Research Department, International Union, United Automobile, Aerospace & Agricultural Implement Workers of America (UAW).

The author wishes to thank UAW research co-workers Sheldon Freidman and George Schwartz for their helpful comments on this paper, as well as Lee Price for contributing suggestions to its content. Any errors or omissions, of course, remain the author's responsibility.

In the last 30 years the UAW amassed an impressive record of collective bargaining gains. As a result of their solidarity and remarkable productivity, UAW members in auto and auto-related companies have achieved good wages and adequate protection for themselves and their families against illness, temporary unemployment, and old age. And beyond the collective bargaining arena, the UAW has always been in the forefront of the struggle for civil rights, the fulfillment of social and human needs through collective action, and the enhancement of workers' dignity.

During the current crisis, the industry lost about 300,000 jobs. The UAW is convinced that if no measures are taken to correct the employment loss off-shore, thousands of additional jobs could be eliminated by mid-decade. The auto industry cuts across America's entire industrial-regional fabric, supporting millions of jobs in the process. No other industry presently offers such levels of employment and community support. Yet public policy is being conducted as if the dislocation suffered by auto workers and auto companies is either self-corrective or too trivial to warrant a search for new policies.

After careful examination of the options, the UAW is sponsoring legislation to stem the drain of auto workers' jobs to other countries by imposing a local content requirement on companies selling relatively large numbers of units in the U.S. In addition, the UAW's future collective bargaining efforts will emphasize job security for its members and a greater involvement in corporate decisions which affect them. Yet in spite of its preoccupation with the crisis, the UAW will continue its progressive tradition, aware that in a political environment of threats to workers' welfare, budget cuts, and "Reaganomics," its strong leadership is needed more than ever.

The Auto Industry

The U.S. auto industry encompasses manufacturing and assembly of complete cars, buses, and trucks, plus production of parts and accessories such as engines, transmissions, brakes and wheels. It is of tremendous importance to the entire economy. Auto and truck production and services consistently account for 6-to-8 percent of GNP; employment in the industry and its suppliers provides for about one-in-nine manufacturing jobs nationwide. Auto enjoyed a solid — if unsteady — annual growth in output up to the early 1970s. High profitability paralleled output; up to 1973 (with the exception of 1967, 1958 and the strike year 1970) auto's yearly rate of profit as a percent of net worth exceeded the comparable rate for all manufacturing.

American auto corporations, their numbers thinned by acquisitions and failures were in firm control of domestic sales through the mid-1960s. The number of imported cars, mostly from Germany, surged in 1958 and 1959, only to fall back to previous levels in the following years. Table 1 shows that it was not until the late 1960s that imports' share of the market became firmly established at over 8 percent and exceeded 15 percent only after the 1973 oil crisis.

Table 1
U.S. NEW MOTOR VEHICLE SALES
(Cars and Trucks)
1950-1980

	Domestic	Imports *(millions)*	Total	Percent Imports
1950	7.5	(a)	7.5	0.3
1951	6.1	(a)	6.1	0.4
1952	5.0	(a)	5.0	0.7
1953	6.7	(a)	6.7	0.5
1954	6.3	(a)	6.3	0.6
1955	8.4	0.1	8.5	0.7
1956	6.8	0.1	6.9	1.6
1957	6.7	0.3	7.0	3.9
1958	5.0	0.5	5.5	8.4
1959	6.4	0.7	7.1	10.1
1960	7.1	0.5	7.6	6.5
1961	6.5	0.3	6.8	4.4
1962	7.8	0.4	8.2	4.8
1963	8.6	0.4	9.0	5.5
1964	9.0	0.5	9.5	5.1
1965	10.3	0.6	10.9	5.4
1966	10.0	0.7	10.7	6.2
1967	9.1	0.8	9.9	8.0
1968	10.4	1.1	11.5	9.2
1969	10.4	1.2	11.6	10.0
1970	8.9	1.3	10.2	13.2
1971	10.7	1.7	12.4	13.4
1972	11.8	1.8	13.6	13.0
1973	12.6	2.0	14.6	13.7
1974	10.0	1.6	11.6	13.8
1975	9.3	1.8	11.1	16.3
1976	11.6	1.7	13.3	13.1
1977	12.5	2.4	14.9	16.1
1978	13.1	2.3	15.4	15.2
1979	11.4	2.8	14.2	19.8
1980	8.6	2.9	11.5	25.2

(a) Less than 51,000.
SOURCE: Facts and Figures, *1952, 1964, 1981. Motor Vehicle Manufacturing Association;* Ward's 1971 Automotive Yearbook.

The table also reveals the industry's cyclical nature — a seesaw pattern of sales of roughly three-to-five years duration. Average total output for each cycle displays an upward trend; the steepest annual gains took place between the early 1960s and the early 1970s. Employment also fluctuated within each cycle, although its cyclical variability was greater and the upward trend more uncertain than for production. During 1960-1973 unit output increased 61 percent, while total auto employment climbed 35 percent, from 724,000 to 976,000. Substantial productivity increases account for the difference between employment and output trends. From 1957 through 1973 annual productivity growth averaged 3.7 percent, about 1.5 times the rate for all manufacturing.

The Union and Collective Bargaining

The UAW was already strong and well established in the auto and agricultural implement industries by the end of the 1940s. With a membership of one million, a vigorous and dedicated leadership, and facing mostly prosperous, growing corporations across the bargaining table, the union was in a prime position to spearhead income and welfare gains which would eventually spill over to many workers in other industries. "Pattern bargaining," the practice of negotiating contracts separately but with terms as similar as possible in each auto company, emerged as a strategy to prevent companies from competing on the basis of labor costs.

In the area of wages, the basic structure was laid out in 1948, when the UAW and General Motors agreed on an annual percentage wage increase based on productivity improvements and a quarterly cost-of-living allowance adjustment to protect the purchasing power of wages. In exchange, the union agreed to accept technological innovations in the workplace and to sign a multi-year contract. Welfare plans came next — medical and life insurance programs — and pensions. These were expanded both in scope and coverage in subsequent rounds of negotiations. Instability of employment was also of particular concern to autoworkers. The pattern was not only cyclical but seasonal. Model changeover months — from June to September — meant long stretches without pay for many workers. In addition, thousands of workers would be recruited during the fall months to work filling up the supply pipelines with new-model cars only to be let go by the end of the year. To the union, this practice was not only inhumane but unnecessary. As a rule, summer shutdowns were also needlessly long. Even when shutdowns were unavoidable, the penalty to the workers — weeks without a paycheck — had to stop. This was accomplished in 1955 when the union negotiated auto's first Supplemental Unemployment Benefit (SUB) with Ford Motor Co. The plan provided for payment of benefits to laid-off members for a number of weeks out of a fund financed by company contributions.

In a review of UAW efforts in the area of job security, the March 2, 1963 issue of *Business Week* described auto employment practices prior to SUB:

> . . . scheduling before SUB first took effect in 1956 was a simple process of hiring 'warm bodies' when the market was up and laying them off when cars weren't selling. The story is always told of how workers came in from the South by the busload during the peak production and sales year of 1955. This helped build up a huge unskilled force, now unemployed, that has made Detroit an economically depressed area for years.
>
> When UAW President Walter Reuther negotiated SUB in 1955 as the beginning of a guaranteed annual wage (GAW), employers had to think twice about mass hirings and layoffs.

Following the 1955 boom period, nearly a quarter of a million production workers were thrown out of work within nine months, not including those laid off only temporarily because of model change. The SUB program helped to put an end to those practices by imposing a price on them.

Auto SUB plans served workers well through two decades, up to the aftermath of the 1973 oil crisis. Then the funds faltered; they were not designed to take care of massive long-term layoffs resulting from as deep and long a slump as the auto industry suffered in 1974-75. In 1975, both GM and Chrysler funds temporarily ran out of money and stopped paying benefits. Rebuilt in the ensuing years, however, SUB benefits were guaranteed for workers with over 10 years of seniority. A guarantee of health care and group insurance coverage for as many as 12-months of layoff was added to SUB income protection.

Job security gains took several forms. Seniority was continued during layoffs of duration and, as the plants became more dispersed, area-wide and company-wide seniority and preferential hiring rights for laid-off employees were negotiated. Better economic and working conditions were negotiated by the union as it continued to accept technological change. These UAW policies helped create a very productive workforce but also became an incentive to keep that workforce comparatively trim. To an increasing extent, a higher demand for output was met by more hours worked rather than more workers. As Table 2 shows, overtime hours in both absolute and relative terms grew remarkably in the 1960s and early 1970s.

Yet overall industry data fail to reflect the true nature of overtime practices in auto. In 1973, one of the Big Four companies[1] averaged over 10 hours weekly overtime in 27 plants; in one-third of them

---

1. The "Big Four" are General Motors, Ford, Chrysler and American Motors.

overtime ranged between 13 and 16 hours a week. Because such schedules bring intolerable pressures on large segments of bargaining units, curbs on overtime were negotiated in 1973.[2]

Table 2
Average Weekly Overtime Hours Worked

Years	Auto Industry	Ratio of Auto Industry to to All Manufacturing
	(hours)	
1959-61	3.0	1.17
1962-67	4.7	1.43
1968-70	4.4	1.28
1971-73	5.0	1.45

The 1973 Oil Crisis

No industry suffered more harm from the 1973 oil crisis than auto. Relatively cheap, available gas was probably the major factor in auto industry growth and in the greater weight and power and larger size which characterized the American automobile. As gas prices jumped and long lines formed at the pump, these characteristics became liabilities. Auto sales slumped and production dropped 20 percent in 1974 with a further 11 percent drop in 1975, as the economy, led by the auto industry, tumbled into the steepest recession since the Great Depression. Layoffs swelled to more than 270,000; employment in the entire industry fell by almost one-third. Auto employment had grown by nearly 20 percent during 1948-1973, when it peaked, but now it became apparent that future job prospects in the industry were grim.

Several factors added up to a substantive change in the employment trend. In response to this drastic change in the oil situation, automobile demand suddenly shifted to smaller, more economical cars; the outlook for gasoline supply and prices suggested this shift would not be reversed. Imported cars, which appealed to auto buyers because they offered economy, captured over 18 percent of domestic sales in 1975, and seemed poised to exceed that ratio. In addition, the smaller Big Four share of the market would consist of a higher proportion of smaller vehicles having less labor content than the large units.

Pointing in the same direction was the pace of technological change. Among domestic producers, the need to "downsize" their entire product line and to build more vehicles in the subcompact-compact range provided the incentive for them to modernize their plant and equipment at faster rates.

---

2. In one of two optional plans negotiated, work beyond nine hours daily on every third Saturday and on every Sunday was made voluntary.

Traditional UAW bargaining goals had emphasized real wages rising along with productivity, the concept of an annual wage, improved health care insurance extending into retirement, and larger pensions. By and large, conditions in the auto industry had assured a worker with seniority of a job, although seasonal and cyclical layoffs were inevitable. Therefore, much of the union's program aimed toward providing workers with stable incomes and benefit coverage during those periods of unemployment. These gains were complemented by increased time off, longer vacations, more holidays and earlier retirement. The grueling work which predominates in auto shops made such provisions imperative. And, while negotiated chiefly for their own virtues, they also served to increase employment opportunities.

Realization that changing conditions translated into fewer auto industry jobs strongly influenced UAW contract demands. The union's 1976 collective bargaining program was a determined effort to open up employment opportunities by reducing worktime. The agreement obtained from the major companies in that year pioneered the Paid Personal Holidays (PPH) program, whereby workers became entitled to a number of additional days off spread throughout the year.[3] To insure the desired employment effect, PPH days could not be traded for compensatory pay.

The PPH program has succeeded in opening up new jobs. Though the companies have refused to release specific information, a reasonable estimate is that about 80 percent of the workers absent on PPH on any given day must be replaced. PPH doubtless was in part responsible for the record employment level reached in the auto industry in 1978.

Declining Sales and Rising Unemployment

In 1980 sales of domestic autos fell to the lowest mark in 10 years — 1981 sales were even lower. For the first time in its history, the entire industry was awash in red ink; General Motors, Ford, Chrysler and American Motors lost $4.2 billion in 1980, and more than $1 billion in the first nine months of 1981. Close to 200 auto and supplier plants have closed permanently since the onset of the current slump. An astounding 2,864 domestic auto dealerships — 12 percent of the total — went out of business between January 1979 and September 1981. According to Department of Commerce estimates, auto-related unemployment came close to one million during 1980: about 300,000 at the Big Four, and the balance at supplier, dealer, and other auto-related companies. At the worst point of the 1979-1980 slump, fully 32 percent of the Big Four's U.S. hourly workforce was on layoff.

---

3. The 1976 contract provided for a total of 12 PPH days; 14 were added in the 1979 contract.

There was some improvement in the next 12 months — about 40 percent of the blue-collar workers on indefinite layoff at the Big Four trickled back to their jobs. (In the 1974-75 recession, 76 percent of the laid-off workers had been reinstated 12 months after the bottom point.) However, even that small upturn proved to be short-lived: the unemployment rolls topped 210,000 again by the end of 1981.

The current crisis is rooted in at least three factors: the energy policies pursued after the 1973 crisis, the recessionary monetary policies to curb inflation, and the onslaught of imports.

The index of gasoline prices relative to those for all items peaked in 1974 at 108.0. From then until 1978 the ratio fell to 100.5. (In contrast, during this time relative gasoline prices in the countries of the Organization for European Co-operation and Development (OECD) rose steadily.) The result was a renewed demand for large cars and an explosive growth in sales of vans and light trucks. Motor vehicle sales increased steadily in 1976 and 1977, and reached an all-time high in 1978. That year's import share declined below that of 1975; for the first time, total average annual auto employment exceeded one million. Healthy levels of capacity and labor utilization pushed productivity forward at an annual average growth rate of 5.3 percent from 1974 to 1978.

This reprieve for the industry was partly responsible for the disaster that followed. Operating on the myopic view that gas would continue to be relatively cheap, the auto companies' earlier interest in downsizing and strengthening the subcompact waned. Meanwhile, demand for subcompacts weakened; the Chevrolet Chevette, and Chrysler's Omni and Horizon lingered in the showrooms while big-car assembly plants worked overtime. Subsequent events proved the fallacy of the "cheap gas" assumption. The worldwide oil shortage of 1979 boosted the retail price of gas 83 percent. There was a 32 percent drop of sales of North American vehicles from early 1979 to mid-1980. Capacity utilization in the motor vehicle and parts industry dropped from 91 to 52 percent.

Imports

This time the foreign auto companies were more ready to meet the demand for smaller, more economical vehicles than they had been during the 1974-75 recession. Imports' share of the car and truck market soared from 15 to 25 percent. Japanese companies took more than 100 percent of this increase; they carved out 21 percent of the U.S. market in 1980, up from their 11 percent in 1978. As UAW President Douglas Fraser stated at the time in testimony:

> These import gains were made at the direct expense of the domestic industry . . . the overwhelming volume and rate of increase of the Japanese cars so saturated the market that domestic car sales plummeted. . . . Aided by undervaluation of the yen, and by a determination to exploit the American market in a period of panic-

buying of small, high-mileage cars following the fuel emergency of early 1979, the tide of Japanese cars and trucks simply overwhelmed the U.S. market. Domestic production and employment plunged. In Japan the auto factories worked overtime and holidays to capitalize on the American dilemma.[4]

Finally, the anti-inflationary policy pursued earlier by the Carter Administration and now, much more unyieldingly, by Reagan, greatly aggravated that dilemma and worsened the auto crisis. Examination of the policy is beyond the scope of this paper, but its consequences for the auto industry have been devastating. High interest rates stemming from the "tight money" stance of the Federal Reserve Board have kept auto and truck sales low due to the negative impact of expensive credit on purchases of durable goods. Other durable goods and housing have been hit similarly; yet another widespread recession is the result — further depressing motor vehicle sales. In the first 11 months of 1981, total new car sales dropped almost 4 percent below the comparable period in 1980; in November the drop was 16 percent.

Public Policy
The UAW's Approach to Import Penetration

The soaring share of the market taken by imports, if allowed to run its course, might permanently damage the U.S.-based industry and shrink it to a fraction of its current size. This opinion is shared by many; for example, William Abernathy, a Harvard Business School professor, cautions that "If the Japanese do not limit imports, a continuing loss of U.S. production and jobs can be anticipated over the next five years far beyond the level of penetration presently realized."[5] At a continuing depressed sale and profit level, the U.S. companies cannot hope to carry through their retooling and modernization plans to meet the competition. They even stand to lose the engineering talent and skilled manpower that have characterized the industry.

On the premise that with some breathing room the domestic industry is capable of meeting the competitive challenge of the Japanese industry, the UAW petitioned the International Trade Commission (ITC) for a ruling of import injury.[6] In his presentation to the ITC, President Fraser remarked that "(the union) is confident that if (the companies) are allowed sufficient time to complete their massive programs to convert their plants, tooling, and auto designs for the production of small, higher mileage cars, the four American manufacturers

4. Douglas Fraser, Testimony before the U.S. International Trade Commission, October 8, 1980.

5. Testimony to the U.S. Senate Committee on the Budget, Subcommittee on Industrial Growth and Productivity, January 27, 1981.

6. U.S. International Trade Commission, Petition for Relief Under Section 201 of the Trade Act of 1974 from Import Competition, June 12, 1980.

will by model year 1985 be able to compete effectively with imports."[7] The Commission agreed that increased imports were indeed causing great injury to the domestic industry, but applying the relatively re-strictive U.S. law, a three-to-two ITC majority found that the industry had been injured by other causes even more than by imports.

Congressional legislation was introduced early in 1981 to limit Japanese car imports for a temporary period. As that was being consid-ered, and after a protracted period of consultation, the Reagan Ad-ministration negotiated voluntary restraint from the Japanese com-panies. The latter committed themselves to exports not exceeding 1.68 million between April 1981 and March 1982, and 1.68 million adjusted by one-sixth of the new-car market change for the following 12 months.

Although less stringent than the UAW had advocated, the voluntary quotas were expected to have some impact on the Japanese share of the market. However, their effectiveness has been eroded by the lack of rebound — in fact, the further deterioration — of the auto market. As noted above, American-based companies, instead of being able to improve their investment financing ability under the shelter of the quotas, have instead been forced to cut back production and are incur-ring huge losses.

The dismal profit picture has resulted in spending reductions on plant and machinery. Ford and Chrysler cut back early in the crisis, seriously jeopardizing the future competitive capability of their U.S. operations. More recently, even General Motors has been trimming its investment plans. In May 1981, the corporation announced that parts of its $40 billion, five-year capital spending program would be delayed, including proposals to postpone construction of two assembly plants — about $1 billion — and renovation of its Baltimore facility for at least a year. GM's new plants were to have been constructed in high-unemployment areas, including Kansas City and Flint, Michigan. Since then, GM has cancelled the Kansas Project and postponed Flint indefinitely. Delay in the startup of yet another plant, at the Detroit-Hamtramck location, was announced in November 1981.

These developments do not suggest that survival of powerful multi-national companies such as GM and Ford is at stake. Rather, what is at issue is whether these companies will continue to be large-scale auto producers and employers within the U.S. The UAW believes that it is the government's responsibility to intervene to ensure that they will. Thus, the centerpiece of the UAW's legislative program to curb the loss of jobs in the industry is Congressional enactment of local content requirements as specified in the Fair Practices in Automotive Products

7. Douglas Fraser, Testimony.

Act.[8] The local content initiative is intended to deal not only with the surge of imported fully assembled vehicles documented above, but also with the increasing volume of parts imported into the U.S.

The value of parts coming in from countries other than Canada has soared in recent years, creating the substantial trade imbalance shown in Table 3. Two disturbing developments account for these deficits. First, as the number of imported cars and trucks on our roads increases, more replacement parts are imported from their countries of origin. Second, foreign auto companies often unfairly deny domestic parts producers the opportunity to sell replacement parts to local dealers of foreign cars. This practice was acknowledged by former Commerce Undersecretary Robert Hergzstein; he added that most U.S.-made parts that replace parts in Japanese cars in this country are sold by non-dealers.[9]

Table 3
U.S. Automotive Parts Trade, Excluding Canada

Year	Imports (000)	Exports (000)	Balance (000)
1970	$ 570,106	$ 951,807	+ $381,701
1971	748,654	942,371	+ 193,717
1972	1,034,181	1,014,651	− 19,530
1973	1,386,852	1,246,335	− 140,517
1974	1,726,136	1,818,653	+ 82,517
1975	1,531,659	2,321,737	+ 790,078
1976	2,155,801	2,496,571	− 218,103
1977	2,761,382	2,543,279	− 1,283,948
1978	3,767,952	2,484,004	− 1,102,578
1979	4,258,999	3,156,421	− 1,102,578
1980	4,572,342	3,882,764	− 689,578

Adjusted for Japanese trucks misclassified as cab-chasis before August 1980.

SOURCE: Tables 2I and 7E *Automotive Trade Statistics,* 1964-1980, U.S. International Trade Commission Publication 1171.

Foreign Sourcing

More importantly, U.S. companies have reduced the domestic content of cars assembled in the U.S. and Canada and plan to continue that trend in the future. According to the companies' own announcements, which are summarized in Table 4, commitments have been made to purchase foreign-made components from their own subsidiaries and other companies in unprecedented volume and scope.

8. *H.R. 5133, introduced in the U.S. House of Representatives on December 8, 1981.*

9. *Wall Street Journal,* September 22, 1980.

Table 4
Foreign Sourcing:
Partial List of Known 1977-1981 Commitments by
Major U.S. Automobile Manufacturers to Purchase
Foreign-Made Major Components For Use in
Domestic Nameplate Vehicles.

Manufacturer	Component	Intended For	Source	Approximate Number of Components	Delivery Beginning
GM	2.8 liter V-6	Cars	GM de Mexico	400,000/year	1982
	2.0 liter L-4 with transmission	Mini trucks	Isuzu (Japan)	100,000/year	1981
	1.8 liter diesel L-4	Chevette	Isuzu	small numbers	1981
	1.3 liter diesel L-4	S-Cars	Isuzu	N.A.	1983
	1.8 liter L-4	J-Cars	GM de Brazil	250,000/year	1979
	THM 180 Automatic transmission	Chevette	GM Strasbourg (France)	250,000/year	1979
	Manual transmissions	J-Cars	Isuzu	250,000/year	1981
Ford	2.2 liter L-4	Cars	Ford-Mexico	400,000/year	1983
	Diesel L-4	Cars	Toyo Kogyo (Japan)	150,000/year	1983
	2.0 liter L-4	Mini trucks	Toyo Kogyo	100,000/year	1982
	2.3 liter L-4	Cars	Ford de Brazil	50,000/year	1979
	Diesel 6 cyl.	Cars	BMW/Steyr (W.Ger./	190,000/year	1983
	Diesel 4 cyl.	Cars	Austria)	N.A.	1985
	Manual transaxles	Front Drive Cars	Toyo Kogyo	100,000 year	1980
	Aluminum cylinder heads	1.6 liter L-4	Europe, Mexico	N.A.	1980
	Accessory Motors	Cars, trucks	Ford-Singapore	N.A.	1984
	Electronic Engine control devices	Cars	Toshiba	100,000+/year	1978
	Ball Joints	Cars	Musashi Seimibu	1,000,000/year	1980
Chrysler	L-6 and V-8 engines	Cars	Chrysler de Mexico	100,000/year	1982
	2.2 liter L-4	K-body	Chrysler de Mexico	270,000/year	1981
	2.6 liter L-4	K-body	Mitsubishi (Japan)	1 million	1981
	1.7 liter L-4	Omni/Horizon	Volkswagen (W. Ger.)	1.2 million	1978
	Manual transmissions	Omni/Horizon	Volkswagen	500,000	1978
	1.6 liter L-4	L-body	Talbot (Peugeot)	400,000 total	1982
	2.0 liter Diesel V-6	K-body	Peugeot (France)	100,000/year	1982
	1.4 liter L-4	A-body (Omni replacement)	Mitsubishi	300,000/year	1984
	L-4 engines	Cars	Peugeot	N.A.	1985
	Aluminum cylinder heads	2.2 liter L-4	Fiat (Italy)	N.A.	1984
AMC	Car components and power train	AMC-Renault	Renault in France and Mexico	300,000/year	1982
VWA	Radiators, stampings	Rabbit	VW de Mexico	250,000/year	1979
	L-4 diesel and gas engines	Cars	VW de Mexico	300,000+/year	1982

N.A. = Figure not available.

SOURCES: *Automotive News, Ward's Engine Update, Ward's Automotive Reports, American Metal Market, Detroit Free Press, Detroit News, Japan Economic Journal,* and *Journal of Commerce.*

Much of the current and potential erosion of North American content in North American nameplate vehicles has been the result of the international standardization of product known as the "world car." This development is comparatively new. Until recently, there was relatively little effort to achieve economies of scale across international boundaries — with the exception of the U.S. — Canada Auto Pact agreement. But with the intensification of worldwide competition ushered in by the vigorous export policies of Japanese companies in a relatively slow-growing worldwide market, all the major companies are scurrying for a competitive edge. Sourcing of Ford's European "Escort" model assembled in England and West Germany, for example, is such that its components come from as many as 17 countries.

Despite fundamental changes in the world auto industry in recent years, the policy of the U.S. government harks back to an era of cheap fuel and rapid economic expansion, when the U.S. accounted for over three-quarters of the world motor vehicle production and other countries were striving to re-industrialize. What may have made sense 30 years ago is clearly unrealistic now, when the U.S. world share has slipped to 21 percent and most major nations have acted to protect their industries in one way or another.

Trade Policies of Other Nations

Table 5 summarizes current auto trade restrictions in 20 countries including the U.S. Five countries impose local content requirements; twelve have non-tariff restrictions — in neither case including the U.S. Nor is the U.S. one of the three countries which has export requirements. The most striking type of restriction affecting relative auto imports and exports among producing nations is the tariff. Except for Japan, which discourages auto imports through other product requirements, every other country has a higher tariff than the U.S., in most instances several times higher.

Adhering to a textbook concept of free trade does not properly address these circumstances. Marina V. N. Whitman, a former Council of Economic Advisors member and currently General Motors' chief economist, has observed that

> . . . countries increasingly act as if comparative advantage were not only dynamic and changing over time, but also endogenous. Countries try to change their comparative advantage over time through deliberate policy. Japan and France have provided two such models; developing countries provide other models. Yet trade theory has not yet assimilated this reality.[10]

Japan, which in 1980 displaced the U.S. as the world's largest motor vehicle producer, is a case in point. The Japanese government pursues an active program of major tax and non-tax subsidies to promote its

---

10. "Automobiles: Turning Around on a Dime," *Challenge*, May-June 1981, p. 44.

auto industry. For many years, imports were subjected to prohibitive tariffs while credit was allocated to the domestic industry on favorable terms. Moreover, Japan's auto industry was — and continues to be — the beneficiary of government policies to stimulate the manufacturing sector at the expense of non-export oriented sectors. Auto makers' energy and raw materials are artificially cheap, they transport their products to foreign markets via subsidized Japanese ships, and escape paying most of the taxes on what they export.[11] Although prohibitive Japanese auto tariffs are no longer in place, an array of non-tariff barriers do push the sticker price of a typical North American-made car sold there to two-to-three times the U.S. level, effectively shutting out North American vehicles from the Japanese market.

Every other nation in the world that has or wants an auto industry has taken definite steps to shape its development. In many cases, the steps taken include strict quantitative restrictions against Japanese auto imports. In the United Kingdom, for example, Japanese vehicles are restricted to a market share of no more than 11 percent. (It is no coincidence that Nissan has announced plans for large scale direct investment in that country, its largest European market.) France limits Japanese imports to a 3 percent market share and Italy to 2,200 cars per year. West Germany recently negotiated limits when the Japanese share of the market started to exceed 10 percent. In each case decisive action was taken well before Japanese import penetration reached half the share it holds of the U.S. market.

Whitman, noting this practice of either explicit or informal restraints on Japanese imports in major countries other than the U.S., warns that:

> The United States may then be in a position of absorbing the bulk of the difference between a growing Japanese auto capacity and the fluctuating demand in its home market. There are always instabilities associated with being a residual market — all the swings hit you because they can't go anywhere else.[12]

In other words, maintaining a laissez-faire policy toward American product markets that are actively cultivated by other countries means risking economic dislocation within our shores.

Local Content Requirements

In choosing a long-term trade component for a U.S. employment-oriented auto policy, requiring a certain proportion of local content appears superior to long-term measures which simply limit imports.

---

11. Frank Stafford, "Automobile Manufacturing in the Great Lakes Region and Japan" in *Michigan's Fiscal and Economic Structure*, by Harvey Brazer, 1981 (preliminary pre-published copy).

12. *Challenge*, May-June 1981, p. 42.

Table 5
Summary of Automobile Trade Restrictions[a]

	Local Content Requirements	Non-Tariff Import Restrictions[b]	Export Requirements	Current Auto Tariff[c] (percent)
Australia	Yes	Yes	No	35-57
Austria	No	Yes	No	20.0
Belgium*	No	Yes	No	10.8
Brazil	Yes	Yes	Yes	185-205
Canada*	No	No	No	14.2
Denmark	No	No	No	10.8
France	No	Yes	No	10.8
Germany*	No	No	No	10.8
Italy	No	Yes	No	10.8
Japan	No	No	No	0.0[d]
Mexico	Yes	Yes	Yes	n.a.
Netherlands	No	No	No	10.8
New Zealand	No	Yes	No	55.0
Norway	No	Yes	No	7.6
South Korea	Yes	Yes	Yes	80.0
Spain	Yes	Yes	No	68.0
Sweden	No	No	No	9.0
Switzerland	No	No	No	10.0 avg.
United Kingdom*	No	Yes	No	10.8
United States*	No	No	No	2.9

a   The measures cited in this chart are for new cars. Trade restrictions on used cars are not reflected.

b   Import restrictions apply to non-tariff measures maintained by a country which deal solely with imports. Tax measures which apply to both imports and domestically produced products are not included. Recent Japanese voluntary export limitation commitments are excluded, but countries receiving such commitments are asterisked.

c   Most European countries impose hefty value-added taxes (VATs) that make the effective tariff rate higher than shown.

d   While no tariff is charged, Japan erects a complicated set of hurdles: e.g., unusual emissions tests; headlight and color rules. These are *not* "import restrictions," however, because they apply to domestic and imported cars alike.

n.a. = Not applicable; imports prohibited except by special arrangement.

SOURCE: UAW Research Department.

Competition among the world's auto companies to provide the American consumer with a wide variety of innovative products built with the most efficient technologies available would be retained under local content requirements. U.S. producers would continue to be pressured by the discipline of the design and engineering innovations of foreign-based manufacturers. Local content requirements would, moreover, lead to increased domestic investment and prevent further job losses, not only in motor vehicle assembly but in the many firms and industries which supply the auto industry.

The content legislation supported by the UAW would require every company with yearly U.S. sales over 100,000 units to produce or buy domestic production worth 25 percent of its automotive sales here by the 1985 model year. A sliding scale would mandate 50 percent domestic production for those with sales over 150,000, 75 percent for those over 200,000, and 90 percent for those companies selling over 500,000 units. Local content requirements tied to sales volume would be phased in beginning with the 1983 model year and credit given for export of parts or vehicles to allow manufacturers flexibility to rationalize production. Another provision would ensure that all vehicle dealers, including affiliates of foreign producers, allow North American producers improved access to their replacement parts market.

Passage of this legislation would immediately affect Toyota, Nissan and Honda because they have been selling in the U.S. at levels for which full-scale domestic assembly can be efficiently accomplished. Indeed, by 1980 both Toyota and Nissan had U.S. sales that approached Chrysler's — a corporation employing about 80,000 people.

A high degree of local content cannot be implemented immediately. But the timetable carried out by Volkswagen (VW) over the last few years can serve as an example for others. VW began U.S. production in 1978. By 1981, it had about 5,500 hourly workers on its employment rolls, an assembly plant in Pennsylvania, a stamping plant in West Virginia, a new multi-plant complex in Texas and plans to start operations in Michigan. The North American content of VW Rabbits is approaching 70 percent.[13]

Collective Bargaining Response
Concession Bargaining

Since the UAW's last collective bargaining round in 1979, thousands of active members have agreed to wage concessions, the most publicized case affecting Chrysler Corporation employees. It should be emphasized, however, that the Chrysler agreement did not result from free collective bargaining, but from the demands made first by the Carter and then by the Reagan Administration through the Chrysler Loan Guarantee Board; that is, the concessions had to be made for the Board to grant Chrysler the funds necessary for survival. Concessions were not a one-way street, either. Chrysler had earlier granted a seat on its board to UAW President Fraser, agreed to allow the union some control over pension fund investment and assured "equality of sac-

---

13. Honda has announced it will operate a small car assembly operation in Ohio by 1982; Nissan plans assembly of small trucks in Tennessee within a few years. Domestic content of vehicles manufactured at either plant is not anticipated to be very high. No other Japanese manufacturer has publicized intentions of investing in the U.S.

rifice" among all Chrysler employees and executives. It then further agreed to set up a stock ownership plan and a profit-sharing plan for UAW employees and to disclose fully financial information (including productivity data) to the union. It also made a commitment to keep certain plants open during the term of the agreement rather than farm the work out to suppliers.

Worker Participation

In the midst of the auto crisis, the corporations, as well as many local unions, have shown increased interest in participatory experiments at the local level. Their focus is generally on product quality, absenteeism, and workers' input into the job process. These arrangements do not replace collective bargaining or substitute for the grievance procedure. At Ford Motor Company, a joint union-management committee on Employee Involvement (EI) is making a major effort to foster creation of local EI committees to enhance product quality.

At General Motors there have been Quality of Work Life (QWL) groups for several years. In some QWL locations the record shows fewer grievances, less scrap, fewer repairs, better product quality, fewer disciplinary actions, and less absenteeism. A QWL at a Buick plant in Flint has been well-received by workers who reportedly do not punch timeclocks; they work in teams, and rotate jobs with the other members of their team. But in other cases, local management has chosen to interpret QWL as a license for speeding up operations, or has been unable to discard the traditional rigid supervisory style and those local programs have either languished or disappeared.

Perhaps due to their individual and flexible nature, it is difficult to make an across-the-board evaluation of QWL experiments. Job security is probably the fundamental variable in whether these programs succeed, fail or are even started. A shop committee is more likely to cooperate with local management in setting up a QWL program if the company can assure the workers of job security at that location. In the Flint Buick case, nearly all of the 16,000 hourly workers are employed, while thousands of their co-workers in nearby plants remain on layoff. The size of the workforce has been maintained there partly because GM chose to convert an obsolete foundry into a modern parts plant. The constructive relationship between management and the union had a bearing on the decision to convert, but there were clearly other considerations pushing in that direction.

Jobs and Technology

Product demand, the market share of imported vehicles, the purchase of parts abroad, and technological change in the industry have the greatest potential impact on employment. Short term changes in demand depend mostly on incomes and interest rates, as well as on the age of the stock of autos in use and the scrappage rate. Demand is certainly expected to increase by 1985 from current rock-bottom levels, but not at the same rate as in previous upturns from deep slumps. In part, this is because the share of replacement demand increases as a larger proportion of the driving-age population owns a vehicle and there are now fewer additions to that population. From 1976 through 1978 fewer than thirteen new cars were sold for every ten cars scrapped; in the mid-1950s, 17 new cars were sold for every ten cars scrapped.[14]

Technological change also determines the number of jobs. In this decade the push for technological innovation is coming from the electronic controls-semi-conductor-microprocessor sector. As they diffuse throughout industry these new technologies reduce costs and create the possibility of increases in real living standards. This is characteristic of all innovation. But there is good reason to believe that more workers will be thrown out of their jobs by current technologies than in the past. It is estimated, for example, that industrial robots such as those used in auto "work" for about $6 an hour (on a three-shift basis), which is about one-third the cost of a live worker.[15] In this way they help managers outstrip their pre-robot plant productivity levels substantially. Knowing the cost of robots, and hence of the upper limit on the amount of labor they embody, the effect on labor generally must be an absolute decline in total labor time, not merely a shift from auto industry labor to robot industry labor.

The mind-boggling potential of microelectronic technology is still largely untapped. Today, annual worldwide robot production stands at about 8,000 units, two-thirds of it Japanese. Of the approximately 20,000 robots operating in the world today, nearly 40 percent were produced in the past 12 months. Of the 5,000 robots operating in the U.S. today, about half are in auto. Cincinnati Milacron's robot division sees a 1990 U.S. robot market of $700 million to $2 billion, implying an annual growth of 24 to 35 percent.[16]

The employment implications are sobering. A recent Carnegie-Mellon University study finds that "Nearly 7% of the total work force do the types of jobs which currently are, or soon will be, in the domain of industrial robots."[17] Nearly half of the jobs at risk are in the metal-working industries sector; as many as 3.5 million of those jobs may be

---

14. *Ward's Automotive Yearbook*, 1980.

15. *Business Week*, June 9, 1980.

16. Daniel Luria, "Technology, Employment and the Factory of the Future," *SME Autofact III Conference*, November 9, 1981.

17. As reported by *Business Week*, August 17, 1981.

on the chopping block. Even if those estimates are wrong by a factor of two, and even if these changes occur in 20 rather than ten years, there are major dislocations on the way. Industries such as auto — and hence workers in Michigan, Ohio and other metalworking centers — are not going to escape major damage unless explicit corrective policies are adopted.

Jobs and Outsourcing

Some forecasters believe imports could take 35 percent of the market by 1985.[18] With respect to parts imports, the Department of Commerce[19] estimates that during any year in the 1982-84 period the domestic companies could be drawing on foreign sources for the quantities of auto components listed in Table 6.

Table 6
Foreign Sourcing Estimates for Domestic Auto Production, 1982-1984

Auto Component	Million Units
Engines	2.5
Transaxles	1.7
Aluminum cylinder heads	1.3
Alternators/starters	1.5
Wiring harnesses	5.0
Rear disk brakes	.5
Constant velocity joints	.6

SOURCE: Transportation Systems Center, Department of Transportation.

The report notes that "the above figures stand totally apart from traditional imports of replacement parts for both U.S.-made and imported vehicles. Rough estimates of what the above list might add up to in dollar terms give a figure of $2.5 billion." But that dollar value, less than 2 percent of motor vehicle and parts shipments, may be too low.

18. Here is William Abernathy's analysis, in his testimony cited earlier: "The Japanese added new capacity last year (1980) amounting to 1,000,000 units over 1979 levels according to published sources. As placed by one government estimate, an additional 500,000 units of capacity has been announced for 1981. There will likely be even more capacity additions that haven't been announced. If only 50 percent of these additions reach the United States this will represent a 30 percent increase over Japanese imports; it is more likely that a 50 percent increase in penetration would be realized in the United States over this two-year period if the Japanese wished. Future years would see even further expansion under such an aggressive scenario."

19. "Status Report on the U.S. Automobile Industry, submitted to the U.S. Senate, Committee on Finance, Subcommittee on International Trade," December 1, 1981.

An alternative estimate by Arthur Andersen and Company[20] is that 85 to 95 percent of total content will be locally produced by 1985. In terms of jobs, that would mean a significant decline from the level implied by the current estimated 98 percent local content.

Those four factors — demand, technological change, domestic share of the market and proportion of local content — account for the bulk of auto industry employment changes. According to the Department of Commerce study, the automotive industry will employ a total of approximately 800,000 workers in the mid-1980s. A UAW Research Department analysis, however, shows that a more realistic figure, assuming nothing is done, is considerably lower because job loss would also occur in the supplier industry. In the seven years between 1978 and 1985 there could be a decline in employment totally without precedent in a basic manufacturing industry.

The U.S. collective bargaining experience offers little guidance as to how to preserve jobs in the face of such profound and rapid changes. Changes stemming from the introduction of new technology, however, have been receiving more attention. For example, the UAW's major contracts now preserve work functions within bargaining units. When new methods or processes are adopted, UAW members are trained in the new skill so they can continue to perform the old work function if not the same task. The company is also required to notify union representatives, as far in advance as possible, of the introduction of new or advanced technologies at any plant location, and has agreed to discuss matters pertinent to new technology in joint labor-management national committees. Due to these relatively new provisions, UAW tradesmen are now loading programs and operating and servicing computer terminals at some locations and installing, maintaining and servicing spray painting robots in others.

As indicated earlier, going abroad for the purchase or production of components — called outsourcing — is a recent phenomenon in auto. Union demands to protect jobs from outsourcing — in its broadest sense — could translate into company agreements that manufacture of a certain product will be kept within a specified country, group of workers, plant or bargaining unit. Just as in the case with technological changes, decisions on outsourcing have long "lead" times; the union is aware that current decisions, if not forestalled, may mean irreversible job losses several years from now.

Too often, companies have been allowed to ignore the cost of job losses for workers and communities when closing, relocating, or drastically automating plants. Industrial workers are increasingly aware

---

20. "U.S. Automotive Industry in the 1980s," Second Delphi Forecast, July, 1981.

that union involvement in technology, outsourcing, and investment decisions may be the only way of curbing these historically exclusive management prerogatives.

Regardless of the reason for their displacement, the jobless have similar needs; an alternative source of income and ultimately another job; health care protection; and acquisition of a new skill. In the evolving federal budgetary climate, even the meager services provided in the past are being cut. There is scant hope of future improvements in aid provided to victims of economic dislocation. More frequently than ever, remedies will have to be found within the collective bargaining process. That employers bear no responsibility for the long-term security of their workers, in particular their high-seniority workers, is a belief that must be reversed.

Lessons from Japan

Frequent comparison is made between the domestic and Japanese auto industries. For workers, auto employment in Japan has certain desirable aspects. Major auto companies there make a commitment of "lifetime employment" to their workers, who therefore do not live in fear of having their livelihood stripped away on short notice. Employers, in addition, usually give transportation allowances and either provide housing or facilitate employee home purchases. Nevertheless, Japanese auto workers have not shared proportionately in the fruits of their remarkable productivity performance. Their industry has enjoyed unprecedented growth, but their wages have remained exceptionally low — when compared not only with the United States, but also with most other industrialized countries. In terms of purchasing power, Japanese autoworkers' wages are close to those of Spanish autoworkers, even though Japanese productivity is much higher.[21]

U.S. auto workers obtained high wages and good fringe benefits over the years because they also were very productive. Although the existence of substantial wage differentials among industries of comparable productivity levels cannot be altogether ignored, neither should American workers be pressured into cutting their wages to match their Japanese counterparts. A depressing effect on the entire industrial wage structure would quickly follow. American workers' living standards should not be reduced to those of the Japanese; rather, the latter should be raised towards those in this country. Japanese workers reportedly are doing this in some areas — for example, the number of annual hours they are required to work.

---

21. "The Purchasing Power of Working Time — An International Comparison," International Metalworkers Federation, 1981.

Conclusion

The crisis in auto has plunged the UAW into the most threatening situation in its history. Scores of thousands of UAW members have been laid off; many of them may never get back their jobs. And for those who remain employed, the outlook is uncertain. Further job loss, more plant closings, and wage or benefit cutbacks are all likely if nothing is done to curb the decline.

The UAW has singled out job security as the most important issue on the bargaining table. But however successful its efforts, there are limitations. The union cannot ensure that domestic industry generally will provide the number of jobs needed to arrest deterioration in the auto-related industrial and regional structure. That deterioration is a direct result of the "free market" orientation that guides public policy in our country — an orientation that is dangerously out of tune with the reality of powerful multinational corporations which can move quickly to that location which offers the biggest profit, leaving displaced workers and depressed communities behind. "Free marketeers" also ignore policies that other governments put in place to curb the multinational powers and defend their industrial and employment bases from an unharnessed flow of imports. As a direct result of this almost unique American posture, U.S.. auto workers are particularly vulnerable to aggressive industrial and trading practices of countries targeting foreign markets for increased penetration — while standing ready to protect theirs.

The problem of domestic manufacturing must be addressed promptly. The past three years demonstrate that the crisis afflicting that sector and its workers — whose well-being is vital to our national interest — cannot be arrested without government action. The local content requirement initiative offered by the UAW could become the first building block of an employment-oriented national policy for the U.S. auto industry.

Response to: Auto Crisis and Union Response

Russ Allen

Although the subject of this conference is labor's response to corporate structural change and technology, Lydia Fischer's excellent paper does not deal with technology (a subject on which she is the first to disclaim expertise) but certainly does relate to the question of changing corporate structure. With the advent of the "world car" and the multinational nature of the automobile companies, the union as an institution has a vested interest in production (and therefore employment) in a particular country, while management does not. Chrysler has even advertised that, to get a Japanese-built car and a cash rebate, the buyer must go to Chrysler!

Ms. Fischer outlines the crisis in the domestic automobile industry and gives the union's program for dealing with the problem in the short run — the proposal for "local content" requirements mandating a certain proportion of domestically-produced components in both original equipment and parts. The proposal stops short of asking for import quotas or prohibitive duties. If anything, one would have to say that the UAW was slow to abandon its essentially "free trade" position, especially in view of the restrictive practices of other Western countries and, of course, Japan.

The most telling part of the paper, to this commentator at least, is the section dealing with the automobile trade restrictions of the other Western, industrialized countries. Ms. Fischer points out, (and I repeat for emphasis since it is largely ignored in Academe), that the United Kingdom restricts Japanese auto imports to under 11 percent; France to 3 percent; and West Germany acted as the Japanese share began to exceed 10 percent. Compare this to the U.S. figure of 22 percent and

Russ Allen is Deputy Director of the George Meany Center for Labor Studies.

1. Robert Cohen, "Brave New World of the Global Car," *Challenge*, May-June 1981, p. 34.

rising. As G.M. economist Marina Whitman so mildly put it, "trade theory has not yet assimilated this reality."[1] The Japanese no longer have in place their heavy duties on imported vehicles, but as Ms. Fischer points out, their non-tariff barriers keep sticker prices at double or triple the U.S. domestic level, thus effectively closing off the Japanese market to U.S. manufacturers. One searches in vain at the U.S. university for this type of information.

It is the changing market share of foreign imports that has had the most devastating and visible impact on the U.S. automobile industry. Also being felt — and to be felt more strongly in the future — is the effect of technology, specifically robotization.

Ms. Fischer lets automobile industry management off too easy for its failure to forecast the market for small, fuel-efficient cars — in spite of the artificially low price of gasoline in the United States. While paying themselves astronomic salaries, top management let the foreign cars — first VW and then the Japanese cars — take a larger and larger share of the U.S. market. As John L. Lewis might say, it ill behooves an industry that has mis-forecast its market for 20 years to ask now for a "breathing space" to prepare itself to meet the competition. The fact of the matter is that all four of the major U.S. car manufacturers make a good product. It strains logic to believe that they cannot make a good, cheap, small, fuel-efficient car that will be accepted by the buying public as being equal or superior to foreign competitors. But they have not done so — in 20 years they have not done so. True, they may have maximized profits in the years 1975 to 1978. But where are their profits now?

It is ironic that it was the union — the UAW — that devoted an issue of its publication *Ammunition* in the post-World War II years to "A Motorcar Named Desire" — the blueprint for an American Volkswagen — small, cheap, fuel-efficient. Auto management would have done well to listen to the union then. Also ironic is the fact that American management which stoutly resists its own government's attempts to regulate (taking this market for granted), readily accepts long-term conditions from foreign governments such as Spain and Brazil, the former because it is "an attractive launching pad for the European market."[2]

But the subject of the paper is not management faults but union response. The author cites the efforts of the union in recent contract negotiations to deal with declining employment in the industry — particularly the personal holiday provisions, for which the union estimates an 80 percent replacement rate thus increasing jobs. While these efforts were clearly in the right direction, as was the effort to eliminate

---

2. Ibid., p. 32.

or reduce compulsory overtime, it can be seen in hindsight how inadequate they were in terms of the real job and income security interests of automobile workers.

Only partial solutions are available at the bargaining table. The rest — a large share — lie in legislative and political action. On this subject, one must speak ideally and not practically. A Congress that allows energy consumers to be billed in advance for a pipeline that has not been built, and will not serve some of them ever, at any time, is indisposed to think at all about social controls in return for public largesse to industry. But social controls there must be. If the federal government is to give specific aid to the automobile industry, what specific commitments should the industry be required to make to the consumer and to its workers? If the risks are to be socialized, as in the Chrysler loan guarantee case, let the benefits be socialized as well. Let there be, for example, a public representative on the Board of Directors, at least for the period of the loan guarantee. Let the union have more than just one director. Let the pension and health insurance funds be jointly administered by company and union. (It is true that the union won a small voice in pension fund investment from Chrysler — 10 percent of "new money" put in the fund). One would have hoped that the union itself had asked for these eminently justifiable concessions from Chrysler in return for the union's (absolutely essential) support of the federal loan guarantee.

If local content is to be required in some proportion by law (and this requirement is by no means unprecedented) what social controls should be enacted along with the local content rule? One is drawn to the Galbraithian solution — monitoring the price and *incomes* (not wage) policies of the major companies and unions by some sort of quasi-public oversight board. The difficulty comes at the point of determining what sanctions would be applied to the malefactors, assuming the ideal situation that one could actually get such an oversight board. In this country, government is not in the habit of disciplining business. But unless there are sanctions, toothy sanctions, the game is not likely to be played according to the rules. It is vexing to think of a detailed plan that would work, and the inclination is to throw up your hands. However, when one thinks of the alternative — letting the automobile companies alone while giving them "relief" or "breathing space" — the will is strengthened. Can you imagine the consumer exploitation that would have occurred in this country if there were not the foreign alternative in the last 15 or 20 years?

It is not hard to go along with the UAW's proposals for local content. The precept is simple: if you want to sell in this market, you have to produce in this market. The difficult part is figuring out what the rest of the country — other union members and the rest of the public — gets in return and how that is secured.

Unions and Technological Change
International Perspectives

Steven Deutsch

Introduction

The purpose of these brief comments is to outline some of the approaches taken by unions in other industrial market economies of the world in the face of rapidly changing and revolutionary new technology. The point is neither to offer in-depth studies of other countries' experiences, nor to imply that there exists somewhere a blueprint which is ready for wholesale adoption in the United States. However, it is useful for American unions to understand how the challenges of new technology are being addressed by other labor movements. Furthermore, it is hoped that such information might help unions reflect on their strategy options, be they collective bargaining approaches with alternative contract language, legislative remedies, the formation of joint labor-management committees, or other possible tacks.

Towards a Trade Union Position

There is no simple summary viewpoint which represents labor, but it is clear that some outlines exist. In the 1950's and 1960's with the advent of so-called "Detroit automation" American unions were especially concerned with the job-displacing potential of production automation. Even then there were diverse reactions to how labor should cope with the problem.[1] But, in fact, the massive growth in public and

Steven Deutsch is a Professor of Sociology on the faculty of the Labor Education and Research Center, University of Oregon.

The author would like to thank Sandra Albrecht, David Lerman and Donald van Houten for helpful comments on an earlier version, and the University of Oregon Office of Scientific and Scholarly Research and the Swedish Center for Working Life for supporting research on labor and technological change.

1. Steven Deutsch, "Perception of and Attitudes Toward Automation: A Study of Local Union Leaders," *Labor Law Journal* 18 (July 1967), pp. 395-405; Steven Deutsch, "Technological Change and Its Effect on Local Union Leadership," in *Industrial Relations: Contemporary Issues*, B.C. Roberts, (ed.), (New York: St. Martins Press, 1968). Steven Deutsch, "Labor, Ideology and Technological Change: Some Sociological Considerations," *International Review of Sociology* 5 (August 1969), pp. 79-92.

service sectors and continued growth in manufacturing in an economy overheated by the Vietnam War, forestalled much of the predicted trauma and the need for confronting the issue of technological change. Structural unemployment due to technology was evident in auto, steel, coal mining, railroads and other industries. However, the simultaneous expansion, expecially in public and service occupations, avoided a widening problem of dislocation and unemployment.

The new realities are that economic growth has been curtailed in the United States and in virtually all industrial countries and that deindustrialization and rising unemployment are international concerns. The newer technologies of microprocessors and computers are having an impact on all industrial societies and in all sectors. The fact that they are being introduced at a time of economic crisis adds urgency to the debate about the future shape of industrial societies.[2] In addition to fundamental issues of job security there are new concerns over job deskilling, workplace safety and health effects of the new technology, and the relationship between technology and quality of working life.

Unions traditionally have not opposed the introduction of new technology; typically they welcome the possible improvements in working conditions in the long run. Yet, ". . . workers are the first group in society to pay the social costs of the application of new technological methods to production. Trade unions, as the representatives of workers, articulate the concern of these social costs."[3] The microelectronics revolution has not generated a union posture of anti-technology, but the devastating employment projections have created widespread concern. The enormous impact which office automation is likely to have has only begun to be addressed by labor. For example, ten typists can be replaced by three word-processors, so it is staggering to imagine that a 2 percent annual reduction of office workers in the United States would displace 25,000,000 workers by the year 2000.[4]

One international trade union staff member has summed up a "trade union view" by suggesting that labor accept the following basic points.[5]

2. Tom Forester (ed.), *The Microelectronics Revolution: The Complete Guide to the New Technology and Its Impact on Society* (Cambridge, Mass: MIT Press, 1981).

3. Organization of European Cooperation and Development, *Microelectronics, Productivity and Employment* (Paris: OECD, 1981).

4. Forester, *Microelectronics Revolution;* Organization of European Cooperation and Development, *Information Activities, Electronics and Telecommunications Technologies: Impact of Employment, Growth and Trade*, Vol. 1. (Paris: OECD, 1981). J. Rada, *The Impact of Microelectronics: A Tentative Appraisal of Information Technology.* (Geneva: International Labor Organization, 1980).

5. David Cockroft, "New Office Technology and Employment," *International Labour Review* 119 (Nov-Dec 1980), pp. 689-704.

1) New forms of microelectronics technology on the factory floor and in the office are likely to cause a loss of jobs in the foreseeable future.

2) A policy of outright opposition to technological change is impractical and/or undesirable.

3) The main responsibility for avoiding large-scale unemployment lies with governments.

4) The smaller number of total work hours available should be translated into shorter working time for more people.

5) Governments should try to discourage labor-displacing use of technology.

6) Industrial democracy and participation schemes should be extended to give workers an effective say over the application of new technology in the workplace.

7) Workers should be protected against deterioration in the content of skill requirements of their jobs and against machinery which could dehumanize their work or adversely affect their health.

8) Trade union representatives should be given training both by their union and their employer in the basic principles of computer and telecommunications technology.

Without debating the correctness of each point and its universal application, it is safe to say that these concerns and viewpoints reflect typical union views. This being the case, it is worthwhile to see how unions in other nations deal with technological change.

Technology as Part of the Work Environment

A major effort has been undertaken by unions in many countries to negotiate so-called technology agreements with employers or employer confederations. These agreements are designed to require employers to furnish workers and their representatives with the information about the impact of new technology on the economy, the working environment, job security, organization and content of work, and education. The purpose is to stipulate employer duty to furnish information in advance to workers and their representatives and to allow the union to help plan the introduction of new technology, to give some assurances in terms of job security and work tasks, and some commitments to job training and education. These technology agreements vary of course, but in many countries they are almost comprehensive due in part to national protective legislation related to the work environment laws of the country (e.g., Norway, Sweden). In other cases there are strong union efforts to gain such collectively bargained agreements along with other items (e.g., England, Australia). In Denmark there is an agreement for the private sector, one with the State as employer, one for banking, one for municipal employees is soon expected, and shortly almost all sectors will be covered.[6]

A major contribution which Scandinavian unions and researchers have made is to address the work environment in holistic terms. Contrary to the tendency in the U.S. to limit discussion to traditional job safety and health factors or physical and chemical hazards, the Scandinavians have understood that the psychological hazards of job stress and the nature of work relations are integrally tied to one another. As a result, the introduction of new technology into the workplace is approached as part of a larger set of worker and union rights to constantly improve the work place. That approach is much needed in this country, as I have argued elsewhere.[7]

Since the 1960's, Norwegian researchers and unionists have worked to increase workplace democracy. The underlying assumption of these efforts has been that increasing worker participation would lead to a more positive work environment, which would both affect productivity and increase worker satisfaction, reduce job stress and result in an overall increase in the quality of working life.[8] By the beginning of the 1970's, the metalworkers' union and the Norwegian Computer Center had initiated some applied projects and by the mid-1970's the union and the Norwegian Employers' Federation has signed an agreement on computer based systems.[9] It was revised in 1978, as the new Norwegian Work Environment Act of 1977 was being implemented.

The Work Environment Act contains several sections that pertain to technology but it is paramount to stress that it was conceived as a law which went beyond setting minimal standards and pushed for the active involvement of workers on the job to monitor and improve working conditions.[10] For example, Section 12 of the Act specifically gives labor rights over the planning of work, production systems and the introduction of new technology. The key is *planning;* labor sharing

---

6. This is outlined in the *Danish Labour News,* July 1981, including the verbatim agreement signed by the Danish Federation of Unions and the Danish Employer's Confederation.

7. Steven Deutsch, "Extending Workplace Democracy: Struggles to Come in Job Safety and Health," *Labor Studies Journal* 6 (Spring 1981), pp. 124-132; Steven Deutsch, "Work Environment Reform and Industrial Democracy," *Sociology of Work and Occupations* 8 (May 1981), pp. 180-194.

8. Bjorn Gustavsen and Gerry Hunnius, *New Patterns of Work Reform* (Oslo: University Press, 1981).

9. David F. Noble, "Social Choice in Machine Design: The Case of Automatically Controlled Machine Tools," in *Case Studies in the Labor Process* (New York: Monthly Review Press, 1979).

10. Gustavsen and Hunnius, *New Patterns;* Deutsch, "Work Environment."

information with management and helping to shape the work environment. The result is not only a process of consultation but a push towards co-determination.[11] David Noble has observed that

> How this technology will actually be employed in a plant depends less upon any inherent nature of the technology than upon the particular manufacturing process involved, the political and economic setting, and the relative power and sophistication of the parties engaged in the struggle over control of production.[12]

A new set of proposed work rules regulating conditions for video display users has been advanced, though not yet approved by the Labor Inspectorate.[13] It has been hailed as ". . . the first comprehensive attempt to introduce legal rather than negotiated standards in this area."[14] Workers in Norway already have the right to negotiate an agreement which limits hours in front of a computer screen, and to participate in the planning and reorganization of the office or shop including the introduction of new technology.

This approach is uniquely Scandinavian and mixes a strategy of both collective bargaining and legislative remedies. Work life reform in Sweden also came through accumulated laws affecting job security, workers on corporate boards, and later laws on codetermination and the work environment.[15] Implicit in the Swedish Work Environment Act is the similar assumption that a healthy workplace is one in which people are actively involved in planning and shaping the work environment, where there is limited monotony and no undue supervisory pressure, where there are controls over job stress and efforts to improve working conditions.

Swedish unions have aggressively moved from efforts to protect job security to demanding the right to be consulted and work with management on the introduction of new technology. This is just as true in the public sector where unions have not only demanded involvement, but argued that it was a matter which affects both the quality of working life for employees and the quality of service given clients in public agencies.[16] The entire matter of computers and worklife, microelectronics and the new technology has been elevated in Sweden to the

11. Gustavsen and Hunnius, *New Patterns*; Max Elden, et al. "Automation and Job Design — the Case of Norway" (Trondheim: Institute for Social Research in Industry, 1981).

12. Noble, "Social Choice," p. 49.

13. Norwegian Labour Inspectorate, "Proposed Rules and Recommendations Concerning Work Stations at Terminals, 1981" (Not yet adopted.)

14. "Norway: New Technology Regulations," *European Industrial Relations Review* (1981), p. 2.

15. Deutsch, "Work Environment."

16. Swedish Union of Insurance Employees. *Electronic Data Processing in the Social Insurance Offices.* 1980.

level of a Parliamentary Commission, set up with the mandate to study the social impact of computerization. Further, the Swedish Labor Federation at its September 1981 Congress adopted a policy statement which not only calls for more worker involvement and better information sharing with the union, but specifically argues that more workers should be trained in computing so as to upgrade the content of jobs and use the new technology to "serve the principle of democracy."[17] In particular, the Swedish Labor Federation has set forth demands including:

> Employees must be guaranteed influence on where and how computerization and electronics are used.
> Local union organizations must be informed in good time of the changes in existing computerization systems or that new data systems are being planned.
> The documentation for negotiations on computerization must indicate clearly the effects on employment, working environment, work organization, training requirements, etc.
> No data system providing for information on individual employees may be introduced without union approval.[18]

To summarize, unions in Norway and Sweden have gained advances by legislative mandate and collective bargaining over the past two decades. This, of course, has been achieved in countries where the labor force is largely unionized, and where the labor movement has a major political party and has even run the government. The labor movements have developed a politics of industrial production which has generated a host of worklife reforms, and helped labor gain more rights on the shop floor, and more control over the working environment and the economy.[19]

Collective Bargaining and Technology Agreements

A major issue of new technology is job displacement. No better illustration exists than in the much heralded "manless factories" in Japan. Japan produced from 2.5 to 3 million automobiles in the early 1970's with 450,000 auto workers. Today that same number of workers produces 10 to 11 million cars. This has been achieved by the use of robots. Japan now leads the world in robot use, currently having 14,000 such programmed robots, 30 percent of which are used in assembly. This compares to 4,100 in the U.S.A., 10 percent of which are used in assembly.[20] However, there are factors tied to job security and the

---

17. *LO Report on Data Processing,* adopted by the Swedish Labor Federation Congress (September, 1981).

18. "Congress Resolution: Computer and Production Technology," *LO, News of the Swedish Trade Union Confederation* (November, 1981).

19. Deutsch, "Work Environment."

20. Steve Lohr, "New in Japan: The Manless Factory," *New York Times* December 13, 1981.

culture which are distinctly different in Japan.[21] While new technology is the major vehicle with which Japan plans to build its economy in the 1980's, and it is anticipated that some workers' jobs will be automated, most of those workers will simply be shifted within their organizations.[22] Matsushita Electric, a "manless factory," expects to have 100,000 robots by 1990, but workers there have not lost their jobs, they have been shifted to other jobs. A system of simply dismissing workers wholesale is unacceptable to Japan. It is not in much of the industrial Western world.

Labor movements in most industrial nations have used their ability to organize workers and bring power to the bargaining table in order to achieve higher wages, limit hours, and improve conditions of work. Perhaps as the economic crisis of high inflation and rising unemployment affects all industrial countries, we will see less stress on wage negotiations, where there is less room to maneuver, and more emphasis on conditions (and security) of work. The European Trade Union Institute has conducted studies on the impact of the new technology, especially microelectronics and the "silicon revolution," which show that there has already been job displacement and considerable economic impact.[23] In the light of these findings and the fact that the predicted future is one of even greater reliance on such technology, it is not surprising that the strongest suggestions for union response all revolve around technology agreements. These agreements should emphasize advance notification and prior involvement for sufficient planning; and, perhaps more importantly, give unions access to information which will help them understand the impact of new technology on work organization and the opportunity to clearly articulate what they want out of such a new work organization. The task is a significant one, for the computers and accompanying systems affect job tasks, communications flows, and decision-making structures, which in turn, affect workers on the job, the sense of solidarity, and the role of the union on the shop floor.

The ETUI report gives illustrations from many European countries and notes that agreements over the introduction of new technology cannot be divorced from union concern over corporate mergers, plant dislocations, shifting investments and the like. As a result, it is pointed

---

21. Koshiro Katzutoshi, "Labor Productivity and Recent Employment Adjustment Programs in Japan — I," *Japan Labor Bulletin* (Dec. 1978) pp. 8-10; Koshiro, "Labor Productivity and Recent Employment Adjustment Programs in Japan — II," *Japan Labor Bulletin* (January, 1979), pp. 4-8.

22. "Japan's Strategy for the '80s," *Business Week*, December 14, 1981.

23. John Evans, *The Impact of Microelectronics on Employment in Western Europe in the 1980's* (Brussels: European Trade Union Institute, 1980).

out that the matter of job security and protection of working conditions links the issue of technology with the broader issue of labor's right to information about such things as capital decisions and plant closings. The lessons for American labor are quite obvious. As someone recently said at a meeting on luring high technology industry to the northwestern U.S., "from silicon valley (California) to Oregon to Micronesia." As we know, a major need for labor in the United States related to corporate disinvestment decisions is advance notification. This point converges with the issue of technology. The bottom line, then, for labor in any technology agreement is to gain early information about all proposed changes, have ample consultative opportunities, gain job protection, and attempt to control the worklife for those affected by the changes.

Some thoughtful work on technology agreements has been done in England where there are similar problems of dislocation, mass unemployment, and high inflation.[24] There is governmental encouragement for management cooperation with labor for effective consultation. A Department of Employment report states that:

> Consultation is not merely an inevitable requirement by trade unionists but something the managements will decline only in their peril, given the widespread apprehensions that have been aroused by possible employment implications of microelectronics.[25]

Others call expressly for a government Agency for New Technology to coordinate and implement a national policy to foster technical and social change and develop labor-management relations which allow more cooperation over the issues of technology.[26] The call for governmental policy is pushed by some British unions such as the Association of Professional, Executive, Clerical and Computer Staff (APEX), which argues that the concern is not simply preserving jobs for those who have them, but the wider issue of total numbers of jobs and work opportunities so that today's problems are not simply pushed into the next generation.[27] They argue for bargaining on shorter hours, output,

---

24. C. Jenkins, "Trade Unions and Technology: The Role of Technology Agreements," in *The Socio-Economic Impact of Microelectronics*, J. Berting et al. (eds.) (Oxford: Pergamon Press, 1980); Association of Scientific Technical and Managerial Staffs, *Technological Change and Collective Bargaining*, 1981; Trade Union Congress, *New Technology: Case Studies* (London, 1980); Trade Union Congress, *The New Technology: Agreements, Samples, Models* (London, 1981); Trade Union Congress, *New Technology and Collective Bargaining* (London, 1981).

25. Malcolm Peltu, "New Technology Without Strife," *International Management*, (November, 1980) pp. 50-52.

26. Greg Bamber, "Microchips and Industrial Relations," *Industrial Relations Journal* 11 (Nov-Dec, 1980), pp. 7-19.

27. APEX, "A Trade Union Strategy for the New Technology," in *The Microelectronics Revolution* (Cambridge, Mass: MIT Press, 1981).

retraining and other dimensions, but ultimately see the need for national or governmental policy-making as an augmentation to collective bargaining. While England has not solved the problem it has provided good illustrative material which can serve a useful purpose for American labor. The joint agreement between the Trades Union Congress and the Confederation of British Industry is provocative for American unions.[28]

Similar efforts have been made in Australia as well. The microelectronics revolution is being felt in Australia and the labor movement is attempting to use technology agreements to increase labor's involvement and halt the job dislocation threat.[29] The Australian Council of Trade Unions is seeking:

> . . . the enactment of a Technological Change (Impact of Proposals) Act. This Act shall require statements of proposals from employers concerning technological change as it applies to an industry and enterprise level.[30]

There is some effort to mobilize attention to the problem as witnessed by the technology research unit in the New South Wales government.[31]

In Denmark there is an agreement for the private sector, one with the state as employer, one for banking, one for municipal employees is soon expected and shortly almost all sectors will be covered.[32]

In all of this material there is the question of what role should be played by government. Suggestions range from governmental "technology taxes" to slow employers' adoption of such changes, to greater governmental involvement in the labor market. In most instances the industrial nations have resisted the latter, and although the economic crisis for the West is felt in all countries, it seems that the primary approach will continue to be technology agreements and labor-management negotiations, albeit with some governmental encouragement and further application of existing and extended laws on work environment and codetermination in its various forms.

---

28. "Joint Accord on New Technology," *European Industrial Relations Review* (1980).

29. Russell Lansbury, "New Technology and Industrial Relations in the Retail Grocery Industry," *The Journal of Industrial Relations* (September, 1980), pp. 275-292.

30. Australian Council of Trade Unions, *Consolidation of ACTU Policy Decisions 1951-1980*, 1980.

31. William Ford, Margaret Coffey, and Dexter Dunphy, *Technology and the Workforce: An Annotated Bibliography* (Sydney, Australia: Technology Research Unit, New South Wales Ministry of Labour, 1981).

32. This is outlined in the *Danish Labour News*, July 1981, including the verbatim agreement signed by the Danish Federation of Unions and the Eanish Employers Confederation.

Some Conclusions and Implications for the American Labor Movement

The interest by American unions in developments in other industrial nations is understandable and logical. First, the international economic interdependence and capital flow patterns make U.S. unions part of a larger international structure. This becomes most obvious when U.S.-based multinational corporations decide to move investments abroad, and serves as one reason American labor wants to increase wages for workers in other countries. Second, some of the discussion in management circles in recent years has been directed towards applications of what *Business Week* calls "The New Industrial Relations," namely, various programs of employee involvement, worker participation, joint labor-management programs, Quality of Work Life programs and so on. Third, there is evidence that international labor organizations have helped increase worker solidarity and develop more unified efforts by labor in the face of global corporate employers. Some of these tactics seem to work. Last, there is evidence that approaches in other countries can have some impact on policy directions here.

Several publications have focused on the issues of technology in various countries and how labor has sought greater influence.[33] A union delegation recently toured several European countries and wrote a report which describes both achievements and policies there and hints at implications for American unions.[34] The American *Business Week* and the English *The Economist* both ran articles in August, 1981 reviewing the impact of robotization and the new technology. The conclusion most easily drawn from these works is that the problems and challenges for labor are very similar on both sides of the Atlantic.

There are interesting international developments. The Nordic Council of Trade Unions and the Confederation of European Trade Unions share information. A recent project in the graphic arts industry has crossed several countries in Europe advancing the idea of a union institute developing new production technology which suits labor.[35] The Graphic Arts International Union urged an International Labor Organization study along these lines.

---

33. American Labor Education Center, *New Technology: Who Will Control It?* (Washington, D.C.: Publication #13, 1981).

34. Dennis Chamot and Michael Dymmel, *Cooperation or Conflict: European Experiences with Technological Change at the Workplace.* (Washington, D.C.: Department for Professional Employees, AFL-CIO, 1981).

35. Swedish Center for Working Life, *Training, Technology, and Products Viewed From the Quality of Work Perspective* (Stockholm, 1981).

The concern with VDTs and office automation is international. Reports are shared and efforts at gaining protective standards diffused from one labor movement to another. In many instances the issues related to new technology are tied closely to feminist concerns, since women were hired last, and still are paid less in most nations, and will be first affected by job displacing technology. Swedish trade union women, for example, see the sex equity laws as relevant to the problem and are utilizing a range of legislation and labor federation agreements to forestall the already marked impact of office automation, grocery electronic scanners, and other such technological changes which disproportionately affect female workers. This too is an international phenomenon where information sharing is useful.

Some American unions have gone in a direction similar to their European counterparts. For example, the Scandinavians pioneered the position of technology stewards comparable to safety stewards. These are unionists with special training and special involvement in technology issues. The Communication Workers of America's move to establish technology agreements and joint labor-management technology committees may create a comparable group of CWA members with specialized skill to engage management on technology questions and assure that union viewpoints are heard all along the line.

One might use other illustrations. But for now, suffice it to say that the experience in other industrial nations is worth looking at and that American unions are in for tough times as the technological revolution advances. All of us who are concerned about the plight of American workers and unions need to apply the best solutions, whether they are truly original indigenous creations, borrowed from elsewhere, or interesting adaptations and hybrids which come from other learning experiences.

Selected Bibliography:
Labor and Technology

Abbott, Lewis F. *Technological Development in Industry: A Survey of Social Aspects.* Manchester, U.K.: Industrial Systems Research, 1978.

American Labor Education Center. *New Technology: Who Will Control It?* 13 (Washington, D.C.: 1981).

Baker, Elizabeth Faulkner. *Technology and Women's Work.* New York: Columbia University Press, 1964.

Bamber, Greg. "Microchips and Industrial Relations," *Industrial Relations Journal,* 11 (Nov-Dec, 1980): 7-19.

Berting, J., ed. *The Socio-Economic Impact of Microelectronics.* Oxford: Pergamon Press, 1980.

Bhalla, A.S., ed. *Technology and Employment in Industry.* Geneva, Switzerland: International Labour Office, 1975.

Blauner, Robert. *Alienation and Freedom.* Chicago: University of Chicago Press, 1964.

Blitz, Herbert. *Labor-Management Contracts and Technological Change: Case Studies and Contract Clauses.* New York: Frederick A. Praeger, 1969.

Bluestone, Barry and Harrison, Bennet. *Capital and Communities: The Causes and Consequences of Private Disinvestment.* Washington, D.C.: Progressive Alliance, 1981.

Braverman, Harry. *Labor and Monopoly Capital: The Degradation of Work in the Twentieth Century.* New York: Monthly Review Press, 1974.

Chamot, Dennis. "Technology: How European Unions Cope," *The Federationist.* November, 1981.

_____ and Baggett, Joan M., eds. *Silicon, Satellites and Robots: The Impact of Technological Change in the Workplace.* Washington, D.C.: AFL-CIO Department for Professional Employees, 1979.

_____ and Dymmel, Michael. *Cooperation or Conflict: European Experiences with Technological Change at the Workplace.* Washington, D.C.: AFL-CIO Department for Professional Employees, 1981.

Cherns, A.B. "Speculations on the Social Effects of New Microelectronics Technology," *International Labour Review*. 119 (Nov-Dec 1980): 705-721.

Cockroft, David. "New Office Technology and Employment," *International Labour Review*. 119 (Nov-Dec 1980): 689-704.

Cooley, Michael. *Architect or Bee: The Human Technological Relationship*. London: John Goodwin and Sons, 1980.

_____ "Computerization — Taylor's Latest Disguise," *Economic and Industrial Democracy*. 1(1980):523-539.

Crozier, Michael. *The World of the Office Worker*. New York: Schocken Books, 1971.

Deutsch, Steven. "Perception of and Attitudes Toward Automation: A Study of Local Union Leaders," *Labor Law Journal* 18 (July 1967): 396-405.

_____ "Technological Change and Its Effect on Local Union Leadership," in B.C. Roberts (ed.) *Industrial Relations: Contemporary Issues*. New York: St. Martins Press, 1968.

_____ "Labor, Ideology and Technological Change: Some Sociological Considerations," *International Review of Sociology* 5 (August 1969): 79-92.

_____ "Extending Workplace Democracy: Struggles to come in Job Safety and Health," *Labor Studies Journal* 6 (Spring 1981):124-132.

_____ "Work Environment Reform and Industrial Democracy," *Sociology of Work and Occupations* 8 (May 1981): 180-194.

Dix, Keith. *Work Relations in the Coal Industry: The Hand-Loading Era, 1880-1930*. Morgantown, W.Va.: West Virginia University, Institute for Labor Studies, 1977.

Edwards, Richard. *Contested Terrain: The Transformation of the Workplace in the Twentieth Century*. New York: Basic Books, 1979.

Forester, Tom, ed. *The Microelectronics Revolution: The Complete Guide to the New Technology and Its Impact on Society*. Cambridge, Mass: MIT Press, 1981.

Garson, Barbara. *All the Livelong Day*. Garden City, N.Y.: Doubleday and Company, 1975.

_____ "The Electronic Sweatshop: Scanning the Office of the Future," *Mother Jones*. July, 1981.

Glenn, Evelyn M. and Feldberg, Roslyn L. "Degraded and Deskilled: The Proletarianization of Clerical Work." *Social Problems*. 25 (October 1977): 52-64.

Gustavesen, Bjorn and Hunius, Gerry. *New Patterns of Work Reform* (Oslo: Oslo University Press, 1981).

Greenbaum, Joan. *In the Name of Efficiency: Management Theory and Shopfloor Practice in Data-Processing Work.* Philadelphia: Temple University Press, 1979.

Hirschorn, Larry. "The Soul of a New Worker," *Working Papers for a New Society* 9(Jan-Feb. 1982): 42-47.

Howard, Robert. "Brave New Workplace," *Working Papers for a New Society* 6(Nov-Dec 1980): 21-31.

Howe, Louise Kapp. *Pink Collar Workers.* New York: G.P. Putnam and Sons, 1977.

Kelber, Harry and Schlesinger, Karl. *Union Printers and Controlled Automation* New York: The Free Press, 1967.

Labor Studies Journal. "Theme Issue: Occupational Safety and Health." 6(Spring 1981).

Labor Studies Journal. "Special Issue: The Impact on Labor of Changing Corporate Structure and Technology." 3(Winter, 1979).

Lansbury, Russell. "New Technology and Industrial Relations in the Retail Grocery Industry," *The Journal of Industrial Relations* (Sept 1980): 275-292.

Levinson, Harold M. et. al. *Collective Bargaining and Technological Change in American Transportation.* Evanston, Ill.: Transportation Center at Northwestern University, 1971.

Lohr, Steve. "New in Japan: The Manless Factory," *New York Times.* December 13, 1981.

McLaughlin, Doris. *The Impact of Labor Unions on the Rate and Direction of Technological Innovation.* Springfield, Va.: National Technical Information Service, 1979.

Meissner, Martin. *Technology and the Worker: Technical Demands and Social Proceses in Industry.* San Francisco: Chandler Publishing Co., 1969.

Montgomery, David. *Workers Control in America: Studies in the History of Work, Technology and Labor Struggles.* New York: Cambridge University Press, 1979.

Murphy, Kevin. *Technological Change Clauses in Collective Bargaining Agreements.* Washington, D.C.: AFL-CIO Department for Professional Employees, 1981.

National Center for Productivity and Quality of Working Life. "The Attrition Clause at *The New York Times*," in *Productivity and Job Security: Attrition-Benefits and Problems.* Washington, D.C.: Government Printing Office, 1977.

National Commission on Technology, *Automation and Technical Progress. Vol. II, Technology and the American Economy.* Washington, D.C.: Government Printing Office, 1966.

Nilles, Jack M. *The Telecommunication-Transportation Trade-Off.* New York: John Wiley & Sons, 1976.

Noble, David. *America by Design: Science, Technology and the Rise of Conglomerate Capitalism.* New York: Alfred A. Knopf, 1979.

Race Against Time: An Overview of Office Automation. Cleveland: Working Women Educational Fund, 1981.

Rachleff, Peter. *Moving the Mail.* Morgantown, West Virginia: The Work Environment Project, 1982.

Rogers, Theresa F. and Friedman, Nathalie S. *Printers Face Automation: The Impact of Technology on Work and Retirement Among Skilled Craftsmen.* Lexington, Mass.: D.C. Health & Co., Lexington Books, 1980.

Rosenberg, Matthew. *Technology and American Growth.* New York: Harper & Row, 1972.

Shaiken, Harley. "Brave New World of Work in Auto." *In These Times.* September 16-25, 1979.

—————————— "Computers as Strikebreakers." *Technology Review.* April, 1982.

—————————— "Numerical Control of Work: Workers and Automation in The Computer Age," *Radical America.* 6(Nov-Dec 1979): 25-38.

Simon, Nora and Minc, Alain. *Computerization of Society: A Report to The President of France.* Cambridge, Mass.: MIT Press, 1980.

Slichter, S.H. *Impact of Collective Bargaining on Management.* Washington, D.C.: Brookings Institute, 1980.

Tepperman, Jean. *Not Servants, Not Machines.* Boston: Beacon Press, 1976.

Thurow, Lester, Bluestone, Barry and Shaiken, Harley. "Reindustrialization and Jobs," *Working papers for a New Society.* 6(Nov-Dec 1980): 47-59.

United States Department of Labor, Bureau of Labor Statistics, *Technology and Manpower Trends,* Bulletin No. 1474. Washington, D.C.: Government Printing Office, 1966.

—————————— *Outlook for Technology and Manpower in Printing and Publishing,* Bulletin no. 1774. Washington, D.C.: Government Printing Office, 1973.

—————————— *Technological Change and its Labor Impact in Five Industries,* Bulletin no. 1961. Washington, D.C.: Government Printing Office, 1977.

Warning: Health Hazards for Office Workers. Cleveland: Working Women Educational Fund, 1981.

Wertheimer, Barbara. *We Were There.* New York: Pantheon Books, 1977.

Zimbalist, Andrew, ed. *Case Studies on the Labor Process.* New York: Monthly Review Press, 1979.

SUBJECT INDEX

Donald Kennedy is a labor educator on the faculty of the Department of Labor Studies, the Pennsylvania State University. He is Editor of the Department of Labor Studies' Publication Series which includes occasional monographs, a quarterly newsletter *Pennsylvania Labor*, pamphlets and reprints.

Charles Craypo is an Associate Professor of Economics at the University of Notre Dame. For several years he was a labor educator at Michigan State University and on the Labor Studies faculty at the Pennsylvania State University.

Mary Lehman holds a Baccalaureate Degree in Labor Studies from the Pennsylvania State University and helped initiate the Publication Series, including co-editing several issues of the newsletter. She is a graduate student at the New York State School of Labor and Industrial Relations at Cornell University and is the recipient of the Dorothy Funt Memorial Fellowship.

The editors gratefully acknowledge the assistance of Cathy Kennedy, David Shelly and Stephen Talbot in the preparation of this book.